Dogs That Know When Their Owners Are Coming Home

Dr Rupert Sheldrake is a biologist and author of more than 80 scientific papers and ten books. A former Research Fellow of the Royal Society, he studied natural sciences at Cambridge University.

He has appeared in many TV programs in Britain and overseas, and has taken part in BBC and other radio programmes. He has written for newspapers such as the *Guardian*, where he had a regular monthly column, *The Times*, *Sunday Telegraph*, *Daily Mirror*, *Daily Mail* and *Sunday Times*, and has contributed to a variety of magazines, including *New Scientist*, *Resurgence*, the *Ecologist* and the *Spectator*. He lives in London with his wife and two sons.

Dogs That Know When Their Owners Are Coming Home

The Unexplained
Powers of Animals

Rupert Sheldrake

arrow books

Reissued by Arrow Books 2011

17 19 20 18

Copyright © Rupert Sheldrake, 2011

First published in Great Britain in 1999 by
Hutchinson
First published in paperback in 2000 by
Arrow Books
Random House, 20 Vauxhall Bridge Road,
London SW1V 2SA

www.randomhouse.co.uk

Addresses for companies within The Random House Group Limited
can be found at: www.randomhouse.co.uk/offices.htm

Random House UK Limited Reg. No. 954009

www.randomhouse.co.uk

A CIP catalogue record for this book
is available from the British Library

ISBN 9780099255871

The Random House Group Limited supports The Forest Stewardship
Council (FSC®), the leading international forest certification organisation.
Our books carrying the FSC label are printed on FSC® certified paper.
FSC is the only forest certification scheme endorsed by the leading
environmental organisations, including Greenpeace. Our
paper procurement policy can be found at
www.randomhouse.co.uk/environment

MIX
Paper from
responsible sources
FSC® C016897

Design/make-up by Roger Walker

Printed and bound in Great Britain by Clays Ltd, St Ives PLC

WITH THANKS TO ALL THE ANIMALS
FROM WHOM I HAVE LEARNED

Contents

PART V:
SENSES OF DIRECTION

PART VI:
ANIMAL PREMONITIONS

PART VII:
CONCLUSIONS

Preface

This is a book of recognition – a recognition that animals have abilities that we have lost. One part of ourselves has forgotten this; another part has known it all along.

As a child, like many other children, I was interested in animals and plants. My family kept a great variety of pets: our dog, Scamp, a rabbit, hamsters, pigeons, a jackdaw, a budgerigar, a terrapin, two tortoises and several goldfish, as well as the populations of tadpoles and caterpillars I would rear each spring. My father, Reginald Sheldrake, a pharmacist and amateur microscopist, encouraged my interests and fuelled my fascination with the natural world when he showed me how drops of pondwater teemed with myriad forms of life, and what the scales on butterflies' wings looked like.

I was especially intrigued by the way that pigeons homed. On Saturday mornings my father took me to see a great liberation of them. At our local railway station at Newark-on-Trent, in the English Midlands, racing birds from all over Britain were waiting in wicker baskets, arrayed in stacks. At the appointed time, the porters opened the flaps. They let me help. Out burst hundreds of pigeons in a great commotion of wind and feathers. They flew up into the sky, circled around and set off in various directions towards their faraway homes. How did they do it? No one seemed to know. Their homing ability is still unexplained today.

At school it was a natural choice for me to study biology and other sciences, and I continued these studies at Cambridge University. But as I proceeded in my education as a biologist, a great gulf began to open up between my own experience of animals and plants and the scientific approach that I was being taught.

The mechanistic theory of life, still the dominant orthodoxy, asserts that living organisms are nothing but complex, genetically programmed machines. They are supposed to be inanimate, literally soulless. As a general rule, the first step we took when studying living organisms was to kill them or cut them up. I spent many hours of laboratory work in dissection, and then as my studies proceeded, in vivisection. For example, it was an essential part of my biology curriculum to dissect nerves from the severed legs of frogs and stimulate them electrically to make the muscles twitch. For the study of enzymes in rat liver, one of the favoured tissues in animal biochemistry, we first had to decapitate the living rats, their blood spurting down the laboratory sink. I heard nothing about how pigeons homed.

These student exercises were mild compared with my experience as a temporary laboratory technician in the Pharmacology Department of a multinational pharmaceutical company, where new drugs were developed and tested. I worked there for six months between leaving school and going to university, when I was aged seventeen. There were rooms full of rats, guinea pigs, mice and other animals waiting to be injected with chemicals to see what dose would poison them. The guinea pigs, their toes pinched until they squeaked from pain, were injected with chemicals being screened for painkilling ability. Cats were operated on. At the end of each day dozens of animals that had survived these various tests and experiments were gassed and thrown into a bin for incineration.

A love of animals had led me to study biology and this was where it had taken me. Something had gone wrong. I began to wonder what was going on. I later came to see that the split I experienced within myself is widespread within and outside the scientific community.

I have come to realize that this split is not inevitable. A more inclusive kind of science is possible. It is also much cheaper.

In 1994, I published a book called *Seven Experiments That Could Change The World* in which I explored well-known but little-understood phenomena, and suggested how inexpensive research could lead to major breakthroughs. One of these experiments concerned the possible telepathic abilities of dogs and cats. In particular, I focused on the ability of some dogs to know when their owners are coming home.

Thus, through trying to find ways in which a broader view of life can be developed scientifically, I have come back to pets. It took me a long time to recognize that they are the animals we know best. I knew this as a child. To many people it is blindingly obvious, but for me it had all the force of a new discovery. I realized that the animals we know best have much to teach us. They can help enlarge our understanding of life; they are not just cute, cuddly, comforting, or fun.

For the last five years, I have been doing research on the perceptiveness of pets with the help of over two thousand animal owners and trainers. I have surveyed over a thousand randomly chosen pet owners to find out how common various kinds of unexplained behaviour are. I and my associates have interviewed hundreds of people with much experience of animals, including dog trainers, search and rescue dog handlers, police dog handlers, blind people with guide dogs, veterinarians, kennel and stable proprietors, horse trainers, horse riders, farmers, shepherds, zoo keepers, petshop proprietors, reptile breeders and pet owners.

If I had quoted from all the accounts and interviews that I have been given, this book would been at least ten times thicker. In some instances, hundreds of people have told me about very similar patterns of behaviour in their pets, like dogs knowing when their owners are coming home. I have had to condense this information, and give only a few examples of each kind of perceptive behaviour in this book. Although many people have contributed to the overall picture, I can acknowledge only a small minority by name. Without all this help from people named and unnamed, this book could not have been written. I am indebted to all those who have helped me, and to their animals.

This research project was initially funded by the late Ben Webster of Toronto, Canada, and has been much helped by grants from the Lifebridge Foundation, New York; the Institute of Noetic Sciences, Sausalito, California; Evelyn Hancock of Old Greenwich, Connecticut; and the Ross Institute of New York. I have also had the benefit of organizational support in the United States from the Institute of Noetic Sciences, in the German-speaking countries from the Schweisfurth Foundation in Munich, and in Britain from the Scientific and Medical Network. I am very grateful for all this generosity and encouragement.

I owe much to my research associates, Pamela Smart in Lancashire, Jane Turney in London, Susanne Seiler in Zurich and David Brown in Santa Cruz, California; and also to my secretary Cathy Lawlor. They have helped me in many ways: in carrying out surveys, in interviewing people, in doing experiments, and in collecting data. All have helped to build up a large computerized database on the perceptiveness of pets, but Pam Smart has had the primary responsibility for maintaining and adding to it. I am also grateful to Anna Rigano and Dr Amanda Jacks for their help with research, and to Helmut Lasarcyk for his labour of love in translating hundreds of reports from the German-speaking countries and adding them to our database.

My special thanks are due to Matthew Clapp for the gift of his services in setting up and maintaining my world wide web site (www.sheldrake.org), beginning when he was an undergraduate at the University of Georgia.

Many discussions, comments, suggestions and criticisms, as well as much practical assistance, have helped me in my research and in the writing of this book. In particular I thank Ralph Abraham, Shirley Barry, Patrick Bateson, John Beloff, John Brockman, Sigrid Detschey, Lindy Dufferin and Ava, Peter Fenwick, David Fontana, Matthew Fox, Winston Franklin, Robert Freeman, Edward Goldsmith, Franz-Theo Gottwald, the late Willis Harman, Myles Hildyard, Rupert Hitzig, Nicholas Humphrey, Tom Hurley, Francis Huxley, Montague Keene, David Lorimer, Betty Markwick, Katinka Matson, Robert Matthews, Terence McKenna, John Michell, Michael Morgan, Robert Morris, John O'Donohue, the late Brendan O'Reagan, Barbara and Charles Overby, Erik Pigani, Anthony Podberscek, my wife Jill Purce, Anthony Ramsay, John Roche, Miriam Rothschild, Marilyn Schlitz, Merlin and Cosmo Sheldrake, Paul Sieveking, Arnaud de St Simon, Martin Speich, Dennis Stillings, Dennis Turner, Varena Walterspiel, Ian and Victoria Watson, Alexandra Webster, Richard Wiseman and Sandra Wright.

In my appeals for information I have been helped by many newspapers and magazines in Europe and North America, and by a variety of TV and radio programmes. I thank all those who made this possible.

I also thank all those who have given me their comments and suggestions on various drafts of this book: Letty Beyer, David Brown, Ann Docherty, Karl-Heinz Loske, Anthony Podberscek, Jill Purce, Janis Rozé, Merlin Sheldrake, Pam Smart, Mary Stewart, Peggy Taylor and Jane Turney. I have been fortunate in having such sympathetic and constructive editors in Steven Ross and Kristin Kiser in New York, and Susan Freestone in London, and the final form of this book owes much to their helpful suggestions.

Finally, I am grateful to Phil Starling for his permission to reproduce the photographs in Figures 2.1, 4.1 and 8.1, to Gary Taylor for Figure 2.2 and to Sydney King for doing the drawings and diagrams.

London, February 1999

Introduction

Kate Laufer, a midwife and social worker in Solbergmoen, Norway, works at odd hours and returns home at unexpected times, but, whenever her husband Walter is home, he greets her with a hot cup of freshly brewed tea. What accounts for her husband's uncanny timing? The family dog Tiki the terrier: 'Wherever he is, or whatever he's doing,' says Dr Laufer, 'when Tiki rushes to the window and stands on the windowsill, I know that my wife is on her way home.'

When the telephone rings in the household of a noted professor at the University of California in Berkeley, his wife always knows when her husband is on the other end of the line. How? Whiskins, the family's silver tabby cat, rushes to the telephone and paws at the receiver. 'Many times he succeeds in taking it off the hook and makes appreciative meows that are clearly audible to my husband at the other end,' she says. 'If someone else telephones, Whiskins takes no notice.'

Julia Orr thought her horses had settled happily into their new paddock when she moved from Skirmett, Buckinghamshire, to a farm nine miles away. But Badger, a 24-year-old Welsh cob, and 22-year-old Tango were merely biding their time. One night six weeks later, when a storm blew open the gate of their field, they took their chance. At dawn they were waiting patiently at the gate of Mrs Orr's old home. They had found their own way back on unfamiliar roads and tracks, leaving tell-tale hoof prints on verges and flower beds as they went.

On 17 October 1989 Tirzah Meek of Santa Cruz, California, saw her cat run up into the attic and hide, which she had never done before. She seemed terrified and refused to come down. Three hours later, the Loma Prieta earthquake struck, devastating the centre of Santa Cruz.

Dogs that know when their owners are returning home, cats that answer the telephone when a person to whom they are attached to is calling, horses that can find their way home over unfamiliar terrain, cats that anticipate earthquakes: these are some of the aspects of animal behaviour that suggest the existence of forms of perceptiveness that lie beyond present-day scientific understanding.

Through five years of extensive research on the unexplained powers of animals, I have come to the conclusion that many of the stories told by pet owners are well founded. Some animals really do seem to have powers of perception that go beyond the known senses.

There is nothing new about the uncanny abilities of animals. People have noticed them for centuries. Millions of pet owners today have experienced them personally. But at the same time, many people feel they have to deny these abilities, or trivialize them. They are ignored by institutional science. Pets are the animals we know best, but their most surprising and intriguing behaviour is treated as of no real interest. Why should this be so?

One reason is a taboo against taking pets seriously.[1] This taboo is not confined to scientists, but is a result of the split attitudes to animals expressed in our society as a whole. During working hours we commit ourselves to economic progress, fuelled by science and technology and based on the mechanistic view of life. This view, dating back to the scientific revolution of the seventeenth century, derives from René Descartes' theory of the universe as a machine. Though the metaphors have changed (from the brain as hydraulic machine in Descartes' time, and as a telephone exchange a generation ago, to a computer nowadays), life is still thought of in terms of machinery.[2] Animals and plants are seen as genetically programmed automata, and the exploitation of animals is taken for granted.

Meanwhile, back at home, we have our pets. Pets are in a different category from other animals. Pet-keeping is confined to the private or subjective realm. Experiences with pets have to be kept out of the 'real' or 'objective' world. There is a huge gulf between companion animals, treated as members of our families, and animals in factory farms and research laboratories. Our relationships with our pets are based on different sets of attitudes, on I-Thou relationships rather than the I-It approach encouraged by science. I experienced this split myself in a particularly intense way, as I describe in the Preface to this book.

Whether in the laboratory or in the field, scientific investigators typically try to avoid emotional connections with the animals they are investigating. They aspire to a detached objectivity. They would therefore be unlikely to encounter kinds of behaviour that depend on close attachments between animals and people. In this realm, animal trainers and pet owners are generally far more knowledgeable and experienced than professional researchers on animal behaviour – unless they happen to be pet owners themselves.

The taboo against taking pets seriously is only one reason why the phenomena I discuss in this book have been neglected by institutional science. Another is the taboo against taking psychic or 'paranormal' phenomena seriously. These phenomena are called paranormal – meaning 'beyond the normal' – not because they are rare or exceptional. Some are very common. They are called paranormal because they cannot be explained in conventional scientific terms; they do not fit in with the mechanistic theory of nature.

Research with pets

The wealth of experience of animals among horse and dog trainers, veterinarians and pet owners is generally dismissed as *anecdotal*. This happens so often that I looked up the origin of this word to find out what it means. It comes from the Greek roots *an + ekdotos*, meaning 'not published'. An anecdote is an unpublished story.

Some fields of research, for example medicine, rely heavily on anecdotes, but when they are published they literally cease to be anecdotes; they are promoted to the rank of case histories.

In the course of the research described in this book, I have found that many people have had very similar experiences of perceptiveness in their animals. And when so many people's accounts point independently to consistent and repeatable patterns, anecdotes are transformed into natural history. At the very least, this is a natural history of what people *believe* about their animals. The next question is whether these beliefs are well founded or not. And that is why experimental investigations are an essential part of this research.

One of my favourite books in biology is Charles Darwin's *The Variation of Animals and Plants Under Domestication*, first published in 1868. It is full of information that Darwin collected from naturalists, explorers, colonial administrators, missionaries and others with whom he corresponded all over the world. He studied publications like *Poultry Chronicle* and *The Gooseberry Grower's Register*. He grew 54 varieties of gooseberry himself. He drew on the experience of cat and rabbit fanciers, horse and dog breeders, bee keepers, farmers, horticulturalists and other people experienced with animals and plants. He joined two of the London pigeon clubs, kept all the breeds he could procure, and visited leading fanciers to see their birds.

The effects of selective breeding in domesticated animals and plants, observed with such attention by practical men and women, gave Darwin his strongest evidence for the power of selection, an essential ingredient in his theory of evolution by natural selection.

Since the time of Darwin, science has increasingly cut itself off from the rich experience of people who are not professional scientists. There are still millions with practical experience of pigeons, dogs, cats, horses, parrots, bees and other animals, and of apple trees, roses, orchids and other plants. There are still tens of thousands of amateur naturalists. But scientific research is now almost entirely confined to universities and research institutes, and carried out by professionals with PhDs. This exclusiveness has seriously impoverished modern biology.

Why has this research not been done before?

The investigation of the unexplained powers of animals that I describe in this book has been facilitated by modern technical devices such as computers and video cameras, but in principle most of these investigations could have been carried out a hundred years ago, or more. The fact that they are only now beginning is a tribute to the strength of the taboos against such enquiries.

I believe there is much to be gained by ignoring these taboos. I also believe there is much to be gained by following a scientific approach. But the word 'scientific' can have quite different meanings. All too often, it is equated with a narrow-minded dogmatism that seeks to deny or debunk whatever does not fit in with the mechanistic view of the world. By contrast, I take 'scientific' to mean a method of open-minded enquiry, paying attention to evidence and testing possible explanations by means of experiment. The path of investigation is more in the spirit of science than the path of denial. And it is certainly more fun.

These different scientific attitudes are illustrated by the tale of a horse called Clever Hans, which is usually employed to justify the dismissal of seemingly unexplained animal powers. I draw the opposite moral from the story, and see it as an example of the need to investigate rather than deny unexplained phenomena.

The tale of Clever Hans

Sooner or later, anyone who takes an interest in the unexplained power of animals will be told the story of Clever Hans. This story has assumed the role of a cautionary tale for scientists.

At the beginning of the twentieth century there was a horse in Berlin named Hans, who was said to be able to carry out mathematical calculations, read German, and spell out German words. He tapped out answers with his hoof. His trainer, Herr von Osten, a former mathematics teacher, was convinced that Hans had mental capacities thought to be confined to human beings. The horse caused a sensation, and many displays were given to professors, military officers and others.

Clever Hans's abilities were investigated by Professor C. Stumpf, Director of the Psychological Institute of the University of Berlin, and his assistant Otto Pfungst. They found that the horse could give the correct answers only when the questioner knew the answer himself and when Hans could see the questioner. They concluded that Hans had no mathematical abilities and he could not read German. Instead, he was reading small body movements of the questioner, and these told him when he had tapped with his hoof the right number of times.

This tale of Clever Hans has been used ever since to justify the dismissal of unexplained abilities of animals, attributing them to 'subtle cues' rather than to any mysterious powers the animal may have. In short, this story has been used to inhibit research, to prevent enquiry, rather than to stimulate it. But to draw this moral from the tale of Clever Hans does not do justice to the investigations of Stumpf and Pfungst. They investigated a controversial claim, rather than dismissing it, and they were brave to do so, because their conclusions went against the beliefs of many of their colleagues.

Clever Hans's abilities were controversial not because they were supposed to involve psychic powers, but rather because they were supposed to show that animals could think. Many scientists, especially Darwinians, were happy to believe that Clever Hans really could carry out arithmetic and understand German. They liked the idea that animals were capable of rational thought because this undermined the conventional belief that the human intellect was unique. They preferred the idea of gradual evolution, of differences of degree between humans and non-human animals, rather than differences of kind.

Conversely, traditionalists were very sceptical about Clever Hans because they thought that higher mental faculties were confined to man. Stumpf and Pfungst's findings supported the traditionalists, and were unpopular with 'disappointed Darwinians who expressed fear lest ecclesiastical and reactionary points of view should derive favourable material from the conclusions'.[3]

Although biologists sometimes talk about the 'Clever Hans effect' as if it were a reason for dismissing any unexplained abilities in animals, the effect is quite specific. It depends on body language, which in horses is an important element in their communication with each other, as it is in many other species. If an animal can respond to a human being when that person is out of sight, this is not an example of the Clever Hans effect, but requires some other explanation.

In the course of research on the unexplained powers of domestic animals, I have found that most animal trainers and pet owners are well aware of the importance of body language. But in any case, many of the phenomena I discuss here, such as the apparent ability of animals to know when their owners are coming home, cannot be explained in terms of the Clever Hans effect. An animal cannot read the body language of a person many miles away.

Three kinds of unexplained perceptiveness

In this book, I discuss three major categories of unexplained perceptiveness by animals, namely telepathy; the sense of direction; and premonitions.

1. *Telepathy.* I start with the ability of some dogs and other animals to know when their owners are coming home. In many cases the animals' anticipations of people's returns cannot be explained in terms of routine, clues from people at home, or hearing familiar cars approaching. In videotaped experiments, dogs can still anticipate their owners' returns at randomly chosen times, even when they are travelling in taxis or other unfamiliar vehicles. Somehow people telepathically communicate their intentions to return home.

Some companion animals also respond telepathically to a variety of other human intentions, and react to silent calls and commands. Some know when a particular person is on the telephone. Some react when their owner is in distress or dying in a distant place.

I suggest that telepathic communication depends on bonds between people and animals that are not mere metaphors, but actual connections. They are connected through fields, called morphic fields. I introduce these fields in Chapter 1, in which I also discuss the evolution of the bonds between humans and animals.

2. *The sense of direction.* Homing pigeons can find their way back to their loft over hundreds of miles of unfamiliar terrain. Migrating European swallows travel thousands of miles to their feeding grounds in Africa, and in the spring return to their native place, even to the very same building where they nested before. Their ability to navigate towards distant destinations is still unexplained and cannot be accounted for in terms of smell, or any of the other known senses, or even a compass sense.

Some dogs, cats, horses and other domesticated animals also have a good sense of direction and find their way home from unfamiliar places many miles away. Animals seem to be drawn towards their desired destination as if by an invisible elastic band that attaches them to that place. These connections may be explained in terms of morphic fields.

Sometimes animals 'home' not to places but to people. Some dog owners who have gone away and left their pet behind are found by the animal in distant places to which the animal has never been before. Tracking the person by smell may explain some cases when the distances are short, but in others the only feasible explanation seems to be an invisible connection between the animal and the person to whom they are bonded. Again, this could be compared to a stretched elastic band, which I attribute to the morphic field linking animal to owner.

3. *Premonitions*. Some premonitions may be explicable in terms of physical stimuli: for example, animals that become disturbed before earthquakes may be reacting to subtle electrical changes, or dogs that alert their epileptic owners to an impending fit may notice subtle muscular tremors or unusual odours. But other premonitions seem to involve mysterious forebodings that challenge our usual assumptions about the separation of past, present and future.

Telepathy, the senses of direction and precognition are examples of what some people call extrasensory perception or ESP. Others attribute them to a 'sixth sense' (or 'seventh sense', or at any rate, an additional sense or senses). Others call them 'paranormal'. Others call them 'psychic'. All these terms agree in pointing beyond the limits of established science.

'Extrasensory perception' literally means perception beyond or outside the senses. At first sight the term 'sixth sense' appears to mean the opposite, because it implies a perceptiveness within the senses, although by another kind of sense not yet recognized by science. This conflict vanishes if 'extrasensory' is taken to mean 'outside the *known* senses'.

Neither the term 'extrasensory perception' nor the term 'sixth sense' suggest what these phenomena are, or how they work. They merely tell us what they are not. They are not explicable in terms of the known senses.

All three types of perceptiveness – telepathy, the sense of direction and premonitions – seem better developed in non-human species like dogs than they are in people. Nevertheless they occur in the human realm too. Human psychic powers or 'sixth senses' seem more natural, more biological, when they are seen in the light of animal behaviour. Much that appears 'paranormal' at present looks normal when we expand our ideas of normality.

Science can advance only by going beyond its current limits. In this book, I hope to show that it is possible to investigate animals' unexplained abilities scientifically in ways that are neither invasive nor cruel. I also suggest a variety of ways in which animal owners and students could make major contributions to this new field of enquiry.

We have a great deal to learn from our companion animals. They have much to teach us about animal nature – and about our own.

PART I

Human-animal bonds

1

The domestication
of animals

Bonds with animals

Many people love their pets and are loved by them. They develop strong emotional attachments. In this chapter I explore the evolution and the nature of such human-animal bonds.

But first it is important to recognize that emotional bonds between people and animals are the exception rather than the rule. For every well-loved cat or dog, there are hundreds of domesticated animals confined to barren environments in intensive farming systems and research laboratories. In many third world countries, beasts of burden are often treated brutally, with humans as the brutes. And traditional societies are not usually subscribers to modern ideals of animal welfare. Eskimos, for example, tend to treat their huskies harshly.

Then there are the animals who are victims of thoughtless neglect and deliberate cruelty. Throughout the industrialized world, organizations for the prevention of cruelty to animals continually uncover and publicize appalling sufferings of animals at human hands: horses with ribs showing through their emaciated skin; dogs tethered and neglected; cats tortured. And many animals are simply abandoned. In the United States alone about five million unwanted dogs and a similar number of cats are put down every year by local authorities or by voluntary organizations.[1]

But in spite of all this exploitation, abuse and neglect, many people form bonds with animals from childhood onwards. Young children are commonly given teddy bears or other toy animals, and like hearing stories about animals. Above all, most like keeping actual animals. The majority of pets live in households with children.[2]

Hearing tales about frightening animals – including fairy tales like Little Red Riding Hood – and forming relationships with friendly ones seems to be a normal and fundamental aspect of human nature. Indeed our nature has been shaped throughout its evolutionary history by our interactions with animals, and all human cultures are enriched by songs, dances, rituals, myths and stories about them.

The evolution of human-animal bonds

The earliest named hominid species, known from fossil remains, are *Australopithecus ramidus*, and *Australopithecus anamensis*, dating back over four million years. The first stone tools were used about two and a half million years ago, and signs of meat eating appear about a million years later, around the time that *Homo erectus* spread out of Africa into Eurasia (Figure 1.1). The use of fire may have begun around 700,000 years ago. Modern humans originated in Africa about 150,000 years ago. The first art, cave paintings, including many of animals, appeared about 30,000 years ago. The agricultural revolution began about 10,000 years ago, and the first civilizations and written scripts about 5,000 years ago.[3]

Our ancestors lived as gatherers and hunters, with gathering far more important than hunting. The old image of Man the Hunter striding confidently out on to the African savannah turns out to be a myth. Even among existing hunter-gatherers only a small proportion of the food they eat comes from animals hunted by the men; most comes from gathering, mainly by women. (The exceptions are the hunter-gatherers of the plant-poor Arctic regions.[4]) Hominids and early *Homo sapiens* generally obtained what meat they did by scavenging the kills left by more effective predators like big cats rather than by hunting for themselves.[5] Big-game hunting, as opposed to scavenging, may date back only some 70,000 to 90,000 years.

In hunter-gatherer cultures, human beings do not see themselves as separate from the realm of other animals, but as intimately interconnected.[6] The specialists in communication with the non-human world are shamans, and through their guardian spirits or power animals, shamans connect themselves with the powers of animals. There is a mysterious solidarity between people and animals. Shamans experience themselves as being guided by animals, or changing into animals, understanding their language, and sharing in their prescience and occult powers.[7]

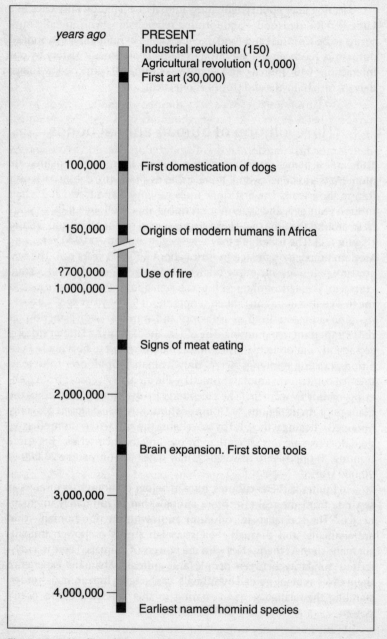

Figure 1.1 A time line of human evolution.

The domestication of dogs

The first animals to be domesticated were dogs. Their ancestors, wolves, hunted in packs as men hunted, and from an early stage dogs were used in hunting, as well as for guarding human settlements. Their domestication predated the development of agriculture.[8]

The conventional view is that the first domestication of wolves occurred between ten and twenty thousand years ago. But recent evidence from the study of DNA in dogs and wolves points to a far earlier date for the first transformation of wolf to dog, over 100,000 years ago. This new evidence also suggests that wolves were domesticated several times, not just once, and that dogs have continued to crossbreed with wild wolves.[9]

If this discovery is confirmed, it means that our ancient companionship with dogs may have played an important part in human evolution. Dogs could have played a major role in the advances in human hunting techniques that occurred some 70,000 to 90,000 years ago. The Australian veterinarian David Paxton goes so far as to suggest that people did not so much domesticate wolves as wolves domesticated people. Wolves may have started living around the periphery of human settlements as a kind of infestation. Some learned to live with human beings in a mutually helpful way and gradually evolved into dogs. At the very least, they would have protected human settlements, and given warnings by barking at anything approaching.[10]

The wolves that became dogs have been enormously successful in evolutionary terms. They are to be found everywhere in the inhabited world, hundreds of millions of them. The descendants of the wolves that remained wolves are now sparsely distributed, often in endangered populations.

The domestication of dogs long predated the domestication of other animals. Indeed dogs may have played an essential part in the domestication of other species, both through their ability to herd animals such as sheep, and by helping to protect flocks against predators.

Some breeds of dog are very old. By the time of ancient Egypt, there were already several distinct breeds: dogs of the greyhound or Saluki type, a mastiff type, a basenji type, a pointer type, and a small terrier-like Maltese type (Figure 1.2).[11] Dogs were venerated in ancient Egypt. Some were even embalmed, and in every town a graveyard was devoted entirely to dog burials. The god of the dead was the dog- or jackal-headed Anubis.

In the modern-day world, there are great variations from culture to culture in the way that dogs are treated. In the Arab world, they are

Figure 1.2 Breeds of Egyptian dogs, from the tombs at Beni Hassan (2200-2000 BC) (after Ash, 1927).

generally abhorred, partly because of the existence of large populations of stray or feral dogs, a source of dangerous diseases such as rabies. Even so, individual hunting dogs are admired and pampered. In other parts of the world, as in parts of Burma, Indonesia and Polynesia, dogs are slaughtered for human food, and are not usually well regarded.[12] But in most cultures, especially where dogs are used for hunting or herding, or kept for no utilitarian reason, they are generally treated affectionately.[13]

The domestication of other species

Francis Galton, Charles Darwin's cousin, was a pioneer of modern thinking about domestication. He pointed out that relatively few species were suitable. Species capable of being domesticated had to meet the following conditions:

They should be hardy, and survive with little care and attention. They should have an inherent liking for man. They should be comfort-loving. They should be useful. They should breed freely. They should be gregarious, and hence easy to control in groups.

Sheep, goats, cattle, horses, pigs, hens, ducks and geese all meet these criteria. But other species, such as deer and zebra, although gregarious, do not, and despite many attempts at domestication they remain too 'wild' to manage with ease.[14]

Cats are the only domesticated species that are not gregarious, but through their territorial and comfort-loving natures form symbiotic relationships with people while preserving something of their independence as solitary hunters. They revert with relative ease to a free-living, feral existence.[15]

Cats were domesticated far more recently than dogs, probably no more than five thousand years ago. The first records of cats are from ancient Egypt, where they were treated as sacred, and it was forbidden to kill them. They were mummified in such enormous numbers that at the beginning of the twentieth century cat mummies were excavated by the ton, ground up and sold as fertilizer.[16]

Horses were also domesticated relatively recently, probably about five thousand years ago in the region around Turkestan. They may first have been used as draught animals. The first record of a horse being ridden is from Egypt, around 1500 BC.[17] Horses soon became important in war and in hunting, when they were more like comrades than slaves.

In early civilizations, although domesticated animals were exploited for human use, there was still a pervasive sense of human-animal connectedness. Several animals were regarded as sacred, just as cows, elephants and monkeys still are in India today. Many of the gods and goddesses took animal forms or had animal helpers.

At first sight, there is little trace of this sense of solidarity with the animal kingdom in industrial societies. Beasts of burden have been replaced by machines; horses, donkeys, mules and bullocks are no longer our daily companions. The intimate familiarity with animals of the peasant has been replaced by modern agribusiness, with animals kept in factory farms and industrial-scale feed lots.

Nevertheless, in our private lives, the ancient affinity with other animals remains. There are many amateur birdwatchers, naturalists and wildlife photographers. Wildlife films are perennial favourites on television, as are stories about animals, especially about dogs like Lassie[18] and the Austrian detective dog, Kommisar Rex. But it is principally and most intimately through the keeping of pets that these bonds are maintained. Even though most people in modern cities no longer need cats for mousing, nor dogs for herding or hunting, these animals are still kept in their millions, together with a host of other creatures that play no utilitarian role: ponies, parrots, budgerigars, rabbits, guinea pigs, gerbils, hamsters, goldfish, lizards, stick insects and many other kinds of pet.

Most of us seem to need animals as part of our lives; our human nature is bound up with animal nature. Isolated from it, we are diminished. We lose a part of our heritage.

The keeping of pets

All over the world people keep pets. As Francis Galton noted in 1865: 'It is a fact familiar to all travellers, that savages frequently capture young animals of various kinds, and rear them as favourites, and sell or present them as curiosities.'[19]

Galton suggested that this kind of pet-keeping was the principal way in which many species had first been tamed, together with the keeping of sacred animals and the maintaining of menageries by chiefs and kings. In some cases, these animals then became domesticated, if they met the necessary conditions (summarized above). I like Galton's suggestion that pet-keeping preceded domestication, and find it very plausible. And if wolves first became human camp-followers and then turned into dogs, Galton's theory suggests a simple way in which this process could have been speeded up, through people adopting cubs or puppies as pets.

In ancient Egypt, and in many other parts of the world, as well as the larger dogs used for hunting, guarding and herding, there were also smaller breeds that seem to have lived in houses as pets. Ancient Greeks and Romans also kept them (Figure 1.3). Indeed, small dogs were found all over the ancient world, and are the ancestors of many pet dogs of today. In Tibet and China it was customary to keep both guard dogs and house dogs; guard dogs were big and fierce and lived outside, while the small dogs lived indoors, in houses and monasteries. [20]

Pet-keeping, as opposed to the keeping of animals for utilitarian reasons, was something of a luxury. Far more people are affluent now, and more keep pets. And pets living indoors, as companions, often become more intimately connected to their human family than animals living outside in a farmyard, barn or kennel. In industrialized countries like France, Britain and the United States, the majority of households contain at least one companion animal. And over recent decades, as urbanization and prosperity have increased, more rather than fewer households have kept pets. In the United Kingdom, for example, between 1965 and 1990 the total number of dogs rose from 4.7 to 7.4 million, and of cats from 4.1 to 6.9 million.

The animal-keeping habits of different nations probably play a large part in the forming of 'national character'. But this is an area where there has been almost no research; there are only bare statistics. Figures for dog

Figure 1.3 Small pet dogs in ancient Greece (after Keller, 1913).

and cat ownership in a range of countries are shown in Table 1. The highest percentages of households with dogs are in Poland and the United States, with France, Belgium and Ireland next. Some of the lowest levels of dog and cat ownership are in Germany. In most countries, more households contain dogs than cats, but in some, notably Switzerland and Austria, there is a striking predominance of cats over dogs as the favourite household animal.

In recent years, there have been some striking changes in the pattern of pet ownership. In the United Kingdom, the number of dogs declined, while the number of cats continued to increase (Figure 1.4). Since 1992, there have been more cats than dogs altogether, but there are still more *households* with dogs than cats, because many cat-owning households have two or more cats. A similar increase in the popularity of cats relative to dogs has also occurred in the United States, and by 1996 cats had over-

Table 1 Percentages of households owning dogs and cats in different countries (after Fogle, 1994).

	Percentage of households with:	
	dogs	cats
Poland	50	33
United States	38	30
France	36	25
Belgium	36	25
Ireland	36	20
Canada	32	24
Portugal	30	14
Czech Republic	30	16
United Kingdom	27	21
Denmark	23	17
Netherlands	22	24
Italy	20	22
Finland	20	18
Norway	17	18
Sweden	16	19
Spain	16	8
Austria	15	26
Japan	12	5
Germany	11	9
Switzerland	10	26
Greece	10	7

taken dogs as the most numerous pets, with populations of 59 and 53 million respectively. But, as in the UK, there are still more households with dogs than with cats.[21]

Social bonds between animals

Most domesticated animals were originally social, as Francis Galton pointed out. They also tend to be animals with dominance hierarchies, which made it easier for human beings to control them. Even cats, although independent and solitary in their hunting habits, grow up with close social relationships between mothers and their offspring.

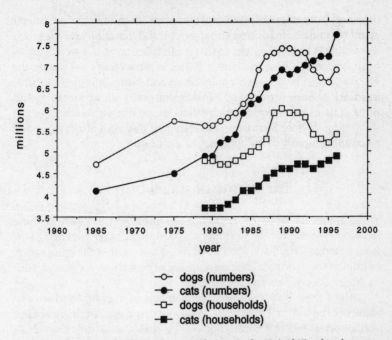

Figure 1.4 Changes in the dog and cat populations in the United Kingdom between 1965 and 1997 (source: UK Pet Food Manufacturers' Association).

The original social nature of domesticated animals reveals itself when they run wild. Charles Darwin, in his *Variation of Animals and Plants Under Domestication*, was particularly interested in this reversion of domesticated animals to their ancestral habits.[22]

In general, feral animals live in groups similar to those of their wild progenitors. Feral horses, for example, usually live in groups of around five, and so do their wild relatives.[23] Feral dogs live in packs and build dens, as do wolves.[24]

Social animals are linked to other members of the group through invisible bonds. The same is true of human social bonds. Our domesticated animals are by nature social, and so are we. The bonds between people and animals are a sort of hybrid between the kinds of bonds that animals form with each other and those that people form with each other.

One difficulty in understanding the nature of these animal-human bonds is that we understand so little of human-human and animal-animal bonds. We know that invisible emotional connections exist between members of a family and we know that these can persist over time and keep people linked together even when they are continents apart. We know animals have social groups, and that somehow the group as a whole is linked together so that it can function as if it were a super-organism, as I discuss in Chapter 9. This is most clearly the case in the social insects, like the ants, termites, bees and wasps. It is plainly visible in a flock of birds turning and banking practically simultaneously, with none of them bumping into each other. And so it is with a school of fish swimming in close formation, but changing direction at any time, and responding rapidly to the approach of a predator.

The nature of social bonds

There are many kinds of social bonds within species, such as those between a mother cat and her kittens, a bee and the other members of the hive, a starling in a flock, a wolf and its pack, as well as the great variety of human social bonds. Then there are social bonds *between* species, such as those between pets and their owners.

All of these bonds connect the members of a group together, and influence the way that they relate. I propose that these bonds are not just metaphorical but real connections. They continue to link individuals together even when they are separated, beyond the range of sensory communication. These connections at a distance could be channels for telepathy.

Bonds between animals exist within a *social field*. Like the known fields of physics, social fields connect things at a distance, but they differ from the known fields of physics in that they evolve and contain a kind of memory. I have suggested in my book *The Presence of the Past* that social fields are an example of a class of fields called *morphic fields*. [25]

Morphic fields hold together and co-ordinate the parts of a system in space and time, and contain a memory from previous similar systems. Human social groups such as tribes and families inherit through their morphic fields a kind of collective memory. The habits, beliefs and customs of the ancestors influence the behaviour of the present, both consciously and unconsciously. We all tune into collective memories, similar to the 'collective unconscious' proposed by the psychologist C.G. Jung.

Termite colonies, schools of fish, flocks of birds, herds, packs and other animal groups are also held together and structured by morphic fields, and these fields are all shaped by their own kinds of collective memory.

Individual animals are linked together through the social fields of their group, and follow habitual patterns of relationships, repeated over

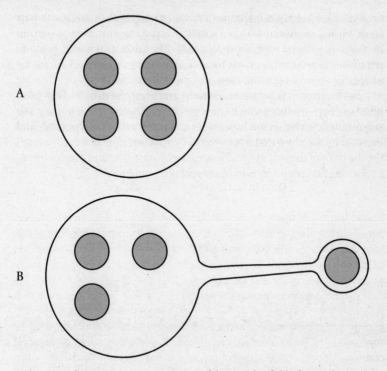

Figure 1.5 A diagrammatic representation of the morphic field of a social group (A), illustrating the way the field stretches out and still connects an individual with other members of the group when they are far apart (B).

the generations. Instincts are like collective habits of the species, or of the breed, shaped by experience through many generations, and subjected to the rigours of natural selection. This view of instincts as the inherited effects of habit and experience is close to the thinking of Charles Darwin, most clearly expressed in his *Variation of Animals and Plants Under Domestication*, and of central importance in *The Origin of Species*. [26]

The process by which this memory is transferred from past to present is called *morphic resonance*, involving an influence of like upon like across space and time.[27] I discuss the nature of morphic fields and morphic resonance in more detail in Chapter 9 and in Appendix C.

Morphic fields link together the members of a social group, and the field embraces all the members of the group within itself (Figure 1.5A). If a member of the group goes to a distant place, it still remains connected to the rest of the group through this social field, which is elastic (Figure 1.5B).

Morphic fields would permit a range of telepathic influences to pass from animal to animal within a social group, or from person to person, or from person to companion animal. The ability of these fields to stretch out like invisible elastic bands enables them to act as channels for telepathic communication, even over great distances.[28]

At this stage, it is not necessary to try and grasp the details of the morphic field hypothesis, of which I have given only the briefest summary. The important point is that this hypothesis makes telepathy seem possible and even likely. But given that it is *theoretically* possible, does it actually occur? On the basis of the available evidence, discussed in the following chapters, I conclude that telepathy is indeed a real phenomenon.

PART II

Animals that know when their people are returning

2
Dogs

The strongest evidence for telepathy between people and animals comes from the study of dogs that know when their owners are coming home. This anticipatory behaviour is common. Many dog owners simply take it for granted, without reflecting on its wider implications.

When Peter Edwards arrives home at his farm in Wickford, Essex, his Irish setters are nearly always at the gate to greet him. Yvette, his wife, says that they often wait for him 10–20 minutes before he arrives, and well before he turns off the road into his drive. She had taken this behaviour for granted for more than 20 years, simply thinking, 'Peter's coming home, the dogs have gone to the gate.'

Yet after reading in the *Sunday Telegraph* about my research on dogs who know when their owners are coming home, Yvette began to wonder. How do the setters know Peter is coming? He works irregular hours in London and does not usually let her know when to expect him. And the dogs respond regardless of which way the wind is blowing or what vehicle he returns in.

The Irish setters' ability to detect Peter's return in advance is typical of many other dogs. In response to queries in Europe and North America, I have collected over 580 reports of dogs that know when their owners are coming home. Some wait at a door or window ten minutes or more in advance of their owner's return from work, school, shopping, or other excursions. Others go out and meet their owners in the street or at a bus stop. Some dogs do this on an almost daily basis; others only when their owners are returning from a holiday or other protracted absence, sometimes showing signs of excitement hours or even days in advance of their return. While some scientists are quick to attribute this phenomenon to routine or the canine's sharp sense of smell and hearing, you will soon discover that in case after case no such simple explanations suffice.

The context for this anticipatory behaviour is the way that many dogs welcome their owners home with great enthusiasm. Unless they are well-disciplined they try to jump up and lick their owner's face, just as puppies greet their parents, with their tails wagging so vigorously that the whole hindquarters become part of the movement.

Wolf greetings are similar. When cubs are weaned, they start soliciting food from their returning parents or other members of the pack. When the adult approaches with food in its mouth, they crowd excitedly around, wag their tails, adopt gestures of submission and jump up to lick the corners of its mouth. In adult wolves, the same kinds of behaviour develop into ritualized greetings. Most attention is directed to the highest-ranking animals.[1]

Thus the greeting behaviour that dogs display towards their owners has a long evolutionary ancestry, going back to the wolves from which our domestic dogs are descended. But many dogs go further than greeting their owners on arrival by actually anticipating their arrivals, seeming to know when they are on the way home even when they are many miles away.

Could it be a matter of routine?

When people return at the same time every day, their dogs' behaviour could simply be a matter of routine. Teresa Preston, of Suffolk, Virginia, assumed this was the case when she noticed that the family dog, Jackson, waited for her children's arrival on the school bus each day. But she had to think again when she realized that Jackson also anticipated the return of her husband, who arrived at unexpected times from his job as Captain of a US Coast Guard buoy tender, stationed 20 miles away in Portsmouth:

> He would arrive home at odd hours. When the ship had come into port, Jackson would get excited, go to the door and want out. Most of the time he would go and sit at the end of the sidewalk, stationing himself to look in the direction he 'knew' the car would travel. He got so good at this, I couldn't help but notice, and sometimes would use Jackson's warning to freshen my hair and make-up before my husband arrived! If I was cooking dinner and was at the point of deciding how many portions to cook or places to set for the meal, I would use his prediction and add accordingly.

Or perhaps the dogs are picking up clues of anticipation from the person waiting at home. In some cases people telephone to say they are coming, and when a person at home knows they are on the way, his or her emotional state might change, giving the dog clues through body language or in other ways. But some dogs' anticipation occurs even when the person at home has no idea when their family member will be arriving. I have received numerous accounts from the families of lawyers, taxi drivers, military personnel, journalists, midwives and other people who do not work fixed hours, who say that it is the dog who tells *them* when their family member is on the way home.

John Batabyal of Stretford, Lancashire is one example. His wife Gloria worked in a hospital on 'flexi time' and often came home at unexpected times, and yet he always had a fresh pot of tea waiting for her. She was puzzled by this until she discovered that at the exact time she left the ward to drive home, both dogs would jump up and sit in the window bay, indicating to her husband that it was time to put the kettle on.

In Manhattan, the West family's Irish nanny benefited from a similar canine early warning system, provided by a blue terrier named Kerry. General Charles West was stationed on Governor's Island in New York Harbour, and his wife worked as a vice president at Time Inc. In General West's words:

> We lived on the fourth floor of an apartment block, and each of us arrived home at varying times from varying directions. Neither the nanny nor our small son knew when we were coming home, but 10 to 15 minutes before our arrival, Kerry would get greatly excited, run to a front window and stand looking into the street, whining joyously, with her tail going like mad. Nanny always knew that one of us was about to arrive, and she always laughed that it was a great warning to clean up the child before the parent got there. And this was not an occasional happening. It went on day after day, week after week for years.

No doubt some dogs are accustomed to waiting for the return of their owner at routine times, but most people do not regard this as particularly remarkable. In most of the 585 reports I have collected, as in these examples, the dog's behaviour is not explicable simply in terms of routine.

Could dogs smell their owners approaching?

Most dogs have a much better sense of smell than we do, and it is likely that they could smell their owners, or their owners' vehicles, from further away than a person could. But just how far?

Dogs normally use their sense of smell for tracking, sniffing the ground and following trails. But to smell someone returning home, they would have to sniff the air. Assuming that the wind is blowing in the right direction and that they are outdoors, or indoors with the windows open, over what range might they be able to smell an approaching person or car?

The best estimates I have been able to obtain suggest that this distance is considerably less than a mile, even with the most sensitive of all breeds, the bloodhound. Malcolm Fish, of the Essex Police Dog Section, is currently conducting trials of bloodhounds for the Home Office to find out if they would be more suitable for some kinds of police work than German shepherds, currently the standard breed. He says that if somebody is hiding in a hedge, a bloodhound up to half a mile down-wind can sometimes pick up the scent of that person, but only if the wind is blowing in the right direction and if the person is stationary. He thinks it highly unlikely that a dog, even a bloodhound, could smell someone travelling home from work. 'If you imagine someone in their car travelling home with a smoke canister, with the windows open and the smoke blowing out, it would blow behind. Scent does not travel forward like sound. Nowadays most cars are sealed too, so there would not be much scent leaving the car, and doors of houses are sealed to keep the draught out, so I think it would be impossible for a dog to smell their owner when they are half a mile away.'

Some dogs react only a minute or two before their owner arrives, and in such cases smell might help explain it. But many react ten minutes or more in advance, when the person is several miles away. Moreover, they do so irrespective of the wind direction, and can still do it when the windows are shut. Their anticipation cannot reasonably be explained in terms of smell.

Could dogs hear their owners approaching?

Most dogs have sharper hearing than we do. They can hear sounds too high-pitched for us to detect, as in 'silent' dog whistles, which emit sounds above the frequency range we can hear. They may also hear sounds further away. One rough estimate is that 'a dog can hear sounds four times further away than a human can'.[2] But this may be unduly generous to dogs. Celia Cox, a British vet who specializes in ear, nose and throat surgery, has tested the hearing of thousands of dogs, and estimates that their sensitivity to noise levels is similar to that of people. She doubts that they can hear their owners approaching from very far away: 'People have told me that their dogs know when they are coming home even before they have turned into their road, but I think it is highly unlikely that this is purely due to hearing.'

Likewise, Kevin Munro of the Hearing and Balance Centre at the University of Southampton has compared the hearing abilities of people and dogs using a sophisticated technique called Evoked Response Audiometry.[3] He was expecting to find that dogs hear much better than people, because this is such a common belief. 'When I got the results I was very surprised that their hearing, apart from being able to hear higher-pitched sounds, was in every other way similar.'

But for the purpose of argument, let us assume that dogs really can hear things about four times as far away as people. If a familiar car or person on foot is approaching your house, how far away do you hear them?

I live in London, and with all the background noise and many passing cars and people, I probably hear familiar cars or people approaching my home less than 20 yards away, and even then only when I am in one of the rooms at the front of the house with the windows open. By contrast, people in isolated parts of the countryside with little or no passing traffic might hear an approaching vehicle more than half a mile away, especially at night. But I estimate that in most urban and suburban settings, most people would not be able to recognize the sounds of a familiar car or person more than a few hundred yards away, and generally much less than that. You can make your own estimate. And then you can test it, with the help of your family and friends. Can you really detect when a particular car or person is approaching when they are that distance away?

Multiply your estimate by four. Then you have a rough indication of how far away a dog could hear its owner's return on the most generous of assumptions. My guess would be that in urban and suburban settings this distance would be less than half a mile, even under the most favourable conditions, with the wind blowing in the right direction. With the wind blowing in other directions, the range would be much smaller. It would be smaller still if the dog was indoors with the windows closed.

All this assumes that the person is travelling on foot, or in a familiar car, but what if the person is travelling in a taxi, a friend's car, or any other vehicle with which the dog is unfamiliar? In spite of the lack of familiar sounds to recognize, many owners have found that the dogs' anticipation still occurs.

For example, when Louise Gavit of Morrow, Georgia, sets off to come home, the family dog, BJ, goes to the door. Her husband has noticed BJ do this over and over again, and by keeping note of the time, they have found that BJ's reactions usually begin when she first decides to come home and starts walking towards whatever vehicle she plans to return home in, even when she is many miles away. 'My method of travel is irregular: using my own car, my husband's car, a truck, or any number of cars driven by strangers to BJ, or walking. Somehow BJ responds to my thought/action just the same. Even when he has seen my car still inside the garage he reacts.'

Returns by bus, train and plane

The idea that dogs' reactions might be explained in terms of distant car sounds is also refuted by the fact that dogs can react in the same way to owners who are travelling by bus or train. Of course, if they always come on the same bus, such as a school bus, the animal might recognize characteristic sounds soon before the vehicle arrived. But when people travel at different times on bus or train services, there is no way that the animal could tell whether their owner was on a particular bus or train from its sound.

Helen Meither, for example, commuted 15 miles by bus to work in Liverpool each day, leaving her Cairn terrier with her family. Depending on when she finished her work, she either came home on a bus that arrived at 6 pm or on one that arrived at 8 pm. 'The bus stop was about quarter of a mile away through a small wood. I never knew whether I would finish work in time to catch the earlier bus but the dog always knew whether I was on it. If I was, he went to the door about 5.45 to 5.50 pm, whatever the weather, and came across the wood to meet me. If I was late he did not stir until about 7.45 and met me at the later bus.'

On the database there are over 60 accounts of animals reacting to people's arrivals by bus that show that the animal somehow knows when the person is coming home in a way that cannot be explained in terms of routine, sounds or smells. The same is true of over 50 cases involving travel by train. Here is one example:

Carole Bartlett of Chiselhurst, Kent, leaves Sam, her Labrador-greyhound cross, at home with her husband when she goes to the theatre or visits friends in London. She returns by train from Charing Cross station, a 25-minute train journey followed by a five-minute walk. Mr Bartlett does not know on which train she will return, which could be any time from 6 to 11 pm. 'My husband says Sam comes downstairs off my bed, where he spends the day when I go out, half an hour before my return and waits at the front door.' In other words, the dog begins waiting for her around the time she is starting her train journey.

In some cases, the absent person tells the person at home that he or she will take one particular train, then in fact takes another. This happened when Sheila Brown of Westbury, Wiltshire, went to London for a wedding and left her dog Tina with a neighbour, telling her that she would be returning on a train arriving at 10.30 pm. In fact she returned five hours early, and was surprised to find some tea waiting for her. Tina had suddenly jumped up and gone to the door and sat there wagging her tail. The neighbour knew that Tina often anticipated Sheila's returns, and rightly concluded that she had an earlier train.

Perhaps even more remarkable than dogs that know when their owners are coming home by train or bus are those that know in advance when they will arrive by plane. There are many stories of this kind from World War II, when some pilots were allowed to keep their dogs at aerodromes. For example, Squadron Commander Max Aitken (later Lord Beaverbrook) kept his Labrador at the base of No. 68 Squadron. Edward Wolfe, who served under him, told me: 'When the squadron was returning in ones and twos from an operation, his black Labrador who would be sitting quietly in the mess would get up and rush outside to meet his master. We always knew when Max Aitken was coming back.'

I received a very similar report of a dog reacting to an owner who was a pilot in a glider squadron, where the returning planes were almost silent.

In at least one case, the possibility that the dog could be reacting to the sound of a particular plane was put to the test. The dog in question was another Labrador, who reacted to the return of his owner, an officer in the RAF. 'He watched his master fly away in a plane, then settled down to wait. When the same plane returned, the dog didn't even get up. The men all thought the dog had failed his test. They were wrong and the dog was right. His master wasn't inside. Later on, a different plane approached from the opposite direction. He jumped up excitedly wagging his tail. His master had returned.' (J. Greany)

Anticipations by dogs belonging to airline staff are similarly impressive. A number of people who work for commercial airlines have found that their dogs know when they are coming home, even when no one else in the house does so. Elizabeth Bryan is one example:

> My whole working life has been as a cabin crew member working out of Gatwick Airport. For ten years my dog Rusty would jump around and bark at the same time I landed and then sit quietly watching the front door until I got home. The astonishing thing is there is no routine to my coming and goings – I could be gone one day or fourteen and no regular time of landing, yet he knew without fail.

Likewise, some people whose work takes them far away from home as passengers on planes have dogs that know when they are returning.

Ian Fraser Ker of Westcott, Surrey, first became aware of this phenomenon when he telephoned his wife on his arrival at Heathrow Airport. She told him she thought he would be coming because their dog, a boxer, was very excited. 'This developed so much that on days when my dog showed signs of excitement and would sit by the front door with his nose stuck as far into the letter-box as it would go, my wife would actually cook lunch for me and lo and behold I would phone from the airport and say I was home.'

In cases like these the dog could not possibly have recognized any familiar sounds or smells, or reacted to routines. And when people at home did not know when to expect the return, the dog could not have picked up its expectation from them. By a process of elimination, telepathy seems the most plausible explanation.

The alternative, as sceptics will hasten to point out, is that evidence based on pet owners' experiences cannot be trusted, either because of tricks of memory, or lying and deceit, or illusion and wishful thinking. Having talked to many pet owners about their experiences and interviewed members of their families, I have no reason to doubt that their accounts of the behaviour of their dogs are generally trustworthy. And, in the absence of any previous scientific investigations, these accounts are the only starting point we have if we want to explore this phenomenon.

It is right to maintain a sceptical attitude, and ask further questions, and realize that people can be mistaken. But some people dismiss all the evidence from dog owners' experience as a matter of principle. This kind of compulsive scepticism stems from the dogma that telepathy is impossible. In my opinion such prejudices are barriers to open-minded scientific enquiry. They are not scientific but anti-scientific. I am more interested in dogs than in dogmas.

Obviously, it is necessary to follow up the study of case histories of dogs' anticipatory behaviour with experimental investigations, as described later in this chapter. But first it is important to find out more about the natural history of dogs that know when their people are coming home. And since the evidence so far points to some kind of telepathic connection, we need to explore in more detail what the idea of telepathy might imply.

Different patterns of telepathic response

Telepathy literally means 'distant feeling', from two Greek roots *tele*, as in telephone and television, and *pathe*, as in sympathy and empathy. If dogs are responding telepathically to their owners, they must somehow be picking up their owners' thoughts or feelings about going home. There are three main ways this might happen:

1. Some dogs might react only when their owners are nearing home, and are of course aware of their own imminent arrival. Another way of expressing this might be to say that dogs feel their owners' approaching presence. The dogs might react, say, two minutes, or ten minutes before their owners' returns, irrespective of when they set off.

2. Some people when travelling homewards may be thinking or feeling very little about going home for much of their journey; they may be fully engaged in conversation or some other activity. But there come stages in journeys at which feelings and thoughts turn homewards with increased intensity: for example when getting off a plane at an airport, or disembarking from a ship, or leaving a train or bus. Some dogs might pick up homeward-bound thoughts and feelings at this stage.

3. The most extreme manifestation of telepathy would occur if dogs were able to pick up their owners' *intention* to return, and react when they are setting off, or even when they are getting ready to set off.

In fact all three types of anticipation are common. Some dogs anticipate their owners' returns only a few minutes in advance. Perhaps the animal could have heard or smelled them, and telepathy might have nothing to do with it. But when the dogs react more than five minutes in advance, the telepathic hypothesis needs to be taken seriously, especially if the dog still reacts when the windows are closed and its reactions do not depend on the wind direction, which would greatly influence the transmission of smells and sounds. And there are many cases where dogs regularly react ten minutes or more before a person comes home, irrespective of the wind direction. One example is Peter Edwards and his Irish setters. Other examples are dogs at aerodromes (discussed above) that reacted when their owner's plane was about to land, or dogs that go to meet their owners at bus stops, setting off when the bus is on the way.

Secondly, there are dogs that react when people get off boats, aeroplanes, trains and buses and start the final part of their homeward journey. We have already seen examples of dogs that react when crew members and passengers on commercial flights arrive at the airport; and there are many others that react when people get off boats, trains or buses.

Finally, there are dogs that seem to react to people's intentions to go home, even before they actually set off. Louise Gavit's dog BJ is one example (see p. 20 above). She has no regular schedule to her comings and goings. With the help of her husband observing BJ at home, she has found that the dog typically reacts as follows:

> As I leave the place I have been, and walk to my car with the intent to come home, our dog BJ awakens from sleep, moves to the door, lies down on the floor near the door, and points his nose toward the door. There he waits. As I near the drive he becomes more alert, and begins to pace and show excitement the nearer I move to home. He is always there to poke his nose through the crack, in greeting, as I open the door. This sensing seems to be unlimited by distance. He does not seem to respond at all to my leaving one place and moving to another, his response seems to become apparent at the time when I form the thought to return home, and take the action to walk toward my car to come home.

There is, of course, nothing new about this kind of behaviour, and it has been noticed and remarked upon for many years. In his well-known book *Kinship With All Life*, J. Allen Boone describes how the dog Strong-heart anticipated his return from lunch at his club in Los Angeles some 12 miles away. A friend looked after Strongheart while he was out. 'There was never any set time for my returning, but at the precise moment when I decided to leave the club and come home Strongheart would always quit whatever he happened to be doing, take himself to his favorite spot for observation, and patiently wait there for me to turn the bend in the road and head up the hill.' [4]

The same pattern of response has shown up in experiments. For example, Monika Sauer, who lives near Munich, Germany, carried out some tests at my request with her dog Pluto, whose reactions were observed by her partner. Pluto reacted not only when she set off to come home in her own car, but also when she set off in friends' cars with which he was unfamiliar. I then asked her to try coming home by taxi. When she did so, Pluto reacted 40 minutes before her arrival. The journey took 30 minutes. She telephoned for the taxi and was waiting for it for ten minutes before setting off. The dog reacted not when she got into the taxi, but when she ordered it.

Advance reactions of this kind are likely to go unnoticed unless people are paying close attention to the times at which they set off and the times at which the dogs react. Among those who do pay attention are Catherine and John O'Driscoll, whose golden retriever Samson is particularly sensitive to John's returns. For example, one day John was at the theatre in Northampton, England, when Samson dashed to the door excitedly, much longer before his return than it took to come home.

Catherine told me: 'I asked John what he was doing at the time, and he said he was looking at his watch wishing he could come home.' On another occasion when John was at a meeting: 'He was looking at this watch and closing his briefcase at the same time as Samson dashed to the door barking excitedly.'

There are many other examples of this kind. Out of the 585 accounts of dogs knowing when their owners are returning on the database, in 97 (17 per cent) they are said to react when the person sets off to come home, or is preparing to do so.

Perhaps some of the dogs who appear to react only a few minutes before a person arrives home do in fact know when their owner sets off, but show obvious signs of excitement only when the person is getting close. Earlier, more subtle responses may pass unnoticed.

Returning from holidays and long absences

Most of the examples I have discussed so far concern dogs that respond when their owners are returning from work or from fairly brief absences. Now I turn to dogs' responses to their owners' returns from longer absences, such as holidays. Some dogs do not anticipate their owners' arrivals when they have just gone out for the day, but they react when they have been away for longer periods, for example the Marchioness of Salisbury's dog Jessie, who lives with her at Hatfield House in Hertfordshire (Figure 2.1).

'Jessie is a very acute and intelligent little dog. She always seems to know what I'm going to do, almost before I do it myself,' Lady Salisbury says. When Lady Salisbury goes abroad, she usually leaves Jessie, a hunt terrier, with her Head Gardener, David Beaumont. He and his wife generally find out when Lady Salisbury is on her way because Jessie becomes restless and waits by the door or the gate of their house, hours before she arrives home. Jessie's behaviour has been documented by Miriam Rothschild, FRS, the distinguished naturalist, who has kindly passed on her observations to me. On one occasion, for example, Jessie's reactions began when Lady Salisbury was packing and preparing to leave a house in Ireland; on another when she was leaving for the airport in Cracow, Poland. Lady Salisbury says that the dog's mother was even more sensitive than Jessie to her homecomings and responded even if she was only away for a day. Jessie does not react unless she has been away for at least three days.

Sometimes the behaviour of the dog seems to be related to the thoughts and intentions of the person well in advance of their actually

Figure 2.1 The Marchioness of Salisbury with her hunt terrier Jessie, at Hatfield House, Hertfordshire (photograph: Phil Starling).

beginning the journey. This was the case with Frank Harrison, who was taken ill with a fever soon after he joined the British Army, and on his discharge from hospital was given a few days' sick leave. He did not inform his parents.

> When I arrived home Sandy (our Irish terrier) was by the door and I was told that he had not moved from the door for two days, except to be fed and exercised. This was about the time I had been told I was being given sick leave. His behaviour had naturally caused concern to my parents. When I unexpectedly arrived home my Mum said 'He knew you were coming. That explains it.' This waiting at the door happened throughout my two and a half years of service in the Army.

Sandy would move to the door about 48 hours before I came home. My parents knew I was coming because Sandy knew.

I have received over 20 other accounts of dogs anticipating the arrival of young men coming home on leave from the armed forces or the merchant navy, and in many cases the families were not informed in advance. Sometimes the dogs reacted one or two days before the young man arrived home, as Sandy did, and sometimes a few hours.

In so far as the anticipatory reactions of dogs depend on telepathy, their reactions when their owners setting off to come home from another continent imply that telepathic communication can occur over great distances. It does not seem to fall off with distance in the way that gravitational, electrical and magnetic phenomena do.

In some cases, the dog's anticipation can be pinpointed to a particular stage of preparing or setting off. Tony Harvey was returning to his farm in Suffolk from a three-week shooting holiday on Dartmoor, 250 miles away, having left Badger, a border terrier, with his wife at home. When he arrived, his wife told him that Badger had jumped up from his basket and up on to the windowsill at 6.40 am. 'This was exactly the time that I had started home from Dartmoor. This was not the time we started to load up, but the exact time that the lorry started along the road for home.' Badger was 'excited all day, standing on the window and looking up the yard', until his owner finally arrived at 9.30 pm.

As in the case of people returning from work, some dogs react when the person is nearing home, rather than at the beginning of their journey. For example, when Larry Collyer is on his way home to Glastonbury, Somerset, after absences of several days, his wife Daphne knows when he is about to return because their chow chow dog goes and waits at the door between half an hour and an hour beforehand. He has also done this when Mr Collyer has returned a day or two earlier than expected.

The people who have the most opportunity to observe the behaviour of dogs prior to the return of their owners from holidays or other journeys are those who work in kennels. I and my associates have interviewed kennel proprietors in both Britain and the United States, and have found that most have noticed that some dogs seem to know when they are about to go home. Typical comments included: 'Some get more alert when it is the day for them to go home.' 'There's an air of expectancy a few hours beforehand.' 'Some of the dogs do act differently on the day when they are going home.' However there was one kennel proprietor in eastern England who firmly denied that anything like this occurred at her establishment. 'Dogs are so happy here that they soon forget all about their owners, and have no interest in their return.' This was, however, an isolated opinion.

Perhaps some dogs in kennels behave differently because the kennel staff give them more attention when they are about to be picked up. But sometimes owners return unexpectedly early, and some dogs still seem to know. Sam Hyers of Rockford, Michigan, described one example as follows: 'A relatively calm dog (lays about most of the time) stood by the door for three hours. I took it out several times but it did not need to relieve itself and then his owner drove in two days early. I had no idea that the owners would be early.'

The bonds between dog and person

Most people whose dogs anticipate their arrival feel that they have a 'close bond', 'strong emotional connection' or are 'very attached' to the dog. In the majority of the cases on our database, 78 per cent, the dogs respond only to one person; 17 per cent respond to two people; and only 5 per cent to three or more. When dogs respond to more than one person, these are usually members of the family. Almost the only other people whose arrival dogs anticipate are friends whom they are particularly fond of, or people who take them for walks or bring them treats.

The only exceptions are cases in which the dog has a strong aversion to a particular person. John Ashton, for example, had a friend who disliked dogs who used to visit him at his home in Lancashire about once a week. At first his Alsatian, Rolf, usually a good-natured dog, showed no unusual behaviour. 'After a few months, my friend Clive visited me one night and about ten minutes before he arrived, Rolf was at my garage waiting and growling and had to be restrained when Clive got there. I can only assume that Clive had smacked or kicked him away on his previous visit. After this night, I always had to go to the garage and meet Clive and restrain Rolf. He always knew ten to fifteen minutes before Clive's time of arrival.'

In one very interesting case, the dog, a springer spaniel, reacted differently depending on the intention with which the person was visiting. The visitor was Christopher Day, a vet in Oxfordshire, and the dog belonged to his mother-in-law:

> The dog used to know whether I was visiting socially or whether I was visiting as a vet. She would be all over me and whooping with delight if I was visiting socially, but if I visited as a vet she was hiding behind the boiler. There was nothing I could see which would give her a clue that I was visiting as a vet, and anyway she would have made the deci-

sion to hide before I came into the house. She got it right every time. I used to visit quite often, pop in and do all sorts of things, although as a vet I'd visit very rarely. And I didn't just visit as a vet because the dog was ill, sometimes it could be routine things. But the dog knew when I was on duty and when I wasn't.

Thus the ability of dogs to know when people are coming depends on emotional bonds, usually positive but sometimes negative, and can be influenced by the intention with which they are coming. But generally speaking, it depends on affectionate relationships with the dogs' immediate human companions, and with visiting members of the family and close friends.

It is of course well known that dogs can form strong bonds with people. James Serpell, who pioneered the study of human-dog relationships at Cambridge University, expressed it as follows: 'The average dog behaves as if literally "attached" to its owner by an invisible cord. Given the opportunity, it will follow him everywhere, sit or lie down beside him, and exhibit clear signs of distress if the owner goes out and leaves it behind, or shuts it out of the room unexpectedly.'[5]

I think that the evidence considered in this and the following chapters suggests that the invisible cord attaching dog to owner is elastic: it can stretch and contract (Figure 1.5B). It connects dog and owner together when they are nearby. And it continues to attach dog to owner even when they are hundreds of miles apart. Through this elastic connection telepathic communication takes place.

Telepathy or precognition?

Many pet owners whose animals know when a member of the family is coming home ascribe it either to telepathy or else to a 'sixth sense', or to ESP (extrasensory perception).

The term telepathy implies that the dog is reacting to the thoughts, feelings, emotions or intentions of a distant person. But the terms 'sixth sense' and ESP are more general, and as well as covering telepathy, are often used in connection with a variety of other unexplained phenomena, including the ability to anticipate danger and the ability to find the way home. And some of the phenomena ascribed to the 'sixth sense' or ESP seem to include precognition, knowing beforehand about future events.

Could it be that dogs know when their owners are coming home because of a precognition of the actual arrival, rather than picking up the thoughts or intentions of their owners?

Perhaps in some cases this is so. But telepathy seems to me a more likely explanation when dogs respond at the time their owners are setting off, or when they are simply intending to set off, before they have actually done so. It also seems a more likely explanation for the responses of animals when their people reach a crucial stage in their journey home, such as disembarking from a plane, boat, train or bus.

One way of teasing apart the possible roles of telepathy and precognition is to look at what happens when people change their minds. If they set off homewards and then their journey is interrupted, what happens? If the animal's response is precognitive, and takes place on the basis of foreseeing the arrival, then it should not react when a person's journey is aborted. If it is responding telepathically, then it should react to the intention to come home, even if the person does not arrive. So what actually happens?

What happens when people change their minds?

One of the first examples I came across of a dog's reactions when someone changed their mind was told to me by Radboud Spruit of Utrecht University, Holland. He was living quite near his parents, about a six-minute drive away, and used to visit them several times a week at irregular times. His mother noticed that the dog usually waited for him at the garden gate about ten minutes in advance, starting to wait a few minutes before he actually began his journey. 'One day my mother called me and asked if I had planned to visit them the day before, because the dog waited for me. I had planned to visit them, but I changed my mind on the way. It was at the same time that our dog was waiting for me. My mother told me the dog got confused after 15 minutes when I didn't arrive. It ran into the house and after some minutes it ran again to the gate. After about half an hour it looked as if the dog had forgotten about it.'

In some cases, the people with the dog are able to tell precisely when the dog's owner set off and when they changed their mind. For example, when Michael Joyce was looking after his sister-in-law's dog while she and his wife went shopping in Colchester, Essex, 14 miles away, he noticed that at 16.45 hours it got up, walked to the window and sat there. 'Just a few minutes later it resumed its former position, sprawled out on the carpet. Then at about 17.15 hours, half an hour later, it became excited and anxious again and remained near the window, waiting/anticipating their arrival. When my wife and sister-in-law arrived I said, "You decided to leave Colchester at about 16.45, changed your minds, and later decided to leave at 17.15."' This was indeed what had happened.

The evidence from these and other interrupted journeys supports the idea that dogs are responding to their owners telepathically, rather than by precognitions of their arrival.

How common are dogs that know when their owners are returning?

The people who have written to me in response to appeals for information tend to be those whose animals behave in particularly impressive ways. Obviously, people whose animals do *not* respond do not write in to say so. Hence my database does not contain a representative sample of all dogs, and does not in itself reveal how common this kind of behaviour is.

From informal surveys of friends, colleagues and people at my lectures and seminars I found that between a third and two thirds of dog owners said they had noticed this anticipatory behaviour in their dogs. Readers can easily carry out their own surveys and see if they come up with similar results.

Although such informal surveys give a rough indication, they are open to a number of criticisms, the most important of which is that the people who are asked represent a biased sample. In order to avoid such possible sources of bias, it is necessary to question a random sample of the population, using standard surveying techniques. I and my associates have now completed four such surveys, which were carried out in very different geographical and cultural environments: in North London; in Ramsbottom, a town near Manchester in northwest England; in Santa Cruz, a beach and university town in California; and in the suburbs of Los Angeles in the San Fernando Valley.

A random sample of households were surveyed by telephone. The percentage containing dogs in Santa Cruz and Los Angeles was 35 per cent, close to the US national average. In Ramsbottom it was 31 per cent, slightly above the British national average. In London it was only 16 per cent, in agreement with the tendency for dog ownership to be lowest in large cities, where more people live in apartments.

The first question pet owners were asked was: 'Have you or anyone in your household ever noticed your animal getting agitated before a family member has arrived home?' Those who answered 'yes' were then asked: 'How long before you/they arrive is the pet agitated?' (They were then asked further questions about their pets which I discuss in Chapters 7 and 8. Readers interested in the details of these surveys can read more about them in our papers published in scientific journals,[6] which are also available on my world wide web site.[7])

In spite of the great differences between the places surveyed and the fact that the surveys were carried out by different people, the results are in remarkable agreement (Figure 3.1). About half the dogs were said to show anticipatory behaviour before their people came home; the overall average was 51 per cent. The highest percentage was in Los Angeles (61 per cent), and the lowest in Santa Cruz (45 per cent). These figures may have underestimated the positive responses, because people who live alone do not usually know whether or not their animal anticipates their return.

Most dogs that anticipated their owners' returns did so less than ten minutes before they arrived, but between 16 and 25 per cent were said to do so more than ten minutes in advance.[8] Such reactions are unlikely to be due to sounds and smells, as I have discussed above, although some might be explicable in terms of routine.

No formal random surveys have yet been conducted in any other countries, but my own informal surveys in Belgium, Brazil, Canada, Denmark, France, Germany, Holland, Ireland, Norway, Portugal and Switzerland have given similar results to informal surveys in Britain and the USA.

Why do so many dogs *not* react?

Even if, as my research indicates, about half the dogs in a given place anticipate their owners coming home, there are still about half that do not. Why not? I can think of five possible explanations:

First, when people live alone there is no one to observe the dog's reactions, so the reactions would pass unnoticed.

Second, some dogs may have reacted in the past, but their owners failed to notice or offer any encouragement. In households where people *do* notice this behaviour, simply paying attention to it may encourage the dog. But in many households there is no incentive for the dog to show what it knows. If more owners paid attention to this behaviour, the percentage of dogs showing it might rise.

Third, the bond between the dog and its owner may not be strong enough to evoke this behaviour. The dog may not be sufficiently interested in the person's return.

Fourth, some dogs may be less sensitive than others. There is a wide variation of sensitivity in all other respects, including smell, hearing and sight, even among dogs that are closely related. So why not in this?

Fifth, some breeds may be relatively insensitive.

These possibilities are mutually compatible, and all could work together.

Too little is known at present to test the first four possibilities. But the fifth can be explored straight away. There is already enough information in the database and from the formal surveys to investigate whether some breeds are more sensitive than others.

Are some breeds more sensitive than others?

I have received reports of anticipatory behaviour by 44 distinct breeds of dog, as well as by many cross-breeds and mongrels of unknown ancestry.

Dog breeds are commonly grouped into several broad categories, and different experts use different systems, which are more or less arbitrary. I use the British Kennel Club classification, with the following categories. The first three groups are traditionally used for hunting, and are often called sporting breeds:

Gun dogs. This group includes Labradors, retrievers, spaniels and setters.
Hounds. The two subgroups are sight hounds, such as greyhounds and
    lurchers, and scent hounds, such as bloodhounds and foxhounds.
Terriers.
Working group. This group mainly consists of dogs originally used for
    working with livestock, such as collies, German shepherds and
    other sheepdogs, as well as draught dogs like huskies.
Utility group. A miscellaneous group that includes poodles, dalmatians
    and bulldogs.
Toy group. Mostly small dogs that have traditionally lived indoors as
    companion animals, including Pekingese, cavalier King Charles
    spaniels and Chihuahuas.

Out of the 415 accounts of anticipatory behaviour on the database where the breed of the dog was given, the breakdown according to these categories is as follows:

Gun dogs	74
Hounds	49
Terriers	46
Working group	135
Utility group	52
Toy group	22
Mongrels	37

The individual breeds that occur most frequently in these reports are Labradors (20 examples), German shepherds (14), collies (12) and poodles (12). But this may not mean they are unusually sensitive; it may simply reflect the fact that these are some of the most popular breeds. Likewise, the fact that most reports concern working dogs and gun dogs may simply reflect the fact that more people keep dogs from these categories than from other categories.

So although no detailed conclusions can be drawn from the reports on the database about the sensitivity of different kinds of dogs, it is clear that anticipatory behaviour is widespread and is not confined to any particular group.

The formal surveys carried out in Britain and the United States give a more reliable picture, because they are based on random samples. The combined results from all four surveys are shown in the table below. As well as the totals for each category, figures for particular breeds are given in cases where there were more than ten dogs of a particular kind.

None of the differences between groups are statistically significant, and they could simply be chance variations owing to the relatively small size of the sample. Therefore not much can be concluded from these differences, but I suspect that the relatively high percentages in the toy and utility groups might prove to be repeatable in other surveys. Many of the breeds in these groups have been bred over generations for human companionship. They may tend to be more sensitive to their owners' intentions both because of their breeding and also because they are more likely to be kept indoors. They may literally be closer to their owners than large dogs, a higher proportion of which are kept in kennels outdoors, or restricted in the parts of the house they can enter.

Kind of dog	Total number surveyed	Number anticipating arrivals	% anticipating arrivals
Gun dogs	58	30	52
Labradors	21	8	38
Spaniels	21	12	57
Hounds	12	6	50
Terriers	41	23	56
Working group	55	24	44
German shepherds	16	6	38
Collies	13	8	62
Utility group	17	11	65
Toy group	20	13	65
Mongrels	82	39	48

These figures confirm that many kinds of dogs seem to anticipate the arrival of their owners. This ability is not confined to any particular breed or group.

Nor is it confined to one sex, although males tend to show this behaviour more than females. Of the 465 accounts on the database of dogs where the gender of the dog is mentioned, just over half concern males. In the random household surveys in Britain, 48 per cent of males were said to show anticipatory behaviour, compared with 44 per cent of females.

Logs of dogs' behaviour

The reports of dog owners about their animals' behaviour are an invaluable starting point for further investigations. In fact they are the only possible starting point, since in the absence of any scientific investigations, they are the only information available.

The next step is the keeping of written records of dogs' behaviour. Much can be learned from such logs, and the only equipment needed is a notebook and pen. For more detailed research, it is necessary to film the dogs' responses on time-coded videotape. Such investigations are the subject of the rest of this chapter.

At my request over twenty dog owners have kept logs of their dogs' behaviour prior to the return of a member of the family, and some have carried out experiments by coming home at unusual times, and travelling in an unfamiliar vehicle such as a taxi.

These logs are extremely illuminating, and reveal details about the animals' behaviour that would otherwise have been forgotten. They confirm that some dogs do indeed anticipate people's arrivals fairly reliably, but not necessarily on every occasion. I would encourage readers whose animals seem to anticipate arrivals to keep logs themselves, noting down:

1. The date and exact times at which the animal seems to show anticipatory reactions, if any.
2. The time at which the person returns, and the time at which they set off to come home.
3. Where they went to and how long they were away.
4. How they travelled home.
5. Whether they arrived at a routine or expected time.
6. Any other comments or observations.

These records are best kept in a special notebook. It is important to note down the animal's failures as well as successes, so that if the dog shows no signs of anticipation before the person arrives home, this is duly recorded. And so should false alarms be noted.

In all but one of the logs I have received, the dogs were regularly reacting ten minutes or more in advance of the person's arrival; some reacted hours in advance, when their person was setting off on a long homeward journey. These reactions cannot be explained in terms of hearing or smelling the returning person. Most cannot be accounted for in terms of routine either. However, in one of the logs, the dog usually anticipated its owner's arrival by only three or four minutes, so it is just possible that on these occasions it could have been hearing her car approaching.

In several cases dogs appeared to give false alarms, but then it turned out that their person had indeed set off to come home, but that they had changed their minds or had been interrupted on the way.

Sometimes the dogs failed to react in advance of their owner's return when they were distracted, sick or frightened. Sometimes they failed to react for no apparent reason. But on the great majority of occasions, the dogs anticipated their people's arrivals by ten minutes or more.

The most extensive set of records concern a male mongrel terrier called Jaytee, who lives in northwest England with his owner Pamela Smart (Figure 2.2).

Figure 2.2 Pam Smart with Jaytee (photograph: Gary Taylor).

The anticipations of Jaytee

Over several years, Jaytee was observed by members of Pamela Smart's family to anticipate her arrival by half an hour or more. He seemed to know when Pam was on her way even when no one else knew, and even when she returned at non-routine times.

Pam adopted Jaytee from Manchester Dogs' Home in 1989 when he was still a puppy, and soon formed a close bond with him. She lives in Ramsbottom, Greater Manchester, in a ground-floor flat, next door to her parents, William and Muriel Smart, who are retired. When she goes out, she usually leaves Jaytee with her parents.

In 1991, when Pam was working as a secretary in Manchester, her parents noticed that Jaytee used to go to the French window almost every weekday at about 4.30 pm, around the time she set off to come home. Her journey usually took 45–60 minutes, and Jaytee would wait at the window most of the time that she was on her way. Since she worked routine office hours, the family assumed that Jaytee's behaviour depended on some kind of time sense.

Pam was made redundant in 1993, and was subsequently unemployed. She was often away from home for hours at a time, and was no longer tied to any regular pattern of activity. Her parents did not usually know when she would be returning, but Jaytee still continued to anticipate her return. His reactions seemed to occur around the time she set off on her homeward journey.

In April 1994, Pam read an article in the *Sunday Telegraph* about the research I was doing on this phenomenon,[9] and volunteered to take part. The first stage in this investigation was the keeping of a log by Pam and her parents. Between May 1994 and February 1995 on 100 occasions she left Jaytee with her parents when she went out, and they made notes on Jaytee's reactions. Pam herself kept a record of where she had been, how far she had travelled, her mode of transport, and when she had set off to come home. On 85 of these 100 occasions, Jaytee reacted by going to wait at the French window before Pam returned, usually ten or more minutes in advance.

When these data were analysed statistically, they showed that Jaytee's reactions were very significantly[10] related to the time that Pam set off, as if he knew when she was starting to go home.[11] It did not seem to matter how far away she was.[12]

However, there were 15 out of 100 occasions on which Jaytee did not react. Was there anything unusual on these occasions? On some, Mrs Smart was away from home or asleep. Jaytee was closely bonded with Mrs Smart, but rather afraid of Mr Smart. When alone with Mr Smart,

Jaytee hid in the bedroom and was not observable. On some occasions, there were major external distractions, such as a bitch on heat in a neighbour's flat. On some he was sick. But on three occasions there were no apparent distractions or reasons for his lack of response. Thus Jaytee did not always react to Pam's returns, and he could be distracted, for example by the bitch on heat.

Jaytee's anticipatory reactions usually began when Pam was over 4 miles away, and in some cases over 40 miles away. He could not possibly have heard her car at such distances, especially when the car was downwind and against the background of the heavy traffic in Greater Manchester and on the M66 motorway, which runs close to Ramsbottom. Moreover, Mr and Mrs Smart had already noticed that Jaytee still anticipated Pam's return when she arrived in unfamiliar vehicles.

Nevertheless, to check that Jaytee was not reacting to the sound of Pam's car or other familiar vehicles, we investigated whether he still responded when she travelled by unusual means: by bicycle, by train and by taxi. He did.[13]

Pam did not usually tell her parents in advance when she would be coming home, nor did she telephone to inform them. Indeed, she often did not know in advance when she would be returning after an evening out, visiting friends and relations or shopping. But it is possible that her parents might in some cases have guessed when she might be coming, and then, consciously or unconsciously, communicated their expectation to Jaytee. Some of his reactions might therefore be due to her parents' anticipation, rather than depending on some mysterious influence from Pam herself.

To test this possibility, we carried out experiments in which Pam set off at times selected at random after she had left home. These times were unknown to anyone else. In these experiments, Jaytee started to wait when she set off, or rather a minute or two before while she was making her way to her car, even though no one at home knew when she would be coming.[14] Therefore his reactions could not be explained in terms of her parents' expectations.

By this stage it was clearly important to start filming Jaytee's behaviour on videotape, so that a more precise and objective record of his behaviour could be kept. And just at this point I was approached by the Science Unit of Austrian State Television (ORF) who wanted to film an experiment with a dog. Pam and her parents kindly agreed to do this filmed experiment with Jaytee.

Together with Dr Heinz Leger and Barbara von Melle of ORF, I designed an experiment involving two cameras, one filming Jaytee continuously in Pam's parents' house, and the other following Pam as she went out and about.

This experiment duly took place in November 1994. Neither Pam nor her parents knew the randomly selected time at which she would be asked to return.

Some 3 hours 50 minutes after she had set out, she was told it was time to go home. She then walked to a taxi rank, arriving there five minutes later, and reached home ten minutes after that. As usual, Jaytee greeted her enthusiastically.

From the videotapes, Jaytee's behaviour can be observed in a detail not previously possible. During the period that Pam was out, he spent practically all the time lying quite calmly by the feet of Mrs Smart. In the edited version produced by ORF for transmission on television, over the period that Pam was told to return, both videotapes can be seen together on a split screen in exact synchrony, so that Pam can be observed on one side of the screen, and Jaytee on the other. To start with, Jaytee is, as usual, lying by Mrs Smart's feet. Pam is then told that it is time to return, and almost immediately Jaytee shows signs of alertness, with his ears pricked. Eleven seconds after Pam has been told to go home, while she is walking across some grass towards the taxi rank, Jaytee gets up, walks to the window and sits there expectantly. He remains at the window for the entire period of Pam's return journey.[15]

There seems no possible way in which Jaytee could have known by normal sensory means at what instant Pam was setting off to come home. Nor could it have been routine, since the time was chosen at random and was at a time of day when Pam would not normally be returning.

This experiment highlights the importance of Pam's intentions. Jaytee started to wait when she first knew she was going home, before she got into the vehicle and began the taxi journey. Jaytee seemed to be responding telepathically.

Videotaped experiments with Jaytee

In April 1995, I received a grant from the Lifebridge Foundation of New York to support my research on the unexplained powers of animals. By then, as a result of the publication of my book *Seven Experiments That Could Change the World*[16] and appeals for information from pet owners, I was receiving hundreds of letters. I read and acknowledged them all personally, but I was unable to cope on my own with the task of organizing them on a database. I needed a research assistant who had the necessary secretarial and computer skills to build up the database, who was interested in animals and who was capable of carrying out experiments on her own. Pam Smart fitted the job description ideally.

So after a year's voluntary research with her own dog, Pam became my full-time research assistant. The experiments with Jaytee continued, but now included the regular videotaping of Jaytee's behaviour throughout the whole period that Pam was out.

The procedure was kept as simple as possible, so that observations of Jaytee could be done routinely and automatically. The video camera was set up on a tripod, and left running continuously in the long-play mode with a long-play film, with the timecode recorded on it. The camera was pointing at the area where Jaytee usually waits, by the French window in Pam's parents' flat. These experiments were only possible because her parents kindly agreed to have their living room continuously monitored for hours on end, and sometimes several times a week. They and the members of their extensive family who often visited them simply got used to it, and carried on life as usual.

Jaytee's behaviour was also videotaped in Pam's own flat while he was on his own, and also in the house of her sister Cathie. The videotapes were scored 'blind' by a third person who did not know any details of the experiment. In most videos, for most of the time, Jaytee is not on camera. But every time he appears by the window, the exact time he does so is recorded, as is the length of time he stays there. Notes are also made about his behaviour. For example, on some visits to the window, he is obviously barking at passing cats, or watching other activities outside. On others he is sleeping in the sun. On others he looks as if he is just waiting. We have now made and analysed over 120 videotaped records of Jaytee's behaviour from the time Pam left home until the time she returned.

Between May 1995 and July 1996 we made a series of thirty videotapes of Jaytee at Pam's parents' flat while Pam went out and about. Pam's parents were not told when she would be returning, and she usually did not know exactly herself. The purpose was to observe how Jaytee behaved under more or less 'natural' conditions. Seven of these thirty videotapes were taken in the daytime, at various times in the morning and afternoon. Twenty-three were taken in the evening, with Pam returning at a variety of times between 7.30 and 11 pm.

The overall results are shown in Figure 2.3. The general pattern is clear. On average, Jaytee waited at the window much more when Pam was on her way home, and his waiting began while she was preparing to set off. He was at the window much less during the main period of her absence. These differences were highly significant statistically,[17] and show that Jaytee was reacting to Pam's intentions. (A more detailed analysis of these results can be found in Appendix B.)

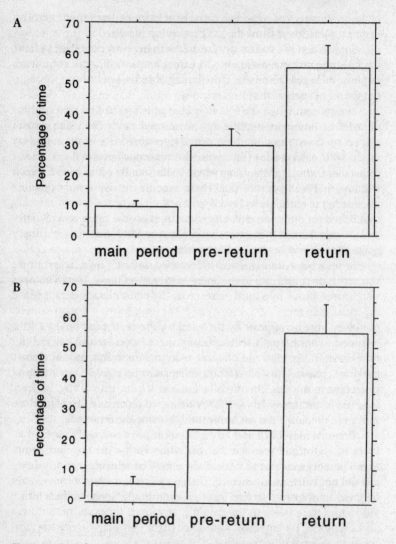

Figure 2.3 Jaytee's reactions to Pam's returns. The bar diagrams show the percentage of time that Jaytee spent by the window during the main part of Pam's absence ('main period'), during the ten minutes prior to her setting off to come home ('pre-return') and during the first ten minutes of her journey home ('return'). (The standard error of each value is indicated by the bar at the top.)

A: Averages from 30 experiments in which Pam returned home at times of her own choice.

B: Averages from 12 experiments in which Pam returned home at randomly selected times in response to being bleeped on her pager.

Jaytee's pattern of response can be seen in more detail in the graphs in Figure 2.4. However long Pam's absence, Jaytee waited by the window much more when she was on the way home than at any other period. He usually began to wait there shortly before she set off, while she was thinking about going home and preparing to do so.

At an early stage in our research, we found that Jaytee anticipated Pam's return even when she set off at randomly selected times, but this was such an important finding that we carried out a further series of twelve videotaped experiments in which Pam returned at random times. I selected a time at random by throwing dice, and when this time came I bleeped her through a telephone pager.[18] She then set off as soon as possible. As usual, a video recording of the area by the window was made throughout the entire period of her absence.

The results, summarized in Figure 2.3B, show the same general pattern as Pam's ordinary homecomings (Figure 2.3A), and confirm that Jaytee's reactions were not a matter of routine nor of expectations communicated by her parents. Jaytee was at the window far more when Pam was on her way home than during the main part of her absence (55 per cent of the time as opposed to 5 per cent). This effect was highly significant statistically.[19]

Following the successful experiment with Jaytee carried out by ORF, there were a number of reports about this research on television and in newspapers. Journalists sought out a sceptic to comment on these results, and several chose Dr Richard Wiseman, who regularly appears on British television as a debunker of psychical phenomena.[20] He is a psychologist at the University of Hertfordshire, and a Consulting Editor of the *Skeptical Inquirer*, the organ of CSICOP (The Committee for the Scientific Investigation of Claims of the Paranormal).

Unlike armchair sceptics, Richard Wiseman has the great virtue of actually doing experiments, rather than simply criticizing other people's. So when he criticized my own research with Jaytee, I invited him to do some tests of his own, and Pam and her family kindly agreed to help him.

Figure 2.4 The time-courses of Jaytee's visits to the window during Pam's long, medium and short absences. The horizontal axis shows the series of 10-minute periods (p1, p2 etc.) from the time she went out until she was on her way home. The last period shown on the graph represents the first 10 minutes of Pam's return journey ('ret'), the point for which is indicated by a filled circle (●). The vertical axis shows the average number of seconds that Jaytee spent at the window in each 10-minute period. The graphs represent the average of 11 long, 7 medium and 6 short experiments. (A minority of 'noisy' experiments were excluded so that the normal pattern could be seen more clearly; but these noisy experiments themselves showed the same general pattern, as can be seen from Figure B.1 B in Appendix B).

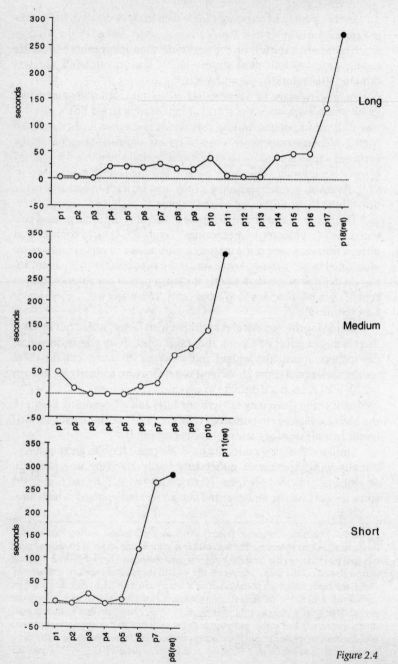

Figure 2.4

DOGS

45

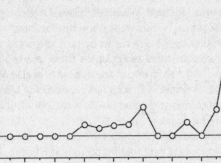

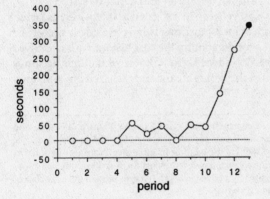

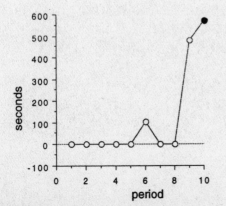

Figure 2.5

In his experiments, Richard Wiseman himself videotaped Jaytee while his assistant Matthew Smith went out with Pam and videotaped her. They travelled either by Smith's car or by taxi, and went to pubs or other places five to eleven miles away. Smith then selected a random number to determine when they would set off home, or else telephoned a third party who had selected a number at random for him. Thus he himself knew in advance when they would be setting off, but he did not tell Pam until it was time to go.

The videotapes of Jaytee's behaviour were analysed 'blind' by someone who did not know when Pam had set off to come home. Pam and I have also analysed them. We all agree about when Jaytee went to the window, and how long he stayed there.[21] These results are shown in Figure 2.5. The pattern was very similar to that in my own experiments, and confirmed that Jaytee anticipated Pam's arrival even when she was returning at a randomly chosen time in an unfamiliar vehicle.[22]

No other animals have yet been investigated as intensively as Jaytee, but several series of videotaped experiments have already been carried out with other dogs. The results confirm the conclusions we have arrived at with Jaytee. The dogs do indeed seem to know when their person is coming home, even when they come at randomly selected times in unfamiliar vehicles.

Figure 2.5 Results of the three experiments carried out by Richard Wiseman and Matthew Smith with Jaytee at Pam's parents' flat in 1995. The graphs show the amount of time that Jaytee spent at the window in successive 10-minute periods. As in Figure 2.4, the final point on each graph represents the first 10 minutes of Pam's return journey, and is indicated by a filled circle (•). (Graphs plotted from the data of Wiseman, Smith and Milton, 1998)

3

Cats

Many cats lead a double life: outdoors they are solitary hunters; indoors they are more or less affectionate companions. In relation to their human keepers, they behave rather like kittens do towards the mother cat that feeds and protects them.

In general, cats are obviously more independent and less sociable than dogs. A cat usually feels no need to be near its owner all the time. While most dogs are person-centred, most cats are home-centred.

Cats have lived in close association with human beings for at least five thousand years. They were probably first domesticated in North Africa, and their wild ancestor was the African wild cat, *Felis silvestris* subspecies *libyca*. The ancient Egyptians revered them, and kept them in their houses. They were embodiments of the cat-goddess Bastet, related to the terrifying lioness-goddess Sekhmet, a slayer and devourer in war.

Rudyard Kipling's famous 'Just So' story, *The Cat that Walked by Himself*, epitomizes feline characteristics. But although cats are solitary hunters, left to their own devices they do not usually live alone, at least if they are female. Recent research on groups of farm cats and feral cats has shown that females are surprisingly sociable.[1] They tend to live in small groups, often containing mothers and daughters from previous litters. Within these groups, litters from different females may be reared in the same nest, with mothers giving maternal care to kittens that are not their own, and suckling them. But males really do lead quite solitary lives, and range over larger territories.[2]

There is a wide range of 'intensities of relationship' between cats and owners, and this helps to explain why cat keeping is increasingly popular in many industrialized countries. Generally these relationships are fairly symmetrical. The more attention owners pay to their cat's wishes, the more attention the cat pays to the owner. And since independence is so important to most cats, 'acceptance of a cat's independent nature is one of the secrets of a harmonious human-cat relationship'.[3] But cats can quite readily adjust to less interaction if their owners have little time for them, or are not interested in forming closer bonds.

Knowing when people are returning

Many cats seem to know when their owners are returning. I have collected 359 accounts of this behaviour from cat owners in response to my appeals for information. And in our random survey of nearly 1,200 households in Britain and America, there were 91 households with cats that seemed to know when their owner was coming home. In other words about eight per cent of households have such cats.

About three quarters of the stories I have received from cat owners concern returns from work, shopping, school or other short absences. Here are some typical observations:

'She is almost always at the window when I come home.'

'He appears from nowhere.'

'Whatever time we come home our two cats seem to be waiting for us.'

'He is always waiting behind the door for us.'

'She is almost always there and I wonder how she knows.'

When people live alone they usually do not know how long their cat has been waiting for them, or if indeed it has been waiting there all day. Even when there are people at home, the anticipatory behaviour of cats tends to be noticed less when the cats are free to roam outside. If the weather is good, some wait outside the house and are therefore less easily observed.

In 70 per cent of the cases I know of, the cat waits for only one person; in 20 per cent it waits for either of two people, and in 10 per cent it waits for three or more. As with dogs and other animals, the people cats wait for are those to whom they are particularly attached, usually members of the immediate family or close friends. Here is an example of a cat living in Washington, DC that responded to two people:

My boyfriend gave me a kitten named Sami for Christmas. Nearly every evening he would stop by my apartment after work. I always knew when he was coming because Sami would sit by the door for approximately ten minutes before his arrival. I had no way of giving the cat signals because I was never aware of the time he would be coming over. He was in real estate and had erratic hours. I doubt Sami could have heard his car as I live in the middle of a very noisy city in a highrise. When my Mum visits she says Sami anticipates my arrival in the same fashion – and I take the subway. (Jeanne Randolph)

In most cases where people have paid attention to cats' waiting behaviour, they have found that the cats start waiting less than ten minutes before the person arrives. Nevertheless, practically all the stories involve behaviour that does not seem explicable in terms of routine, familiar sounds, or other straightforward explanations. For example, when the teenage son of Dr Carlos Sarasola was living with him in his apartment in Buenos Aires, Argentina, he often came home late at night, after his father had gone to bed with their cat, Lennon. Dr Sarasola noticed that Lennon would suddenly jump off the bed and go and wait by the front door about 10 to 15 minutes before his son arrived, having travelled by taxi. Intrigued by this behaviour, Dr Sarasola made careful observations on the time the cat responded to see if the cat could be reacting to the sound of the taxi door shutting. It was not, because the cat responded well before the taxi arrived. 'One night I paid attention to several taxis that stopped at the front of my building. Three taxis stopped and Lennon remained quiet with me in bed. Some time later, he jumped down and went to the door. Five minutes later I heard the taxi arrive in which my son was travelling.'

Some cats make a point of meeting their owners on their way home from work or school, and a few even wait for them at bus stops or railway stations.

As with dogs, in some households the cat's reactions are a signal for preparing food or making cups of tea: 'My father's cat went down to the front gate and sat on a stone gatepost waiting for him about ten minutes before he returned home. As a journalist, his hours were very variable. My mother said that she knew to put the potatoes on when the cat looked up, apparently listened, then trotted off. It can't have been the distant sound of the car, however, because it went on even when he had no car and returned by bus and on foot.' (Joyce Collin-Smith)

In some cases the cat's warning of returns helps people to break up illicit parties. That was the case with Bryan Roche:

During my time as an undergraduate psychology student, I took a working holiday on Nantucket Island, USA. The guesthouse in which I worked and boarded was inhabited by a Persian cat named Minu. Its owner (my employer) insisted that she had a psychic relationship with this cat, such that, whenever she was driving home, the cat would 'growl' for up to 20 minutes prior to her arrival. She often illuminated this fable with amusing recollections of her feline's psychic antics and I regularly took to jesting with the residents about her unlikely stories.

One night, however, unbeknown to my absent employer, I held a small party in the guesthouse. As the party was in full swing I noticed that the cat was acting rather strange. She was arching her back, as cats do, but also growling quite loudly as if she were a dog. Given the gravity of being apprehended in the act of partying in my employer's house, I decided to heed the cat's warning and end the party. The guests were more amused with my superstition than with the cat's imitation of a dog. Sure enough, the cat's owner arrived home about six or seven minutes later. The psychic cat had saved my job.

I was still not convinced of the psychic nature of what had happened and I took to observing the cat very carefully. It quickly emerged that Minu could 'sense' the arrival of her owner even when she arrived in a different car or at an unusual time. Her predictions even proved reliable when her owner was returning to the island from the mainland by boat! I became so convinced of the reliability of the cat's predictions that I held several more parties to which the cat was cordially invited. On each of these occasions, the cat proved to be a fail-safe 'employer arriving alarm'.

Although many cats respond to their owners' returns on a regular basis, some do so only under certain conditions, most commonly when the owner's return is linked to their being fed. And some people have noticed that their female cats respond most when they are pregnant, but lose interest in their owner's return when they have kittens to attend to.

Of the 274 reports of anticipatory behaviour on the database where the gender of the cat is given, there are slightly more reports about males than females.[4] In the random household surveys we carried out in England, slightly more females than males were said to respond: 26 per cent as opposed to 24 per cent. These differences are not statistically significant, and we can conclude that, on average, males and females behave very similarly in this respect.

Keeping logs

Cats free to roam outside usually change their behaviour according to the weather. On sunny days, they may wait outside in a sunny place near the door or gate; on rainy days indoors, on a windowsill looking out; and on cold days, somewhere warm.

This variability has so far frustrated the carrying out of videotaped experiments with cats, because if the camera is set up and left running pointing at a particular place, the cat may wait in another place, off camera. Dogs, by contrast, tend to go to the same place to wait, usually against the door or gate, and can be filmed more simply. To work effectively with cats would either require a more sophisticated surveillance system than has yet been employed, or else require the experiments to be restricted to cats that wait in one predictable place.

The behaviour of cats that move freely in and out of doors is more natural, and more varied. It can be studied most simply and directly through the keeping of logs by cat-owning families.

The most detailed log so far is that kept by Judith Preston-Jones of Tonbridge, Kent, and her husband. Their two Siamese cats, Flora and Maia, usually reacted to her return after short absences, from shopping or swimming, by waiting by the garage or on the doorstep. After longer absences, or in the evening, they anticipated her return by about ten minutes, waiting in a variety of places.

In the log that she and her husband kept over a two-month period, there are 28 entries covering returns at a range of times in the afternoon and evening. On 15 occasions Mr and Mrs Preston-Jones went out together and so there was no one to observe the cats, but on all but one of these occasions the cats were waiting for them at one of their usual places on their return. The exception occurred when it was very cold, and the cats were sitting on the boiler. On eight occasions Mr Preston-Jones observed the cats showing signs of excitement and anticipation 10–15 minutes before his wife returned. Their waiting places varied according to the circumstances. When it was raining they were indoors, either by the door or watching from the kitchen window; and when it was fine they waited outdoors, either in the garden, on the doorstep, or by the garage. On four occasions the cats were already outdoors with him in the garden and showed no special signs of anticipation. And at one homecoming the cats were nowhere to be seen, and were found hiding upstairs while a repair man worked on the washing machine.

The most interesting observation occurred one evening when Mrs Preston-Jones came home at 9.40 pm, following a meeting in a village church about three miles away. Her husband greeted her with: 'Well, the cats got it wrong this time! They got restless at 9 pm so I expected you home half an hour ago.' In fact, what had happened was that she had left the church and got into her car, and then remembered something she wanted to discuss with a friend, returned to the church and stayed there until 9.30 pm. The cats reacted when she initially set off and got into the car.

Aversions

Just as some dogs anticipate the arrival of people to whom they have a strong aversion (p. 29), so do some cats. Mosette Broderick, who lives in

Manhattan, became an object of aversion through helping her former professor, who told her that his cat Kitty hated him for days after he took her to the vet. Mosette volunteered to take Kitty to the vet herself, so Kitty started hating her instead.

> As the years passed, Kitty developed her disgust towards me to a degree that my professor always knew when I was on the block. When I turned down 62nd Street, from Lexington Avenue, some 200 feet and much noise away, Kitty would run and hide behind the stairs which she only did when she expected my arrival. The curious fact here is that I would be out of hearing, sight and smell range. In a crowded city like New York, she could not have heard me over the din of traffic. She certainly could not have seen. Smell in winter in New York with the doors shut and the heat on in the house could also not have been a factor. I was also not always there on the same day or time so schedule was not possible either.

At first, Kitty behaved like this only when Mosette was arriving to take her to the vet, but as time went on she hid before even the most innocent of visits.

Cats compared with dogs

Fewer cats than dogs anticipate their owners' arrivals. I have received 359 cat stories, and 585 dog stories. Of course these figures are only a rough guide, but a similar picture emerges from the random household surveys carried out in England and the United States. Out of a total of nearly 1,200 households surveyed, there were 91 households with cats said to know when someone was returning, and 177 with dogs that did so. The total number of dogs and cats in these surveys was practically the same. Overall, 55 per cent of the dogs were said to show this anticipatory behaviour, compared with 30 per cent of cats. This difference between dogs and cats showed up in all four locations we surveyed: London and Greater Manchester in England, and Los Angeles and Santa Cruz in California (Figure 3.1).

The figures for anticipatory behaviour by cats were higher in California than England. I do not know why. Perhaps the Californian cat-owners tend to form closer bonds with their animals than the English. But even in California, dogs significantly outperformed cats.

Are cats therefore less sensitive than dogs? Not necessarily. They may simply be less interested in their owners' comings and goings. And some may be only weakly bonded with the person returning. Nevertheless,

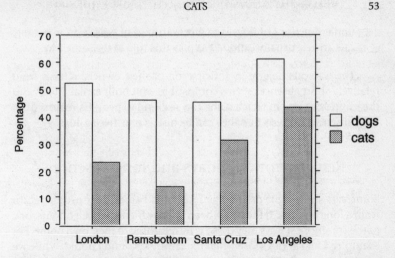

Figure 3.1 The percentages of cat and dog owners who said their animals anticipated their returns. The surveys were carried out with a random sample of households in London; in Ramsbottom (Greater Manchester in northwest England); and in Santa Cruz and Los Angeles, California.

many cats *are* interested in their owners' arrivals and seem to anticipate their return.

The patterns of anticipation shown by dogs and cats also show characteristic differences. With dogs, a considerable proportion (17 per cent) react when their owners are setting off to come home, or are intending to set off (as discussed on pp. 24–26). With cats, this proportion is only about one per cent. Also, with dogs a sizeable percentage react when the person reaches a crucial stage in their journey, such as disembarking from a train or plane (see pp. 22–23). Some cats do this too, but again the proportion is very low, around two per cent. Nearly all cats that respond to their owners returning from work or shopping trips do so when their people are actually in transit. Why should this be so? I can think of two possible reasons:

1 Cats may be less sensitive than dogs, or for some reason unable to detect their owners' returns until they are quite close to home. They may not be able to pick up their owners' intentions from many miles away in the same way that many dogs seem to.
2 Cats may be capable of knowing when their owners are setting off, but have no motivation to respond very long in advance. If their aim is simply to meet and greet the returning person, there is no need to start waiting when they are still far away. And while one of the tradi-

tional functions of dogs is to give warnings of people approaching, cats are not usually expected to play this role in the same way.

The way cats behave in anticipation of their owners' returns from relatively short absences seems compatible with both explanations. But the impressive way in which some cats respond to people's returns from long absences suggests that they can be just as sensitive as dogs.

Returns from holidays and long absences

Some cats show signs of anticipation hours before their people return from a long absence. If they have been kept by friends or neighbours, one of the commonest ways they do so is by returning to their own home. For example: 'Our cat can sense when the family is coming home. While we were away the animal was with our neighbours. At the moment when we set off in Greece, Turkey or Italy (shorter distances, of course, too) the cat insisted on staying in our house again for the night.' (Dr Walther Natsch, Herrliberg, Switzerland)

Sometimes this behaviour is unexpected, and causes alarm to the person caring for the cat: 'We went on holiday and left our cat with my aunt, just over two miles from our flat in the centre of Brighton. When we returned two weeks later, the cat was sitting on the gate pillar waiting for us, and we were grateful to my aunt for having saved us the trouble of fetching him. When we rang to thank her, she was frantic; the cat had slipped away that very morning and she had been searching ever since.' (John Eyles)

Another way in which cats show this anticipation is by turning up to meet a member of the family who is returning for a visit. This is what happened to Elisabeth Bienz when she left her home in Switzerland to move to Paris, leaving behind her beloved cat Moudi:

> A few days later he disappeared from my parents' home and was not seen again. Every two or three months I came home for a visit, and the cat reappeared – well fed and cared for. My parents never learned where he was in the meantime. A few days after I had gone he disappeared again. The biggest surprise came when I turned up for an unannounced visit one day. Some hours before my arrival the cat showed up. My mother was puzzled and thought he had made a mistake. But then I showed up too.

On my database there are over 50 examples of anticipatory behaviour by cats prior to their people's returns from holiday or long absences.

In most of them, as in these examples, the cats seemed to know of the impending returns long in advance. And in some cases there is no possibility that they picked up this anticipation from the people who were caring for them.

Such cases refute the argument that cats have only a short-range awareness of impending returns. Their excitement and motivation are probably much enhanced after long absences or holidays, especially when they have been taken away from their familiar surroundings. They are anticipating not only their favourite person's return, but a return to living in their own territory.

Although cats anticipate returns in a characteristically feline way, it seems clear that their anticipation cannot be explained simply in terms of routines and sensory clues. As in the case of dogs, it seems to be telepathic and depends on close bonds between cat and the person. I suggest that these bonds involve connections through morphic fields, and that these are stretched, not broken, when a person goes away and leaves the cat behind. The bonds are the channels through which telepathic communication can occur, even over hundreds of miles.

Cats and dogs are not the only species kept as pets that anticipate the returns of their people. As we see in the following chapter, this ability is found in other species too, and even in humans. As with cats and dogs, it seems to depend on the formation of close bonds that can act as channels for telepathy.

4

Parrots, horses and humans

Among dogs and cats, the anticipation of their owners' arrivals depends on strong social bonds between the person and the animal. We would therefore not expect to find this telepathic ability in species that are inherently solitary, as most reptiles are, or which do not form strong bonds with humans, like stick insects. And even among species that are both social and do form strong bonds with people, it may well be that some are inherently insensitive to human feelings and intentions.

However, although there is much less information available about species other than dogs and cats, there is enough to suggest that animals of at least 17 other species also appear to anticipate people's returns. Some humans do it too, especially in traditional, rural societies.

Anticipations are shown not only by mammals but also by birds, and of the 33 stories I have received about return-anticipating birds, 20 concern parrots.

Parrots

Parrots have the advantage over dogs that they can talk, and some of them announce their owner's arrival well in advance, like Suzie, a green Amazon, who lived with the Lycett family in Warwick from 1927 to 1987. The father, a money collector for a hire purchase company, used to travel to his collecting round in Coventry on an autocycle.

> As he did not have regular hours he could come home at all different times. My father's name was Cyril which the parrot could not pronounce very well. In the evening the bird would be sitting quietly on

her perch when suddenly she would get all excited and shout 'Werril' and we would know that we could put the kettle on because my father would be home in half an hour. (John Lycett)

Pepper is a youthful Amazon parrot who lives in Pennsylvania. He belongs to Dr Karen Milstein and her husband Philip, to whom the bird is closely bonded. 'Our bird frequently starts calling "Hello" and calling my husband by name shortly before he arrives home, even though the time may vary significantly from day to day,' she told me in 1992. By 1994, when Pepper was seven, she noticed that he was often reacting to her husband's intention to come home. In October 1994, Dr Milstein kept a log, and here, for example, is the entry for 17 October:

5.40 pm Pepper is quiet
6.14 Pepper started calling 'Hello'
6.16 Philip called to say he was leaving. Said he formed intent to leave two minutes earlier
Pepper continued to call 'Hello Philip' until Phil came home just after 6.30 pm

But although on most occasions Pepper became excited when Philip formed the intention to come home, and did so at non-routine times, sometimes he did not respond at all until Philip pulled into the driveway.

Parrots can form very strong attachments to particular people and can show strong signs of jealousy, especially towards people of the opposite sex. Oscar, a blue-fronted parrot belonging to David and Celia Watson, in Sussex, is strongly attached to David: 'When he sees my husband, sometimes I can't go near him at all, he wants to attack me. I can't even touch his cage or give him his food. He is quite jealous. And he flings himself against the side of the cage when my husband leaves the room.' Not surprisingly, Oscar is very excited when David returns. His excitement begins ten to twenty minutes beforehand: 'We thought he might be responding because David was coming home at a regular time, but it hasn't worked that way,' Celia says. 'With the job that my husband has now he never comes home at the same time and Oscar is still waiting for him. He runs in his cage and starts fluttering his wings and makes little noises.'

Most of the stories about parrots anticipating their owners' returns concern returns from work or shopping, or other daily trips from home. But some are about reactions to the person's return from longer absences. For example, when Peter Soldini went on holiday to France from his home in Switzerland, he left his parrot with his mother, telling her that he intended to return in four weeks. Without informing his mother, he decided to come home early, after only three weeks, and took three days on the return journey. 'When I entered my mother's house the first thing she said was, "You won't believe how this bird has been acting these last three days. All day long he has been talking and singing. He is so excited."'

Other members of the parrot family

Other members of the parrot family also seem capable of anticipating owners' returns. I have received three accounts of budgerigars that show unmistakeable signs of excitement five to ten minutes in advance; three of parakeets; and two of cockatiels.

Kathy Dougan lives in Santa Cruz, California, with six cockatiels. Friends who had been in her apartment when she was out had noticed that they became more active and chirped loudly before she returned. She kindly agreed to my colleague David Brown carrying out a series of ten experiments, in which the birds were videotaped during her absence. She returned at randomly selected times, when she received the signal through a bleeper.

An analysis of these videotapes shows that on some occasions the birds chirped loudly when she was not on her way home, for example when the telephone rang or someone knocked on the door. But in seven out of the ten experiments the birds did indeed chirp more when she had set off to come home, a journey taking over 20 minutes on foot. On average, over the whole series of experiments, they were chirping loudly for 15 per cent of the time when she was out, and 49 per cent of the time when she was on her way home. These results were statistically significant.[1]

From the point of view of experiments, birds that announce their owner's return by name, as some parrots do, are more likely to give unambiguous results than less specific behaviour, like the excited chirping of cockatiels or budgerigars, but we have not yet found an opportunity to do any videotaped experiments with an owner-announcing parrot.

Judging from the reports I have received, almost the only caged birds that anticipate their owner's arrival are members of the parrot family. This impression is confirmed by the random household surveys carried out in Britain and the United States. Thirty-eight of the households surveyed contained pet birds, four of which were said to anticipate the return of their owners: a parrot, a parakeet, a cockatoo and a cockatiel. No finches, canaries or other species were said to do so.

However, there is one exception to this generalization: a talking mynah bird called Sambo, belonging to the Rolfe family of Sutton St Nicholas, Herefordshire (Figure 4.1). Sambo had a great rapport with the

Figure 4.1 Suzanne Rolfe with the mynah bird Sambo (in the photograph against the cage) and Sambo's successor Jacko, in Sutton St Nicholas, Herefordshire (photograph: Phil Starling).

Rolfes' elder son Robert, and used to tell the Rolfes when he was coming home from boarding school. 'Two or three days before he was due to come home, Sambo would start chattering about "Robbie"', says Suzanne Rolfe. The family assumed that this was because they had been mentioning his name more often than usual, but when he left school and started work, he was stationed in East Africa. 'Sometimes he would let us know when he was coming on leave, but more often than not he'd arrive without warning. We always knew he was coming, though, because Sambo would start calling "Robbie" a few days before he arrived.'

Chickens, geese and an owl

The other stories of anticipatory behaviour by birds that I have received concern a pet tawny owl, chickens and geese.

Owl: An owl called Joggeli lived with the Koepfler family in their flat in Zurich, Switzerland, for 25 years:

> When something happened that was delightful to it the owl made a characteristic sound, a high-pitched grr-grrr-grrrr, like a bell. At the same time it closed its eyes. When our sons came home from school or university we always heard Joggeli's joyful sound when it could not see or hear them yet. My brother, who lives at another place and rarely visits us, did not take Joggeli seriously and laughed about the bird. One day Joggeli made angry, aggressive sounds and flew against a window pane. I thought, 'What is wrong with it? It does this only when Ralph comes.' And really, my brother paid us a surprise visit. (Heidi Koepfler)

Chickens: A common feature of accounts of the anticipatory reactions of chickens is that they react to the person who feeds them. For example, when Roberto Hohrein was at school in Germany, his family kept ten chickens. It was his job to feed them when he came home from school. His mother found that ten to fifteen minutes before he arrived, they seemed to be waiting for him, standing in the corner of their chicken run from which they could see him as he approached.

> What surprised my mother was that they did not stand there at the same time every day but at different times, according to my timetable. German schools do not finish at the same time every day. Sometimes I did not come by public transport but found a car to pick me up. But no matter when it was, the hens always stood there and waited for me because they were hungry. Only when I came extraordinarily early they did not pay attention. That was when they were not hungry yet.

Geese: If chickens' responses are motivated more by a desire to be fed than by personal attachment there is one story about geese that suggests that a bond with a particular person was their principal motive. Herr K. Theiler, living near Thun in Switzerland, had three pet geese with whom he had a particularly close relationship: 'Even my mood, happiness or sadness, was reflected in their behaviour.' His wife was able to tell from them when he would be coming home from his office. 'The geese waited impatiently at the entrance to the garden. Usually I was home at 12.15, but if something had come in between she saw that I would be late because the geese were quiet.'

Birds from a wide range of species are known to form strong attachments to people, especially if they have been raised by them from an early age,[2] and it may well be that other species are capable of this kind of anticipatory behaviour, over and above those I have already heard about.

The wild ancestors of most domesticated birds, including geese, chickens and birds of the parrot family, lived in flocks. Maybe their ability to anticipate the arrival of a human companion is derived from an ability to know when separated members of the flock are approaching. Or perhaps it is more related to an ability of young birds to know when their parents are returning to the nest with food. But nothing seems to be known about this kind of anticipatory behaviour in the wild.

If further investigations of pet birds confirm that members of some species can indeed anticipate the arrival of their owners through a kind of telepathy, then it would be worth observing birds in the wild. Do they seem to anticipate the return of other birds with whom they are closely bonded? Do young birds in the nest anticipate the arrival of their parents with food?

It should also be possible to do experiments with domesticated birds, such as geese, to see if they can anticipate the return of a bird that has been taken away beyond the range of sight and hearing and is then brought back again, or allowed to return by itself. Experiments should also be possible with homing pigeons. Do birds left behind in the loft show any signs of anticipation before their mates and other companions return from a race?

Reptiles and fish

I have not heard of a single tortoise, lizard, terrapin, snake or other pet reptile that anticipates the arrival of its owner. I have received no accounts of this behaviour through my general appeals for information on psychic pets, nor have any examples been uncovered by random household surveys in Britain and America. Appeals in specialist publications like *Reptilian International* have also failed to reveal a single case. Perhaps anticipatory reptiles exist, but if so they seem to be very rare.

This is surely a significant finding, albeit a negative one. It suggests either that reptiles are incapable of picking up when their owners are on the way home, or that they have little or no interest in their comings and goings. I suspect that their lack of social bonding may be crucial.

In the wild, most reptiles are solitary, coming together only to mate. Moreover, in most species when the females have laid their eggs, they abandon them to their fate, and the young have to fend for themselves. Think, for example, of baby sea turtles hatching on beaches thousands of miles from their ancestral feeding grounds, which they have to find on their own with no adults to guide them. The brood-tending behaviour of crocodiles provides a notable exception. Female Nile crocodiles, for

example, guard the nest in which they have laid their eggs, and also protect their young brood and lead them to the water. But the young soon
scatter and keep away from older members of the species, whose canni-
balistic tendencies they have good reason to fear.[3] So even here, there is
not much scope for bonding. And if wild reptiles do not form strong
bonds with each other, captive reptiles will have little inherent capacity
to form bonds with their human keepers.

These negative conclusions about reptiles are reinforced by one of
the most experienced of my correspondents, Jeremy Wood-Anderson, a
naturalist and reptile collector who lives in Pakistan where he has kept a
wide variety of reptiles for over 30 years. While he is convinced that 'psy-
chicness' exists to varying degrees among mammals and birds, he does
not think it exists in reptiles in any recognizable form. He is convinced
that they cannot pick up their owner's thoughts telepathically: 'Beyond
reactions to habits they have got used to, there is absolutely no connection between the mental processes of reptiles and humans.'

I have come to similarly negative conclusions about amphibians.
Relatively few people keep pet frogs, newts and other amphibia, but
there are no reports to suggest that they form psychic bonds with
humans, or respond to them telepathically. The same goes for pet insects,
such as stick insects.

Many fish species are more social than reptiles or amphibia. They
swim in schools or shoals. And some species, including some kinds of
chiclids popular with keepers of tropical fish, build nests and protect the
eggs and the fry. But even in species where there is some degree of
parental care there is little scope for human beings to substitute for fish
parents and form bonds with the young.

The keeping of fish is far more common than the keeping of reptiles,
amphibia and insects. In Britain alone, there are about 19 million pet
goldfish and 10 million tropical fish.[4] About ten per cent of households
keep fish. There are plenty of opportunities for people to notice whether
their fish get excited before a particular member of the family comes
home. But I have not heard of a single instance, nor observed anything of
this kind with our own family goldfish, nor found any evidence for any
other kind of telepathic connections between people and fish.

Guinea pigs, ferrets and other small mammals

By far the commonest mammalian pets are dogs and cats, but a variety of
other species are quite widely kept, including rabbits, guinea pigs, rats,
mice, gerbils, hamsters and ferrets. I have received no reports at all of

psychic gerbils, hamsters, rats or mice. I have received only one inconclusive report about a house rabbit, and four about guinea pigs, but none is said to have reacted more than two or three minutes beforehand, and it is impossible to rule out the possibility that they were reacting to familiar sounds.

Of all the small mammals I have heard about, the only one that seems promising from a telepathic point of view is a ferret in the East End of London. This animal is strongly bonded with its owner, while his wife and the ferret share a mutual dislike. Joan Brown has noticed that the ferret waits for her husband at the front door before he arrives home:

> If the ferret is in the lounge, she either hears the car before I can or she somehow knows my husband is on his way, because she races to the door a good ten minutes before he arrives. Sometimes he will come home late but she still knows. If he stops off for a drink with work-mates he could be an hour late, but she will be waiting for him an hour later than normal too.

Monkeys

John Bate of Blackheath, South London, had a return-anticipating squirrel monkey:

> When I was commuting between Coventry and Blackheath, the monkey would let my wife know when I was north of the Blackwall Tunnel [under the River Thames] by chuckling in a distinctive manner. Entertaining a friend one Friday afternoon my wife announced that I would be home within 15 minutes. 'How do you know?' asked her friend. 'The monkey has just told me' replied my wife. Within a quarter of an hour they heard my key in the door. However acute and discriminating the hearing of an animal, it seems doubtful that it would be possible to distinguish one car from another in heavy London traffic, four or five miles away, either across or under the water of the River Thames.

I agree with this conclusion. I have heard of several other return-anticipating monkeys, but they are so rarely kept as pets nowadays that there is little scope for further research with them, fascinating though this would be.

Horses

Together with dogs and cats, horses are the non-human species with which people form the strongest relationships. Many riders feel themselves closely bonded with their horse, and some are convinced of a psychic link. I discuss more general evidence for person-horse telepathy in Chapter 8. Here I am concerned specifically with the ability to know when their owners are coming home.

Many people have found that their horse seems to know when they are approaching its stable. It may become more alert, show signs of excitement, or whinny. But most are not sure how long in advance the horse responds, or to what extent its reactions are a matter of routine, or whether the response is due to sharp hearing. Moreover, since horses do not live in houses, they are usually less closely observed than dogs, cats and other house animals.

Those who have the best opportunities to notice anticipatory behaviour in horses are people who work in stables or who care for other people's horses while they are away.

When Adele McCormick and her family went away from their ranch near Calistoga, California, they usually left their 13 horses in the care of people who knew when they would be returning. Their horses did indeed seem to anticipate their return, but conceivably they could have picked up this anticipation from the people looking after them. But on one occasion they were looked after by a stranger who did not know when the family would be coming back.

> When we arrived home the man greeted us and said 'I knew you were on your way home because the horses started acting strange.' He said that while he was feeding them, 'Instead of looking at the food like they normally do all thirteen horses kept looking down the road, running and whinnying.' He said this started at 4.30 pm. We arrived at the ranch between 5.15 and 5.30 pm.

Sometimes horses show anticipatory behaviour hours in advance, especially when their person has been away for a long time. This happened over and over again with Elliott Abhau who, because of her work, had to leave her two cherished horses with her best friends on a farm in Maryland. Over the next ten years, she came to visit every few weeks at irregular intervals. She did not usually tell her friends when she was coming, but they told her that they always knew because of the way the horses behaved: 'The day before, they pick on each other (which never happens otherwise) and then on the day stand at the fence together looking down the driveway.' This happened hours before her arrival by car, the journey taking four to six hours.

Herminia Denot grew up on a ranch in Argentina, and learned to ride almost before she could walk. She was very attached to her horse Pampero, but she had to leave him behind when she went to secondary school in Buenos Aires, returning to the family ranch for her vacations. The *gaucho* (cowboy) who looked after her horse noticed that as the time of her return drew near, 'Pampero would go crazy. He galloped around the ring neighing.' The day before her arrival he would stop in front of the corral gate, looking northwards in the direction of the train station. But on one occasion her parents brought Herminia home by car, and this time Pampero surprised the *gaucho* by looking to the southeast, and not to the north where the trains ran. The direction he was looking in was in fact the direction from which she was approaching by road.

Finally, an English example: Fiona Fowler got her New Forest pony, Joey, when she was 12 and broke him in herself. When she went away to study nursing in London, she had to leave Joey with her mother near Winchester. She went home on days off about twice a month. Her mother noticed that Joey always seemed to know when she was on her way home, making his way from a lower paddock, where he spent most of his time with other horses, to wait at the gate. He continued to do this over a period of years whenever she was returning. 'There was one particular occasion when I wasn't expected home and my mother was surprised to find Joey waiting at the gate as usual. Ten minutes later I phoned from the station requesting to be picked up.'

Stories like these show that some horses seem to know when their owners are coming in a seemingly telepathic way. The next stage in this research would be to carry out videotaped experiments with such a horse, recording its behaviour while the owner sets off home at randomly selected times.

Sheep

Sheep are not often kept as pets, but when lambs are raised by people they can form close attachments, as in the nursery rhyme 'Mary had a little lamb'.

Margaret Railton Edwards and her husband Richard found themselves the owners of a lamb when some sheep-farming friends left a sick one, still on the bottle, at their home in Cheshire. They nursed the lamb back to health and he lived with them in the house for about four months:

> Shambles was almost house trained and would sit on my knee watching TV in the evening. My husband Richard would come home between 5 and 7 pm. About ten minutes prior to his arrival Shambles would sit by the front door and wait for him. Even if Richard was in a

friend's car he would still wait at the door. Occasionally Richard would come home at lunchtime and the same thing would happen.

I have heard from two other people who have kept pet sheep who have had similar experiences. One lamb, Augustus, was adopted by the Ferrier family on Whidbey Island, Washington, and formed a particularly strong attachment to Grant, then aged 14, who fed him, took him for walks, and played butting and ball games with him. Grant's father Malcolm told me that Grant came home from school in the afternoon at irregular times because of various extra activities, but the family could always tell when he was on his way: 'Augustus perked up, baaed, ran about his pen and showed every sign of an event about to happen. And then five minutes later Grant and his pals would appear.' Could Augustus have known by any normal means? Malcolm Ferrier does not think so:

> We talked often about his sequence, and were completely convinced that there was no normal physical method by which Augustus could be aware of Grant being on his way. He couldn't see him (much vegetation), nor hear him when he started his welcoming routine, particularly over the suburban traffic noise. It was very clear to us all, in an amateur and non-experimental way, that some sort of strange communication was taking place; the neighbours often remarked upon it too. Grant often tried, unsuccessfully, to creep up on the beast.

These stories about sheep, though few in number, agree well with the pattern of behaviour shown by dogs, cats, horses, parrots and other kinds of animals. The ability to anticipate a person's return seems to occur in a wide range of mammalian and bird species. In every case, it seems to depend on the formation of close bonds between the person and the animal.

Those species that do not show this kind of anticipation, including fish, reptiles and small mammals like hamsters and mice, may not do so either because they are inherently insensitive to telepathic influences, or because they are incapable of forming bonds with people that are strong enough to act as channels for telepathic communication.

Presumably this ability has not evolved simply in the context of pet-keeping, but occurs between animals in the wild. I return to a discussion of animal-to-animal telepathy in Chapter 9.

If anticipation of returns is so widespread among non-human animals, we might expect that some people might also have a capacity to know when other people are about to arrive.

Humans

Stories abound from people who have lived or travelled in Africa about the way in which some Africans can anticipate arrivals in the absence of any known means of communication. For example, Laurens van der Post found that bushmen in the Kalahari desert of southern Africa could tell when members of their group had killed an eland 50 miles away from their camp, and when they would be returning. The bushmen who hunted it were travelling with van der Post, and as they drove back towards the camp in Land Rovers laden with meat, van der Post wondered how the people there would react when they learned of their success in hunting. One of the bushmen replied, 'They already know'. Sure enough, as they approached the camp they heard the song that was used to celebrate on such occasions. When the eland was killed, they immediately knew 'by wire', as the bushman put it. Van der Post found that they were 'evidently under the impression that the white man's telegraph also worked by telepathy'.[5]

Many people familiar with Africa have had similar experiences. A young European man named Sinel who lived among the tribesmen of the Southern Sudan remarked that 'telepathy is constant'. They always knew where he was and what he was doing, even when he was far away. On one occasion when he got lost, men came out to collect him, as if sensing his plight. On another when he had picked up an arrow tip and brought it back with him, two tribesmen came to ask him if they could examine it.[6] I have heard similar stories in India. Probably such abilities were better developed in traditional societies than they are in the modern industrial world.

Even in some parts of Europe they seem to have been widely recognized. The 'second sight' of the Celtic inhabitants of the Scottish Highlands included 'visions of "arrivals" of persons remote at the moment, which later do arrive'.[7] In Norway there is even a special name for the phenomenon, *vardøger*, which literally means 'warning soul'. Typically, someone at home hears a person walking or driving up to the house, coming in and hanging up their coat. Yet nobody is there. Some ten to thirty minutes later, similar sounds are heard again, but this time the person really arrives. 'People get used to it. Housewives put the kettle over as the *vardøger* arrives, knowing that their husband will arrive soon.'

Fortunately, this phenomenon has been studied by Professor Georg Hygen of Oslo, who investigated dozens of recent cases. He has concluded that this phenomenon is more telepathic than precognitive: in other words the *vardøger* is not so much a pre-echo of what will happen in the future as something related to a person's intentions. For one thing, the sounds are not always identical to those heard in advance. A person might be heard going up to the bedroom whereas when they arrive they go into the kitchen.[8] Moreover, the *vardøger* phenomenon can still occur when a person does not arrive, having changed their mind.

One example concerns a man who had arranged to meet his wife in a store. He then decided to pick her up at her office instead, but he was unable to do this because he was delayed, so he went to wait for her at the store as originally planned. She did not arrive; and after waiting for an hour he went home. When she came back home herself, she complained that he had not come to her office. She had heard his *vardøger*, and from previous experience trusted this so much that she waited at the office for an hour before she gave up.

In the English-speaking world, there is no equivalent word for *vardøger*. Nevertheless, some people spontaneously notice and comment on anticipations of arrivals, although none has mentioned the sound effects typical in Scandinavia. Of these accounts, most concern parents and children, and the remainder husbands and wives.

In some cases a child seemed to anticipate a parent's arrival. Here is an example of a baby doing so:

> Until my son was about eight months old I always knew when his father was on his way home. About seven or eight minutes before he arrived my baby would become very alert and then expectant. As we lived on an active air base at the time I don't think he heard anything and my husband rode a bicycle some of the time. He used to return home unexpectedly at any time of day or night as he was a pilot used to 'scrambling' his aircraft. (Belinda Price)

Other parents have told me that when they go out in the evening leaving their baby with a baby-sitter, quite often their baby wakes up shortly before they arrive home. And when children are old enough to talk, some actually announce the arrival of a parent. This happened when Sheila Michaels was looking after a three-year-old boy in New York while his mother was hospitalized. 'I did not expect his mother to be released for another day. I was reading a favorite story to him when the boy got off the bed and went to the door, calmly saying "Mommy, Mommy", but in a way that upset me terribly. I tried to get him to come back and read the book with me but he could not be budged, repeating, "Mommy, Mommy", endlessly. I told him she would be back tomorrow, and his father was due in a couple of hours. He was immovable. Then his mother walked in.'

I have heard of no cases of fathers anticipating the return of their children, but several of mothers. Here is a dramatic example from World War II. 'During the war my brother Jack served in the Royal Navy, and during active service was not allowed to write home. One evening – when Jack had been away for more than two years – my mother suddenly stood up and said "I must get Jack's bed ready – he'll be here tonight." "What on earth makes you think that?" we asked, laughing at her. "I just KNOW he'll be here," she said and went upstairs to attend to the bed. Later that evening Jack arrived!' (Charles Lawrence)

Most anticipations are more mundane. Bonnie Hardy, who lives in Victoria, British Columbia, as the mother of teenage boys found this phenomenon wore her out through lack of sleep. When the older boys returned home very late at weekends, despite their efforts to be as quiet as possible, she found she was still being disturbed. 'Nothing worked and then I realized that it was not just their movements in the house that disturbed my sleep, but the fact that I woke up when they got in their car to head home.' She woke up first, and then heard them arrive.

In a similar way, some women find they wake up before their husband comes home. Cindy Armitage Dannaker, who lives in Pennsylvania, is one of them: 'It has happened so often that now I just say to myself "He's coming", and wait. Usually within five minutes or so I hear my husband's jeep pulling up our road. I feel like he thinks of me or something and I pick this up in my sleep. All I know is that suddenly for no apparent reason I am wide awake and I feel he is coming.'

Sometimes this anticipation occurs well in advance, particularly when people have been separated for long periods. And sometimes people act on these feelings in an appropriate way, for example by going to meet a particular train or plane.[9] Here is a particularly striking account:

> I was employed by the UN for 14 years, during which time I had to do much travelling. But on only one occasion did I return early to Geneva because of illness, during the 1970s when I was in Abidjan. I did not inform my wife that I was returning, as I didn't want her to fuss and she was at the time on holiday in Austria with our four sons. However, when I arrived back in Geneva she was waiting for me at the airport. She said that she had had an overpowering feeling that she must meet that particular flight so had packed up the family and returned. (O.S. Knowles[10])

If such cases of anticipation by people are viewed in isolation, they seem like scattered anomalies. But in the context of anticipatory behaviour by a wide variety of animal species, they fit into a larger pattern. The anticipation of arrivals seems to be an important aspect of the natural history of telepathy. The fact that these anticipations can occur in babies and when people are asleep shows that they are not dependent on the higher mental faculties. They work at a more fundamental level, and are rooted in our long biological and evolutionary heritage.

PART III

Animal empathy

5

Animals that comfort and heal

Empathy

The word empathy means 'a sympathetic understanding or suffering'.[1] As we have seen, it shares the Greek root *pathe*, feeling or suffering, with the words sympathy and telepathy. However, I am not suggesting that empathy and telepathy are necessarily linked. People no doubt pick up other people's feelings through body language and other sensory information, and animals are sensitive to people in the same way. What is of interest here is not so much the way the feelings are transmitted as the fact that the animal responds to them so sympathetically.

Mutual help is an essential aspect of social life in many animal species. Even those who believe all animal behaviour is shaped by 'selfish genes'[2] acknowledge the importance of altruistic behaviour in ant colonies, in parental care in birds and mammals, and in social groups of every kind.[3] For example, when a member of a herd or flock gives an alarm signal, alerting other members of the group to danger, it may be endangering itself by drawing the attention of a predator towards it.[4]

The selfish-gene theorists acknowledge the reality of altruism in animal social groups, but explain it in terms of selfish genes working for their own survival and reproduction. An individual animal may lay down its life for the greater good of the genes that it shares with its offspring and close genetic relatives.

Altruism between pets and human beings cannot be explained in terms of selfish genes in any straightforward way. A person helping a sick pet, caring for it and paying veterinary bills, is behaving altruistically, but not because of selfish genes shared by the pet and the person. Pets and people have very different genes; they belong to different species. And just as people help pets, so pets help people, not least through their emotional bonding.[5] People form the closest bonds with species that show the greatest empathy towards them: above all, dogs, cats and horses.

Keeping pets can keep us well

Our own cat was called Remedy because my wife Jill soon found that she was just that. Her warm, purring presence was indeed a remedy. She seemed to sense when she was really needed, and sit or lie on Jill or me, working her healing magic.

On my database there are over 200 stories about animals that comfort and heal. Most of them are about cats and dogs staying close to people who are sick or sorrowful, as if to comfort them. Indeed, there is no 'as if' about it. They *do* comfort people, and even help to heal them. A number of scientific research projects have quantified their beneficial effect.

In one American study, elderly people who adopted cats were compared with a similar group of elderly people who did not adopt cats. Regular follow-up interviews and tests showed that within a year there were striking differences between the two groups. As measured by standard psychological tests, the cat owners felt better, while the non-owners felt worse. And although the owners and non-owners did not differ significantly to start with, after a year those with cats felt less lonely, less anxious and less depressed. The cats also had a favourable effect in reducing blood pressure in people with hypertension, and in reducing the need for medication.[6]

Of course, the benefits conferred by the cats were not simply because the cats were in the house, but depended on the bond that developed between the person and the cat. Companion cats provided fun, company and affection, and helped take people's minds off their troubles and their ailments. The stronger the bond, the greater the positive effects seemed to be.[7]

Likewise, relationships with dogs can reduce blood pressure and confer other physiological benefits.[8] These benefits may also be experienced by the dogs themselves, as their heart rates drop while they are being petted.[9]

In a study by Erika Friedmann and her co-workers at the University of Pennsylvania, pet owners who had been hospitalized with heart disease, including heart attacks, showed an improved survival rate a year later than a control group of non-pet owners.[10] The presence of a pet at home was an even stronger predictor of survival than having a spouse or extensive family support.

Pets can also help people who are bereaved. Several studies of people who have recently lost a spouse have shown that pet owners were less depressed, and less prone to feelings of despair and isolation. They also had better general health and needed less medication.[11]

But it is not only sick, elderly, bereaved and vulnerable people that can benefit from keeping pets. These effects are quite general, both for adults and for children.[12] Dogs in particular help people make friends. And research by James Serpell at Cambridge University showed that most people who had recently acquired dogs developed a greater sense of security and self-esteem. Their general health improved, partly because of the increased amount of exercise they took in walking the dog. They also suffered less from minor ailments like headaches, colds and flu.[13]

Pets can help children to develop a better sense of mutuality or involvement with others. The animals not only provide them with acceptance, company and fun, but may also help develop their social skills and a sense of responsibility, as they care for the pets and respond to their needs.[14] And there is evidence that families that acquire pets tend to argue less, feel closer and spend more time playing together.[15]

Although most studies have reinforced the message that pets are good for you, this is not always the case.[16] Pets are not magical, they are good, bad or indifferent, like people. And some people acquire a pet precisely because they want benefits from it, and the heavy weight of expectation can lead to the animal being unceremoniously abandoned or killed because it develops behavioural problems, or fails to make the owner feel better.

As well as the dogs that are kept simply as pets, there are many that help people in very practical ways, including sheepdogs and other working dogs, and the service dogs that play a vital role in the lives of many thousands of people. The best known are guide dogs for blind people, but there are also hearing dogs for deaf people, dogs that assist disabled people, and dogs that alert epileptics to oncoming seizures.

There are also many programmes – over 2,000 in the US alone – in which animals visit people in hospitals, hospices and homes for the elderly. These animals usually belong to volunteers and are often called PAT ('pet as therapy') animals. They are helpful for children, especially for the chronically sick, many of whom eagerly await their animal visitors.[17] They also are very popular among elderly people and among people in hospices, where they can have a relaxing effect on both patients and staff, lighten the mood, provide affection and physical contact, and act as social lubricants.[18]

Some prisons allow animals to visit prisoners, or help prisoners to keep pets themselves, and have found reductions in violence, suicides and drug-taking, as well as improved relationships between prisoners and staff.[19]

How can animals be so beneficial to humans? Attempts to categorize their influences include words like 'empathy', 'acceptance', 'companionship', 'emotional security' and 'affection'. These are the same words that are often applied to the healing effects of other people. The secret of this healing power is the same whether it comes from people or from animals: unconditional love.

Loving unconditionally seems to come more easily to many dogs and cats than it does to most human beings. The loving behaviour of pets is both a cause and effect of the bonds they form with people. It is expressed most notably when their owners are in need.

Comforting cats

One of the most consistent features of accounts of the comforting and healing behaviour of companion animals is that they respond to people's needs. They are not simply behaving in a generically affectionate manner. For example:

> My Kitty always seems to know when I need comfort. One night as I lay down for bed after a very stressful day with the world's troubles heavy on my mind, Kitty jumped up on me, ran up my chest, meowed and placed her paw gently on my face. She seemed to say, 'It's okay, Mom, I love you.' Then she snuggled up under my chin. That was the best medicine I could ever have. (Jahala Johnson, Antioch, Tennessee, USA)

The responsiveness of cats is especially striking in animals that normally cherish their independence.

> For 15 years Baerli, a yellow male cat, was my loyal companion, the joy of my life. He was a gorgeous cat who loved his freedom. When I did not feel well or was sad, though, he never parted with me. Instead he lay on my lap purring and pressing himself closely to me. When I was well again he was off as usual, especially at night. (Gertrude Bositschnick, Leoben, Austria)

When there is more than one cat in the household they sometimes take turns. Karen Richards of Stourbridge, in the West Midlands, lives with five cats and when she was very unwell for months on end, unable to go to work, one of the cats stayed close while the others roamed free.

'The cats had a rota for going out, so I was never left completely on my own.'

Several people have reported that their cats comforted them when they were grieving over the death of a loved one. For example: 'Both cats stuck with me as if they didn't want to leave me alone with my sorrow, and this lasted exactly the time I was mourning. After that the cats were more aloof again.' (Murielle Cahen, Paris)

Many people have commented that their cats behave in an unusually considerate manner when they are ill. A common feature of these stories of considerate and comforting behaviour by cats is that it happens when needed, and goes on as long as necessary. But when the person has cheered up, calmed down or got better, the cat reverts to its usual, more independent behaviour.

Devoted dogs

Many dogs, like many cats, seem to sense when their people are in need of comfort. For example, Jeanette Hamilton of Redwood City, California, finds that her standard poodle, Marcus, is extremely sensitive to her emotions. 'Whenever I cry (silently) he comes to me and licks away my tears. He tunes in whether he's at my feet or in another room, whether he's asleep or awake.'

Out of over 120 accounts of such behaviour by dogs there are many comments like these: 'My dog senses exactly when I do not feel well or am sad.' 'When I am sad, she does not leave me and puts her head on my knees.' One of the simplest yet most eloquent is from Sue Norris of St Helens, Lancashire: 'I am autistic and have a dog Nickita, she knows how I am. She comforts me before I have told her. Sometimes I have bad days. She is there with me where I am.'

Many dogs also seem to know when their person is ill and behave very considerately, staying close and behaving in a truly comforting way. Rosemarie von der Heyde of Achern, Germany, has a dachshund who usually greets her enthusiastically on her return home. 'But once I had injured my heel and when I came home he reacted very differently. He just stood there without moving and looked at me. Slowly he came to me and held out his paw. I lay down on the sofa and contrary to his normal behaviour he did not start jumping on me. He quietly lay down next to me as if to console me.'

Sometimes dogs also seem to know what part of the person's body is painful, and comfort them where it is needed. John Northwood of Poole, Dorset, is a retired policeman who believes dogs should not be allowed on to beds. He often takes out his daughter's collie Ben for walks, but on one occasion when he was visiting he had a bad back and had to lie down.

> As my head hit the pillow, the bedroom door opened and in came Ben. He jumped up on to the bed and stretched out against my back. I felt too ill to say anything but the feel of him against my back was good. He must have sensed that I was unwell and needed warmth.

Some people who suffer from migraines have dogs that come and lie with them while they are suffering. Frau R. Huber of Horgen, Switzerland, found that her dog Nero also knew on which side of her head she had the migraine. 'If it was the right side he excitedly and vigorously licked my right eye and my right forehead with a low whimper. If the pain was on the left he did the same on the other side. It was like a massage.'

Animals preventing suicide

As we have seen, both dogs and cats can be very sensitive to their people's moods and emotions. In some cases their responses go beyond comforting; they can literally save people's lives.

In the midst of a stressful marital problem, a woman in the North of England decided to end her life. Leaving her dog and cats 'sleeping contentedly in a pile in front of the fire', she went into the kitchen for water and paracetamol tablets. Suddenly William, her beloved English springer spaniel, jumped up, ran in front of her, and for the first time in the 15 years of his life, 'He snarled! His jowls were pulled completely back so that he was almost unrecognizable,' she says. 'Horrified, I replaced the bottle top and genuinely afraid of the dog, I went back into the room and sat on the sofa. William bounded after me, leapt on to me and began frantically licking my face, his whole body wagging.'

In some cases dogs have prevented a suicide by alerting others. A German dog called Rexina was shut in the house one day by her owner while he went to a shed in the garden. The dog waited by the door, but after a while she howled and came running to the other members of the family.

> She was very excited and we noticed that our father had been gone for quite a while. We let her out and looked for him. When we found him he said, 'Thank God you came!' Later he admitted that he had intended to commit suicide. Rexina had felt it, and if she had not been there we would have been too late. (Dagmar Schneider)

Cats too have stopped people from killing themselves, like a Swiss cat called Pamponette.

> I was feeling really low and wanted to kill myself. My cat must have felt the state I was in. That day she did not leave my side for one moment. She, who normally never meows, meowed all day, and she rubbed her head against mine each time I sat down. In the afternoon Pamponette usually slept with my other four cats, but she never left my side, and during the night she slept next to my pillow, where she does not normally like to stay. (P. Broccard)

Her behaviour was very like that of cats who comfort their owners when they are sick or upset, but here the stakes were higher.

Animal as therapists

The ancient Greeks thought that dogs could cure illness, and kept them as co-therapists in their healing temples. Asklepios, the chief healing divinity, extended his power through sacred dogs.[20] Although they have no such acknowledged part to play in modern medicine, in practice they have found their way back into a healing role through pet-as-therapy programmes run by volunteers.[21]

Some effects of animals taken to visit sick or elderly people are generic: they have a comforting and cheering influence and take people 'out of themselves'. But sometimes the animals show a remarkable sensitivity to the needs and condition of particular people. For example Chad, a golden retriever, goes almost every day with his owner, Ruth Beale, to visit a hospice in Birmingham, England:

> He seems to know which patients are really poorly compared to the others who he acts the clown with. He will just sit there with his head on their lap or on the bed, or stand there quietly with them. There was one particular lady he came very close to and we had a telephone call at 10 pm saying she was dying and she wanted Chad with her. And he stood with her for three hours while she actually died with his head on the bed.

Chad won the PAT Dog of the Year award in 1997 for his hospice work.

Deena Metzger used to keep a wolf called Timber when she was working as a counsellor, living in the country near Santa Monica, California. He too showed a remarkable sensitivity. 'I watched him discern my patients' needs and come to them, laying his head quietly in their lap, when they were experiencing pain too great to be comforted by a human. His intuition was infallible.'[22] Other counsellors and therapists have also found that their dogs or cats can be very perceptive about their patients' needs and even act as co-therapists. Even Sigmund Freud was assisted by his dog, a chow, who was no mere ornament but part of the process, the 'petting cure', as he called it. She would 'sit quietly at the foot of the couch during the analytic hour'. But towards the end of the session, she helped Freud more than the patient by 'unfailingly beginning to stir', showing that time was up.[23]

Horses have a remarkably therapeutic effect on people with mental or physical problems, including people with Down's syndrome. For many years there have been programmes in Britain and other countries of riding for disabled people, enabling them to gain a new confidence and sense of freedom. In addition to the psychological benefits, they can also achieve improved balance and coordination.[24]

In Calistoga, California, Adele and Deborah McCormick, a mother and daughter team, work as therapists with people with serious mental illness, criminal behaviour and drug addictions. But their work as psychotherapists took on a new dimension when they enlisted the horses on their ranch in the healing process.[25] 'The size, strength and physical presence of the horse make people become more aware, quite literally bringing them to their senses . . . Equine therapy is for anyone who feels down, demoralized, frightened, worried or lost. It is for those who are looking for an alternative means of healing physical illness or who wonder how to handle the pressure of each coming day.'

Many people ride just because they like it, and are receiving many of these benefits without even thinking of their horse as a therapist.

Pets as counsellors

People often talk to their animals, and some confide in them on a regular basis. This can often be of great help. It is as if the animal acts as a counsellor. A woman in Chicago wrote to me about her Bernese Mountain dog as follows:

> When I was sad he came and nudged me as if he wanted to say, 'Don't forget I'm still around!' When he lay down and I told him my troubles he looked at me understandingly with his big eyes and suddenly put his paw on my hand. From then on he has been doing that regularly.

Dr Mary Stewart, of Glasgow University Veterinary School, is a lead-ing researcher on human-animal interactions and also an experienced counsellor. Her familiarity with both these areas has enabled her to com-pare pets, especially dogs, with counsellors.

It is generally agreed that the important attributes of a good coun-sellor are being 'genuine, honest, empathic, nonjudgemental, able to listen, not talking too much, and ensuring total confidentiality'. Mary Stewart points out that these are the very qualities that owners of dogs and other companion animals say they value so highly. It is as if these animal companions are quietly providing a kind of counselling service to their owners without anyone being aware of it. She suggests that one of the reasons that some dogs and other animals increase their owners' self-esteem and encourage feelings of well-being is that they embody 'the core conditions of congruence, empathy and unconditional positive regard, the necessary conditions of any counsellor who endeavours to provide a "growth producing climate" in which clients may get in touch with their own inner resources for development'.[26]

Of course there are major differences. The very fact that animals live so much in the present and are unable to speak means that they cannot help to explore the past, or look at personal relationships and at self-destructive patterns that keep repeating. Here good human therapists are irreplaceable.

But as well as obvious limitations, animals have advantages. Humans, like other primates, find physical contact comforting. Espe-cially when they are young they need to be touched and held lovingly to feel secure. Animals can comfort us by touching us, and we can stroke or cuddle them, but a counsellor has to be careful in offering this kind of reassurance, to avoid possible accusations of abuse.[27]

Perhaps the greatest advantage of animals is their capacity for love. For clients with low self-esteem, it is difficult to accept that any human can have much regard for them, and so it is hard to feel counsellors really accept them, rather than just seeming to do so. Some fear that if all were revealed, the acceptance would be withdrawn. By contrast, they can easily believe that their animals love them unconditionally. And, as Jef-frey Masson shows so vividly in his book of that title, 'dogs never lie about love'.[28]

Dogs faithful after death

The devotion of some dogs continues after their person has died. Some-times their devotion is so striking that they unwittingly achieve not only fame and a place in popular mythology, but have monuments erected to them. There is one by the lonely waters of the Derwent Dam in Derbyshire, erected by public subscription and inscribed as follows:

IN COMMEMORATION OF THE
DEVOTION OF
TIP
THE SHEEPDOG WHO STAYED
BY THE BODY OF HER DEAD
MASTER, MR JOSEPH TAGG,
ON THE HOWDEN MOOR FOR
FIFTEEN WEEKS
FROM 12TH DECEMBER 1953
TO 27TH MARCH 1954

Tip's master was a retired gamekeeper, aged 81, who was found dead on the high moors fifteen weeks after setting off with Tip from his home in Bamford for a ramble over the hills. Search parties failed to discover them, snow had covered the hills, and they had long been presumed dead. Three and a half months later a couple of shepherds came across the body of Joseph Tagg with Tip beside it, in a piteous condition but still alive. She rapidly became a national heroine and spent her final year in luxury at the home of her master's niece, who had to protect the dog from hosts of admiring visitors. A vast crowd assembled for the unveiling of her memorial, and pilgrims still visit her shrine.[29]

A similar celebrity attended the terrier belonging to a young man called Charles Gough, who died in a remote part of the Lake District in 1805. His remains were found months later by a shepherd, attracted to the spot by the emaciated dog still hovering around the corpse. Sir Edwin Landseer immortalized the scene in a painting, and a host of poets and artists added their own tributes.[30] The greatest of them, William Wordsworth, commemorated the dog in his poem 'Fidelity', which ends with these lines:

Yes, proof was plain that, since the day
When this ill-fated Traveller died,
The Dog had watched about the spot,
Or by his master's side:
How nourished here through such long time
He knows, who gave that love sublime;
And gave that strength of feeling, great
Above all human estimate!

Countless other dogs never achieve such fame yet show deep devotion to their people after death. They are often grief-stricken, and go through what can only be described as a period of mourning. Some lose all will to live. For example: 'Immediately after the death the dog refused all food and itself died about a fortnight later.' A few bereaved dogs even seem to commit suicide, by jumping out of windows or running out under lorries.

Some somehow find their owner's grave and stay there, like Greyfriars Bobby, the famous faithful dog of Edinburgh. Others visit regularly, but still come home, if they have a home to come to:

> My husband suffered a severe stroke in 1988, and died in hospital after having been there for two weeks. After his burial in a churchyard near our house, Joe, the dog, would disappear for hours and we discovered that he was sitting by my husband's grave. How did he know when my husband died, and where he was buried? (Molly Parfett, Wadebridge, Cornwall)

Such stories of enduring devotion illustrate how strong the bonds between dogs and their owners can be, and reinforce their age-old reputation for loyalty.

6

Distant deaths and accidents

If there are invisible bonds between animals and owners that enable them to respond to each other's needs, and also enable some pets to know telepathically when their owners are heading home, it would be surprising if these bonds were not affected by the distress or death of the owner.

The effects of death and distress are not subjects that lend themselves to experimental investigation. Obviously, no one can be asked to have an accident for the sake of science, or die at a randomly selected time so that the reactions of their pet can be observed. The evidence necessarily comes exclusively from spontaneous cases.

On our database there are currently 108 accounts of dogs apparently responding to distant accidents or deaths of their human companions, 51 accounts of cats doing so, and ten of humans knowing when their pet was in distress or had died at a distance. What can we learn from these cases?

Dogs and distant accidents

Sometimes dogs show unmistakeable signs of distress for which no immediate reason can be found. It later turns out that their owner was at that very time in danger, or had an accident:

> One day our dog acted like mad, jumped at the door and wanted to get out. We locked her in. But she continued howling, scratching, was not herself. Suddenly my husband came home. He was injured because there had been a fight in the bar. The dog had known it. We do not know how. (Hilde Albrecht, Limbach, Germany)

In a case such as this it is scarcely conceivable that the dog could have known about her owner's experience by sight, smell or hearing. Nevertheless, sceptics might argue that the bar must have been close enough for the normal senses to have detected some clue. But often the accidents occur many miles away from home, beyond the range of all known senses.

One summer evening in 1991, a young British soldier left his home in Liverpool to return by train to his barracks in southern England. Later that evening, the family dog Tara started whining and shivering violently. The boy's parents thought she must be ill, gave her some paracetamol and tried to comfort her. But she would not calm down for over an hour. She remained alert and restless until the telephone rang:

> The phone call was from a Birmingham hospital to say that David had fallen from the train in the Tamworth area [80 miles away]. His injuries, though severe, were not serious and they allowed him to speak to us. Tara showed her delight during the phone call, then lay down and went to sleep. We learned afterwards that she first got upset at the moment he fell off the train, and calmed down when he was in hospital having been examined and made more comfortable. (Margaret Sweeney)

There are eleven cases on the database of dogs reacting to distant emergencies in a comparable way, by showing signs of distress or restlessness. As well as the two examples given above, five involved car or motorbike accidents; one a capsized kayak; one a fire; one a heart attack; and one took place when a woman was giving birth in a maternity hospital 16 miles away.

Remarkably, while I was writing this chapter, I personally experienced a dog's reactions coinciding with a distant accident. During the school half-term holidays in February 1998, we were looking after a yellow Labrador named Ruggles, belonging to some friends and neighbours, the Beyer family. The son, Timothy, was away on a school skiing trip in the Italian Alps; his parents had gone on holiday in Spain. Ruggles settled in well, and spent most of his time in our family room. But one morning when he returned from a walk at 11.30 am, he would not leave the entrance hall. All persuasion failed. He remained by the front door until he was taken out for another walk at 3 pm. So striking and unusual was his behaviour that I thought that Timothy's mother and father must have decided to come home early. I was expecting a telephone call from them to say that they had just arrived.

There was indeed a telephone call that afternoon, but it was not from Timothy's parents. It was from Italy, to say that Timothy had fallen off a chair-lift that morning and broken a leg; he had been flown by helicopter to hospital. The accident happened at 11 am British time. (Curiously enough, when Ruggles returned from his afternoon walk, he was limping. He had jumped into a pond and landed on some broken glass, and had a bleeding paw and a severed tendon. He had to spend the night at a veterinary clinic. So he and Timothy were both in hospital at the same time with bandaged legs.)

Obviously it is impossible to know for sure whether the dog's reactions between 11.30 am and 3 pm were really due to the boy's accident. Ruggles did not seem particularly distressed when he was waiting by the door. Rather, it was as if he knew something important was happening and felt he had to be at the ready. But his reaction was so definite, and the coincidence so remarkable, that I think there could well have been a causal connection.

In this case, as in most cases, the dog's reactions were of no use to the injured person. Apart from anything else, the animal was too far away. But in some cases dogs have helped save their owner's life, or tried to do so.

In one, the dog's owner had fallen out of a kayak in the middle of the river Rhine, and was struggling: 'In my weak condition I saw my friends running towards me with my dog. She was pulling them with her and barking loudly. They asked whether I had any trouble because the dog had suddenly started to tear at the lead and wanted to go down to the river – at exactly the moment when I had almost given up my struggle against the water.'

In another, in Northern Ireland, a German shepherd, Chrissie, saved the life of his owner, Walter Berry, who got covered in petrol while repairing a car and then accidentally set himself alight with a welding tool. The dog was 200 yards away with Walter's wife Joan when this happened, through a couple of double garages and a yard. 'Chrissie went berserk – and made noises that he had never made before', Joan said. She realized something was wrong, and let Chrissie out. He rushed straight towards Walter. Joan followed, and fortunately arrived in time to put the fire out. Chrissie saved Walter's life.

In these two cases, precisely because the dogs were close enough to be of help, it is hard to rule out the possibility that they were alerted by sound or other sensory clues. However, this objection cannot apply to a dog in San Francisco named Lupé, who saved her owner's life when she was over 40 miles away:

When Lupé was about two years old, I had taken an overdose of drugs on a day when she was visiting with friends in San Jose. It was reported to me afterwards that Lupé had suddenly gone to the end of the property and begun to howl 'uncannily' and her agitation could not be relieved. After some time, my friends thought 'Something must be wrong with Leone', and they rushed to San Francisco and found me. (Leone Katafiasz).

In many cases where dogs howl for no apparent reason, or show other obvious signs of distress, it later turns out that their owner was not just in danger but actually dying. Nothing that the dog can do can save them.

Dogs that howl when their owners die

Out of 40 accounts I have received about the reaction of dogs to the death of an absent person to whom they were attached, 36 (90 per cent) involved vocal responses. In 21 cases the dogs howled; in five they whimpered or whined; in four, barked in an unusual way; in three, 'cried'; and in three growled. In the four cases where no sounds were mentioned, they were said to be 'upset', 'miserable', 'shivering', or 'distressed'.

The most impressive cases are those in which the animal shows clear signs of distress at unexpected times, especially when the person and the animal are far apart. In the following example, from the Falklands War, they were separated by over 6,000 miles:

> My son was very close to our West Highland terrier. He joined the Royal Navy in 1978 and being shore-based much of his time until 1982, was home regularly for weekends. He travelled by train. We gradually came to realize that the dog would start getting excited about 20-30 minutes before he walked in the door, so as soon as she started running backwards and forwards to the front door, I would start getting him a high tea so that when he walked in (always hungry) his meal was ready. We used to laugh about it at the time. In April 1982 his ship, HMS *Coventry*, was drafted to the Falklands. Early evening May 25th the dog leapt on to my knee shivering and whimpering. When my husband came in, I said 'I don't know what's wrong with her, she's been like this for more than half an hour. She won't be put down off my knee.' On the 9 o'clock news, it was said a 'Type 42' had been sunk, we knew it was HMS *Coventry* although the name wasn't given out until next day. Our son was one of those lost. Our little dog pined away and died in a few months. (Iris Hall, Cowley, Oxford)

Typically, the dog's distress or its howling can only be understood in retrospect:

> My brother Michael was a co-pilot in a Wellington bomber during the war. He went on many raids over Germany in 1940. At that time we

had a dog Milo who was half spaniel, half collie, and was particularly fond of Michael. One night in June, Michael was on his way home from a raid when he radioed to base to say that he was just off the coast of Belgium and would soon be back. That same night, Milo, who slept in a stable at the back of the house, howled so much that my mother had to get up and bring him into the house. Michael never returned from his mission that night. He was reported missing, believed killed, 10 June 1940. (Stephen Hyde, Acton, London)

My husband and I were on holiday in County Cork in Eire in April 1968, and on Easter Saturday my husband died very suddenly. Our seven-year-old standard poodle was staying with friends in St Albans. At just after midnight the poodle howled and rushed upstairs to my friend, who was in the bath. At just after midnight my husband died. (Mrs G. Moore, St Albans, Hertfordshire)

If the bond between person and animal is indeed a real connection, linking them together invisibly even over thousands of miles, then the disruption of this bond through the death of one, or through severe danger, might be *expected* to affect the other. To take a simple analogy, if two people are connected by a stretched elastic band, and one of them shakes it or lets it go, the other feels a difference. Even if they do not know exactly what is happening to the other person, they know *something* is happening.

It seems very unlikely that dogs form such bonds only with people. They are social animals and can form strong connections with each other. Do dogs react when other dogs to whom they are attached die in distant places? Sometimes they do. Here is one example, out of seven cases in our database in which the death of the other dog took place unexpectedly and at a distance:

I have a Beance sheepdog, Yssa, two years old, who came with me to France at the age of three months from the island of La Réunion in the Indian Ocean, 10,000 km away. There, I left her mother, Zoubida, aged ten. On 13 February this year, she was sleeping in my son's room. About 3 am she came scratching at my door, whining, crying and excited. She didn't want to go outside. At 9 am my brother-in-law called from La Réunion. The guard of our house had found Zoubida dead. She had been poisoned. (Dr Max Rallon, Châteauneuf le Rouge, France)

The existence of so many independent accounts of this type persuades me that this is a real phenomenon, even though it is not possible to do experiments. But further research is needed through the collection of more well-documented stories, the most convincing being those involving several witnesses of the dogs' behaviour.

Why do dogs howl when their person dies?

Howling is not found in all the species of the dog family – foxes do not howl, for instance – but is restricted to members of highly social species, such as domestic dogs, dingoes, coyotes and wolves.[1]

The literature on wolf ecology suggests that they howl for two main reasons: first and foremost, to help assemble the pack, particularly before a hunt. Second, lone individuals howl either to seek contact with other pack members or to attract other wolves during the breeding season.[2]

Some wolves and dogs howl at the moon or the sky: no one knows why. And some howl in response to the sound of singing or the violin, as if they are trying to sing along. But like lone wolves, domestic dogs most often howl when they are on their own, deprived of the company of humans or other dogs, especially if they are shut away. Desmond Morris says this 'howl of loneliness' is a way of saying 'join me'.[3] So what about their howls when a close companion dies?

Of the accounts I have received of dogs that howled when their owners died, some were shut outdoors, and their howling caused them to be brought inside, as in the case of Milo. In this limited sense their howling worked, and brought them companionship and comfort. But in many cases the dogs howled when they were not shut out, and the attempts of people to comfort them were unsuccessful, at least to start with. Perhaps this kind of howl is a way of expressing grief. And it may have a long evolutionary ancestry, because several observers of wolves have observed that 'wolves howl in a particularly mournful way when a beloved companion has died'.[4]

The animals that did *not* howl were clearly very disturbed or upset. They obviously felt something was wrong. Perhaps they did not know what: they may simply have been in an apprehensive or fearful state. If human companions were nearby, they usually went to them for comfort.

The responses of cats to distant accidents and deaths

Although fewer cats than dogs seem to react to accidents and emergencies, the situations in which they do so are similar, as the following examples show:

In May 1994 I sat outside on the verandah, and our three-year-old Persian cat, Klaerchen lay beside me, purring comfortably. My 11-year-old daughter had gone out with her girlfriend on her bicycle. Everything seemed wonderful and harmonious, but suddenly Klaerchen jumped up, uttered a cry that we had never heard before and in a flash ran into the living room, where she sat down in front of the shelves with the telephone. The phone soon rang and I got the news that my daughter had had a bad accident with the bike and had been taken to hospital. (Andrea Metzger, Bempflingen, Germany)

The ways cats respond to distant deaths are similar to the way they react to emergencies. Most commonly, they make unusual sounds, such as howls, plaintive meows or whining, and show other signs of distress.

We had a beautiful Carthusian tomcat that we all loved, but he loved my husband most of all. In the summer holidays we went camping in Denmark and left the cat at an animal home in Switzerland. In Denmark my husband, who was 48 years old and had never been ill, died of a heart attack. When we went to pick up our cat, the lady told us she knew exactly when a tragedy had happened to us and then gave us the exact day and hour – which she could not have known! Our tomcat had withdrawn into a corner and whined in a way he had never done before, staring at a certain point in front of him as if he observed something special, his whole body shaking. (Hedwig Ritter, Zurich, Switzerland)

But while most cats seemed to respond vocally to the death of a distant person, some reacted silently. One cat simply hid on the night the father of a family was dying in hospital: 'Nobody could find him, he never went out. He only came out of hiding when we came back for the burial.'(Mme Charlin, Lyons, France) Other cats changed their sleeping places.

The effect of the person's death does not seem to fall off with distance. In some of the cases in our collection the person dying was thousands of miles away, yet their cat still seemed to know. For example, a tomcat belonging to a family in Switzerland was very attached to their son Frank, who went away to work as a ship's cook. He came home irregularly, and the cat used to wait for him at the door before he arrived. But one day, the cat sat at the door and meowed in extreme sadness. 'We could not get him away from the door. Finally we let him into Frank's room, where he sniffed at everything but still continued his wailing. Two days after the cat's strange behaviour we were informed that our son had died at exactly that time on his voyage, in Thailand.' (Karl Pulfer, Koppingen, Switzerland) The distance was over 7,000 miles.

Human reactions to distant
deaths of animals

If, as I have suggested, the bond between animal and person can be thought of as being like an elastic band, then it should allow influences to pass in both directions, from person to animal and from animal to person. We have already considered influences passing from a person to an animal. What about influences in the other direction? Do some people react to their animals when they have had accidents or are dying at a distance?

Judging from the numbers of reports in the database, humans are generally less sensitive to their animals than animals are to their people. We have 54 reports of animals reacting to the distant death of people and only seven the other way round. All seven came from women. Five concerned dogs, and two cats. Five took place when the women were awake, and two in dreams.

The waking experiences typically involved feelings of worry and distress, and some involved physical symptoms as well. For example, on 20 May 1997, Dianne Arcangel was leaving a hotel to go to the airport to catch a plane home to Texas. Soon after the car journey began, at 4.05 pm Texas time, she began to feel agitated, but could find no reason for it.

> As we continued the drive, I began to feel nauseated and to perspire. After about 15 minutes I was feeling that my stomach and intestines were being torn so intensely that I held my stomach and bent over. By the time we arrived at the airport, I felt physically sick and in deep grief. Fearful that something was very, very wrong at home I called my daughter. 'We just had a terrible storm with lightning, but it is over now,' she said, and she told me everything was fine. But I cried all the way home. When I arrived at Houston airport at 10 pm I found my husband in tears. He explained that lightning hit our house at 4.08 pm (all our clocks were stopped at this time). Kitty, one of my eight cats, was so terrified of the storm that she ran outside. When my husband got home, he saw two large dogs in the back yard, standing over her lifeless body. As he pulled them away, he could see they were both covered with her blood and hair. The trauma to her body was where I felt excruciating pain at the same time it was occurring to her. (Dianne Arcangel, Pasadena, Texas)

Some other women have also experienced physical distress, but in a less specific way. In this case of Mary Wall, who lives in Wiltshire, it occurred when she was over 2,000 miles away from her Shi Tzu dogs, on holiday with her husband in Cyprus:

At 4 pm Cyprus time on a Friday I was overcome by an intense sensation, so much so that I eventually mentioned it to my husband. Something was desperately wrong with the dogs. The sensation was so strong it was physically distressing. On arriving at Heathrow airport a few days later I was told the boy dog died the previous Saturday. I would never have believed a dog or any animal could 'get through' to a human, though I have experienced 'knowing' what was happening two or three times in my life, but only concerning close relations.

Sometimes there was a feeling that something was wrong, but not specifically connected with the dog. For example, a Swiss woman working in her office in Basel had a strange feeling one morning. She mentioned to her workmates but could not explain it. 'After about one hour the thought went through my head, "You should ring up home." I learned that an hour before our Alsatian dog had been hit by a car and died.' (Lotti Rieder-Kunz)

In other cases, the knowledge that the dog had died was quite explicit. Nancy Millian of New Haven, Connecticut, had gone on vacation leaving her dog Blaze at home. 'About five days into the trip, I became incredibly agitated and heard the words, "Blaze died" in my head. I told my friend who responded that I was probably just experiencing normal worry. I called home and was assured that all was well.' Two days later she arrived home to learn that her dog had indeed died the day she felt agitated. His caretaker had not wanted to upset her, knowing there was nothing to be accomplished by her early return.

Finally, here is an example of explicit information coming through in the dream of a teenage girl:

In the summer of 1992 I was away from home the month of July. One night I had a nightmare that my cat had been run over by a car in our road (we were living in Belgium at the time and I was in Holland). I remembered the dream the next morning and since I kept a diary at the time, I wrote down my dream. When I got home I was told that my cat had been run over. I checked my diary and it was the same night that I had had my dream. (Laura Broese)

In all these cases, the people and their animals were far apart and there could have been no transfer of information through normal sensory channels. Telepathy, or something like it, seems to me the only plausible explanation. Just as animals can react telepathically when their owners are in distress or dying, people can be influenced in a similar way by their animals' distress or death.

People who know when other people have died

The phenomena described in this chapter so far concern people and non-human animals. Yet similar reactions to distant deaths and accidents can occur between people and people. Indeed, some of the most impressive cases of human telepathy concern people at a distance who are in danger or who are dying. The pioneers of psychical research, starting over a century ago, built up impressive collections of such cases, authenticated through careful enquiry and attested by witnesses.[5] In just over half these cases, people dreamed of the person who was dying or in distress. Of the cases that occurred when people were awake, the majority involved an impression or intuition without a visual image. About 20 per cent of the total number of cases involved images or hallucinations.[6]

Of the cases in the database in which people seemed to know about the distress or death of distant pets, one involved visual imagery – the dream about the cat being run over. The others involved feelings, impressions or intuitions. So the same kinds of experience seem to occur with pets as with other people, even though the proportions of dreaming and waking, or visual and non-visual communications may differ. Just as most cases of person-to-person telepathy depend on close relationship, so do the person-to-pet and pet-to-person cases discussed in this chapter.

PART IV

Intentions, calls
and telepathy

7

Picking up intentions

Bonds between dogs and people have been built up over tens of thousands of years, and between cats and people, and horses and people for at least five thousand years. They are inter-species social bonds that have evolved subject to natural selection and to deliberate human selection over many generations.

The social bonds between people and domesticated animals are similar to the bonds that exist between animals of the same species, for example between a pair of wrens and their nestlings; or members of a school of fish; or wolves in a hunting pack, or members of an Australian aboriginal tribe. They are bonds within the morphic fields of the social groups. Through these fields, members of the group can remain connected even when they are far apart, and can communicate telepathically with each other.

We have already seen how this kind of communication at a distance enables pets of many species to know when their owners are coming home. In some cases, the animals seem to detect their person's intention to come home even before they have set off. Some human beings have a similar capacity, but it is better developed in traditional rural societies than in modern ones, and in our urban civilization is more evident among young children than adults. With people, as with non-human animals, these telepathic anticipations occur only when there are close emotional bonds with the person returning.

These close bonds, whether between humans, or for our purpose here, between animals and humans, are emotionally resonant as well. Animals can comfort and heal their people. Even when far apart, some of the bonded partners can tell when the other partner is in distress or dying. This too involves a kind of telepathy, and works both ways, from people to animals and from animals to people.

This leads to a discussion of the ways in which people's intentions, calls and commands can affect their companion animals, and ways in which animals can likewise affect people. In some cases, these intentions, calls and needs seem to be communicated telepathically. This telepathic ability exists within animal societies in the wild, demonstrating that telepathy has a long evolutionary ancestry. Telepathy is natural, not supernatural, and is an important aspect of animal communication. Human telepathy needs to be seen in this broader biological context.

I start here by considering the ways in which animals pick up their owners' intentions, and people pick up their pets'.

Animals 'reading minds'

Many people have noticed that their animals seem to 'read their minds'. The perceptiveness of pets may well depend on a combination of influences, such as the observation of body language, hearing particular words and learning the owners' routines. In addition, they may be able to pick up intentions directly by a kind of resonance or telepathy. As we have seen in Parts II and III, some animals pick up people's intentions and feelings when they are miles away, so it would be surprising if they could not do so when close by.

Many people experienced with animals take telepathy for granted, and there is a wealth of anecdotal experience that points to the reality of telepathic influences. On the other hand, committed sceptics believe that any mysterious connections currently unknown to science are impossible, or too unlikely to merit serious attention.

The only way to resolve this issue is to take a close look at the evidence from people's experiences with their pets, and then to carry out experiments to clarify what is going on.

Cats that disappear before visits to the vet

Some cats strongly dislike going to the vet. Dozens of cat owners have told me that their cats simply vanish when they are due to be taken for their appointment. Experienced owners of such cats try to avoid giving away any clues, but often their efforts are in vain:

> The cat always knows hours ahead of time when I am going to take him to the vet, long before I actually fetch his basket from the attic. I try to act as naturally as possible so he won't notice, but he can see

> through me at any time and will yowl to go out. (Andrea Künzli, Starr-
> kirsch, Switzerland)

This is inconvenient not only for the owners but also for the vets. Some advise people to keep their cat shut up indoors before the appointment, especially when injections or operations are involved. But some cats still escape.

How common is this kind of behaviour? We carried out a survey of the veterinary clinics listed in the North London Yellow Pages Telephone Directory. We interviewed the vets themselves, or their nurses or recep-tionists, asking whether they found that some cat owners cancelled appointments because the cat had disappeared. Sixty-four out of 65 clinics had cancellations of this kind quite frequently. The remaining clinic had abandoned an appointment system for cats: people simply had to turn up with their cat, and thus the problem of missed appoint-ments had been resolved.

Although there was general agreement that some cats do indeed pick up their owners' intentions, there was a variety of opinions as to how they might do it:

> It is not always the cat basket. The clients know that once they produce
> the basket there is not a hope in hell of catching the cats, so it is usu-
> ally before the baskets have been brought out. People say they get
> home around 5.30 pm and the cat is always on the doorstep, but the
> day of the appointment he is not there. I think they have definitely
> read their thoughts because the owner has not been in all day so they
> cannot have seen that the owner is upset or behaving any differently.
> They say 'I don't know why he hasn't come back for his tea. It's very
> odd.' (Veterinary Receptionist, East Barnet)

> Sometimes people say they have gone to get the basket out and the cat
> has stayed in the bushes in the garden, or cats don't always come back
> in the morning and that's before they have seen the basket. They are
> expected to come in for their breakfast and they stay in a tree. Or for
> evening appointments, the people go out to work and in the mean-
> time the cat goes and hides. (Veterinary Nurse, Wembley)

> Sometimes the cats see the cat basket and sometimes they disappear
> for no apparent reason. It happens quite often. Animals do have extra
> senses we do not understand particularly. I would not go so far as to say
> this is telepathic, but they are very finely tuned to different situations.
> They can pick up on people's behaviour and feelings, but I would not
> go as far as to say on their thoughts. (Veterinarian, Eastcote)

It is usually hard, if not impossible, to disentangle the ways in which animals pick up their owner's intentions when they are nearby. But what if at the moment a person decides to take the cat to the vet the cat is not present? For example, if a person rings the vet from her place of work to make an appointment for that same evening, will the cat have disappeared when she goes home to collect it? And would this still happen if the day for visiting the vet was chosen at random by a third party, and the cat owner was informed only after arriving at work? In this way, the possibility of a telepathic component in the ability of some cats to read their owners' intentions could be put to the test experimentally.

Other feline aversions

Visits to vets are not the only thing cats try to avoid. Some also run away when they are going to be given medicine or sprayed for fleas, or subjected to other procedures they dislike.

> My cat Ciggy knows where a lot of his food comes from and often takes up a position nearby waiting expectantly for his next meal. When, however, I go to the same cupboard to get his spray to treat his coat, even before I get hold of the spray he makes a dash to go out through his cat flap into the garden to avoid being sprayed. I never tell him when I am going to spray him and I have even tried thinking of something else whilst going for the spray but he always seems to sense my intention. (Sheila Howard, Wandsworth, London)

Cats also tend to disappear before they are going to be taken away for good. For many years Pauline Westcott of Roehampton, Surrey, did rescue work with cats, collecting them in response to telephone calls from their finders or from people who no longer wanted them. In nine out of ten cases the cats had to be destroyed.

> We continually found that if an appointment was made to collect them, even with strenuous efforts on the part of the keeper, the animals would in many cases not be found at all. We were told the cat disappeared within minutes of the call being made to make an appointment, or even just before the call was made. Only by boarding up a room and literally shutting every single entrance, crack, ventilator, etc. could we be sure of finding the animal. So much time, petrol and man hours were wasted that our system had to be altered time and time again. There were inevitably visits when a cat was never captured.

The cats' awareness of imminent danger is obviously of survival value, and if wild animals have comparable abilities, they would presumably be favoured by natural selection. But even less is known about such intuitions in wild animals than in pets.

Compared with cats, dogs rarely disappear or try to hide before going to the vet. However, some seem to know when they are on the way to the clinic. Maxine Finn, a Veterinary Receptionist in North London, described their reactions as follows:

> A lot of clients have dogs that know when they are coming to the vet. When they are driving the dog starts shaking and whining as if they know they are on their way. About one client a week says that. Sometimes we have clients that come back a few years after their last visit and the dogs still start to shake on the way. They either seem to remember the route or they somehow pick up where they are going to.

Some dogs, like cats, also anticipate when they are about to be subjected to procedures they dislike, such as being washed or having their nails or fur clipped.

> On the day our poodle Snowy was going to be clipped (about every six weeks) no matter what precautions we took to stop her knowing she always crawled under the piano or a bed to hide – to this day I shall never know how she knew other than reading my mind. (Sylvia Scott, Goostrey, Cheshire.)

The commonest way in which dogs respond to their owners' intentions is not through aversions, but through their enthusiasm for walks.

Dogs that anticipate going for walks

Most dogs are excited by the prospect of a walk and react with eager anticipation when they see their owners preparing to take them out, or hear words such as 'walk'. Some are taken as a matter of routine at the same time every day, at which time they get excited. For example, if they are usually taken out after a particular TV show has ended, when they hear the end-title music or see the set being switched off, they show signs of anticipation. In this respect their reactions are like the 'conditioned reflexes' studied by the Russian physiologist I.P. Pavlov, who found that when dogs were repeatedly given meat after they heard a bell ring, they came to associate the bell with feeding and salivated when it rang, before they even saw the meat.

But many dog owners do not take their dogs out at routine times, and some have found that their dog's excitement begins *before* they have given any obvious signs, such as putting on their coat or getting out the lead. For example:

> Because of work and family commitments I take my dog Digby for walks at different times of the day, but he always seems to know when I'm thinking of taking him. He can be lying down quietly and I'll be doing something in the house and I'll think to myself, 'I'll just finish this and then I'll take Digby out.' Then up he gets and follows me about with that expectant look on his face, wagging his tail. I don't know if it's body language or my thoughts he reads, but it can be as long as half an hour before we actually go out but he still knows that thought is on my mind. He doesn't take his eyes off me or leave my side. This has often amazed me (and irritated me! – I keep falling over him). I keep thinking 'How does he know?' (Mrs R. Kellard, Abington, Northamptonshire)

Many other people are puzzled by the way their dogs seem to read their thoughts even when they are not giving any sign of their intention. We have over 50 such reports on our database. Like Mrs Kellard, most informants are well aware of the possibility that body language could give the game away, but some have come to the conclusion that this cannot always be the explanation, because their dogs still react when sleeping or out of sight:

> I just cannot understand how my dog Ginny, a mongrel I have had for seven years, can know when I am going to walk him (and the other two dogs). Only thinking of it is enough for him to jump about joyfully. Here I should add that my animals can move freely on our estate, whenever they feel like it. I have performed this experiment several times with him. In order to exclude any possibility of eye contact and information through the other senses I left the dog outside in the garden and behind closed windows and doors when I thought of taking him. And still the same result every time: he behaves like mad from sheer joy and expectation. When I dress to leave for work, however, he remains totally quiet. My other two dogs are not like him. (Liliane Hoschet, Cessange, Luxembourg)

> I could be doing anything or nothing, just sitting sewing or baking, and the thought would come in my head, 'Go for a walk, take the

dogs, it's nice out', and the dachshunds would be there at my feet wagging their tails. They could not tell from my expression or movements as this happened when they were in the garden or fast asleep. I deliberately tested this theory and no way could they see me. Once the thought was in my head, my dogs knew, no matter what they were doing at the time. (Mary Rothwell, Arnold, Nottingham)

With dogs that respond in this way, it is possible to do simple experiments in which the dogs are kept where they cannot hear, see or smell their owner, and are filmed continuously on videotape. Then at a randomly selected time the owner starts thinking of taking them for a walk, and after a delay of, say, five minutes, actually does so. Does the videotape show that the dogs show signs of excitement before going on the walk, and after their owner had formed the intention to take them?

Some preliminary experiments of this kind have already been carried out at my request by Jan Fennell of Winterton, Lincolnshire. She is an animal behaviourist and well aware of the way in which animals can pick up routine patterns or clues from their owners' behaviour. She has six dogs, and had already observed that the dogs seemed to know when she was intending to take them out at non-routine times, and when she tried to avoid giving them any clues.

For the purpose of the experiment, the dogs were shut up in an outbuilding where they were filmed continuously by a video camera on a tripod, pointing towards the door. She thought about taking them for walks at randomly selected times during the period that the video was running. The experiments were carried out on five different days: once in the morning, twice in the afternoon and twice in the evening.

The videotapes show that most of the time the dogs lay around, or played together, while now and then some of the dogs reacted, briefly, with pricked ears to sounds from the outside, such as passing motorbikes. But after Jan had decided to take them for a walk, in four out of five videotapes, the dogs moved closer to the door and sat or stood in a semicircle around the door, some with their tails wagging. They remained in this state of obvious anticipation for three to five minutes before Jan came and opened the door to let them out for their walk. By contrast, in the remaining videotape, they showed no such advance reaction, and showed interest only 13 seconds before she entered the outbuilding, probably in response to the sound of her approaching.

In addition, in a control experiment Jan shut the dogs up and visited the outbuilding at a randomly selected time but with no intention of taking them for a walk. When she went to the outbuilding, only one of the dogs went to the door before she opened it, a mere 12 seconds in advance. When she opened the door, the other dogs got up and moved around, but remained quite calm and showed none of the excitement that preceded a walk.

These pioneering experiments suggest that the dogs could indeed anticipate their owner's intention to take them out on most, but not all, occasions, without being able to see her.

Dogs that know when they are being taken out by car

Some dogs anticipate when they are going to set off with their owner in a car. This phenomenon is similar to the anticipation of walks. Although routines or normal sensory clues may often account for the dogs' reactions, this is not always the case. Here is an example from Australia:

> My wife and I leave home at irregular intervals to go shopping, etc. In general we take the dog along in our car. On departure the dog will sit next to the tail gate to be let into the rear compartment of the car. If I come out of the house with the intention to go away the dog will dash to the tail gate. But if I leave the house with the car keys in my hand only to pick up something which I have left in the car, the dog will not respond. Today when we were at the table for morning tea, my wife said she would like to go shopping in about five minutes. Looking out of the kitchen window, I saw the dog already sitting next to the tail gate, facing the door of the house in expectation. At this point of time I had not left the house and had no prior contact with the dog. There was absolutely no physical element, to our knowledge, that could have indicated to the dog that we were about to go away. (Dieter Eigner, Powelltown, Victoria)

On our database there are over 30 such examples, but there is no need to discuss them at length because of their general similarity to anticipation of walks by dogs. The same considerations apply to experiments designed to eliminate normal sensory clues. The decision to go in the car should be taken at a randomly selected time with the owner separated from the dog in such a way that the dog could not receive any information by sight, hearing or smell. The dog's reaction should be recorded on a continuously running videotape, with the camera pointing to the area where the dog usually waits (in this example, by the tail gate of the car).

Pets that know when their owners are about to leave them

It makes a big difference in the lives of domestic animals when their owners go out, especially when they go away on holiday or on other protracted journeys. Many dogs and cats seem to pick up their owners' intention to leave. No doubt this often happens because the animals see obvious preparations such as the packing of suitcases. But on our database there are over 100 reports from pet owners who think the animals know even before they have seen any tell-tale signs. For example: 'Our Labrador, if anyone was going on holiday, would go round looking miserable for three or four days before they actually left and before any packing started. Once they left he reverted to normal.' (Mary Burdett, Blackrock, Ireland)

In the four surveys I and my colleagues carried out in Britain and the United States (p.32), one of the questions we asked was: 'Would you agree or disagree that your pet knows you are going out before you show any physical sign of doing so?' This question covers several different phenomena: going away on a journey, going out and leaving the animals behind, and going out and taking the animals with them. On average, 67 per cent of dog owners and 37 per cent of cat owners agreed (Figure 7.1). These were the highest percentages of positive answers to any of the

Figure 7.1 The percentages of dog and cat owners who said their animals knew when they were going out before they showed any physical sign of doing so. The surveys were carried out with a random sample of households in London and in Ramsbottom, northwest England; and in Santa Cruz and Los Angeles, California.

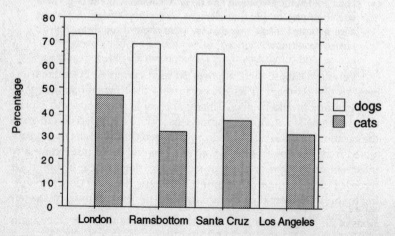

questions we asked about the perceptiveness of pets. But although this is the one of the commonest ways in which animals react to people's intentions, it is one of the hardest to test experimentally, because it is difficult to keep the person away from the pet for hours, or even days, before the time of departure.

Animals that know when they are going to be fed

Many animals seem to know when they are going to be fed, often showing their anticipation through excitement. This expectation may often be a matter of routine, or seeing, smelling or hearing the person preparing the food, or responding to some other signal from that person. But it may also depend on a more subtle detection of intent.

The most striking examples concern not regular meals, but treats or titbits.

> The older my German shepherd Maxi gets, the more he appears to be telepathic. I only have to think 'sausages' or 'chocolate' or 'biscuits' and he appears. He can be in the garden, with the door closed and he 'knows'. I can open the fridge a dozen times and no reaction, but then, if sausages or chocolate is taken from the fridge, he is at the door and 'knocking' to come in. (Frank Bramley, Telford, Shropshire)

Cats show very similar behaviour. Here is one out of many examples:

> Tiger, who was a tabby, used to weave in and out of my legs picking up scraps of meat that fell to the floor – common enough – but she always seemed to *know* when I was just *thinking* of getting the mincer out for meat (no reaction if I was going to mince fruit or vegetables), and would be under my feet, though previously curled up asleep or out in the garden – before I even opened the drawer in which the mincer was kept. This was also before I got out the meat (otherwise I would have assumed that she'd smelled it). She just seemed to read my mind, as she never reacted when I opened that same drawer to get out other items of equipment. (Joan Hayward, Dorchester)

How do they know? In some cases, senses of hearing and smell that go far beyond the human range may be involved; or they may respond telepathically to human intentions, even at a distance. These are the familiar alternatives that have presented themselves in previous discussions of the responses of animals to their owners' intentions. Once again the only way to try and resolve the question is to separate the animal from the owner so that sound, smell and hearing can be ruled out.

Horses

Many horse owners and stable-keepers have found that their animals seem to anticipate being fed, but it is difficult to separate the direct effects of intention from routine, or from hearing or seeing the food being prepared and fetched. However, some people who keep horses live miles from the stable or paddock, too far away for the horse to see, smell or hear them, and in these circumstances, some horses still seem to anticipate their arrival, as if they know they are on the way, even if they come at non-routine times.

Olwen Way, who lives in Brinkley, near Newmarket, used to keep a stud farm and racing stables, and has had many years of experience with horses. She now keeps a pony named Freddy near her son's house in the next village, Burrough Green, a 2.5-mile drive from her home. Because Freddy suffers from laminitis (an inflammation of the foot exacerbated by eating young grass), he has to be kept in a starvation paddock, and Olwen goes to Burrough Green to feed him daily. Her daughter-in-law and grandchildren often noticed that Freddy went to the fence in his paddock and seemed to be waiting for Olwen before she actually arrived, even though she came at irregular times.

Over a period of six months, Olwen and her family kept a log of Freddy's waiting behaviour on the days when there was someone to observe it. Usually Freddy reacted two to three minutes before Olwen arrived in her car, but sometimes eight to ten minutes in advance, when she was setting off from home. On one occasion she came from a more distant village, a 20-minute drive away, and Freddy reacted 20 minutes before she arrived. We have also videotaped Freddy's behaviour in experiments in which Olwen set off in response to telephone calls at randomly chosen times and travelled by taxi. Freddie still reacted in advance, ruling out the possibility that he was responding to routines or to sounds from Olwen's car.

Bonobos

We have enquired about anticipation of feeding times by monkeys and apes at various zoos in Europe. In most cases the animals are fed at regular times, so it is hard to distinguish the effects of their keepers' intentions from routine. Also, like most zoo animals, they tend to be well fed, so they are rarely very hungry.

My favourite ape story is from Betty Walsh, senior chimpanzee keeper at Twycross Zoo in Warwickshire, England. It concerns her bonobos (pygmy chimpanzees):

> One bonobo had a long bamboo cane, which she was poking members of the public with, so we wanted it off her. I had a bag of four cakes which we were going to have for our tea, and I thought I would give her a cake if she gave me the stick. But she saw I had four cakes and she broke the bamboo stick into four pieces, one piece for each cake. It was more than clever. She worked it out in a split second.

Here it is impossible to separate telepathy, subtle cues and sheer intelligence. The ape somehow picked up her keeper's intention to reward her with a cake for giving up the stick, and having seen the four cakes immediately thought of a way of getting all of them.

In spite of the difficulty of separating telepathic anticipation from routine, some apes react in a way that suggests they do pick up their keeper's intention to feed them. For example, Jacqueline Ruys, a head keeper at Apenheul Zoo, Apeldoorn, Holland, looks after three bonobos. She prepares their food in the early afternoon and keeps it in a building 100 metres away from the bonobos' cage, with trees and another building in between. The animals are usually fed between 3 and 5 pm, but not at a fixed time:

> When I am leaving our building with the food bucket in my hand, they cannot see me but the males immediately start to scream. They start screaming when I have one foot out of the door. Yet when I go out to throw a bucket of trash in the can outside, without their food, they don't scream. I go in and out of the building where we prepare their food about fifty times a day. I don't know how they know, but they know when I am coming with the food instead of something else.

In situations such as this, it should be possible to set up experiments in which the animals are videotaped and the feeding times selected at random. Since being fed is of such fundamental importance to all animals, experiments of this kind could be done with a wide range of species, and could provide a way of finding out which species are capable of bonding with their human keepers and responding to their intentions telepathically. Here, as elsewhere, there is a great potential for empirical research.

8

Telepathic calls and commands

In the previous chapter, I discussed ways that animals respond to people's intentions. Many animals seem to pick up intentions whether their owners like it or not, without any deliberate effort on the owner's part.

In calling an animal or giving commands, the owners are deliberately trying to influence their animals' behaviour. A person calling a cat wants it to come. A shepherd wants his dog to herd sheep in accordance with his intentions. A rider wants her horse to jump a hedge. Through calls and commands, people actively *will* their animals to do something. Sometimes these calls and commands appear to be communicated telepathically, and can go in both directions, from people to animals and from animals to people.

Telepathy also seems to occur in connection with calls by telephone. Some cats and dogs seem to know when their owner is calling, or about to call. And many people have had seemingly telepathic intuitions that a particular person is calling, before they actually answer the phone.

How common are telepathic experiences with animals?

Among those who work with dogs and horses, the existence of telepathic influences is usually taken for granted. 'No one in their senses disputes them', said Barbara Woodhouse, the formidable British dog trainer:

> You should always bear in mind that the dog picks up your thoughts
> by an acute telepathic sense, and it is useless to be thinking one thing
> and saying another; you cannot fool a dog. If you wish to talk to your

dog you must do so with your mind and will power, as well as your voice. I communicate my wishes by my voice, my mind and by the love I have for animals . . . A dog's mind is so quick at picking up thoughts that, as you think them, they enter the dog's mind simultaneously. I have great difficulty in this matter in giving the owners commands in class for the dog obeys my thoughts before my mouth has had time to give the owner the command.[1]

When I began asking pet owners, dog handlers, blind people with guide dogs and horse riders about their communication with their animals, I soon found that Barbara Woodhouse's opinions on the subject are widely shared. This impression was confirmed by formal surveys.

I and my associates carried out surveys of randomly selected households in England and the United States in which we asked animal owners the following question: 'Would you agree or disagree that your pet responds to your thoughts or silent commands?' An average of 48 per cent of dog owners and 33 per cent of cat owners agreed.[2]

We then asked a further question: 'Would you agree or disagree that your pet is sometimes telepathic with you?' The pattern of answers was broadly similar to that for the question about thoughts and silent commands. On average, 45 per cent of dog owners and 32 per cent of cat owners believed that their animals' responses were not simply a matter of picking up sensory clues, but involved a telepathic influence.[3]

We also asked people about their experience with previous pets: 'Would you agree or disagree that any of the pets you have known in the past were telepathic?' Forty-five per cent of pet owners and 35 per cent of people currently without pets agreed.[4]

These surveys suggest that at least a third of the adult population believe they have had or still have telepathic connections with animals. In Britain, that would mean over 15 million people, and in the US over 65 million!

What kinds of experiences lead so many people to think that their animals can respond to them telepathically? I have already discussed the way in which animals seem to react telepathically to people's intentions (Chapters 2, 3, 4 and 7) and distress (Chapter 6). I now turn to various kinds of calls and commands.

Summoning cats

Of all the seemingly telepathic phenomena described by cat owners, the ability to summon a cat mentally is one of the commonest. For example, Nancy Arnold of Kalamazoo, Michigan, has five cats and has often noticed that when they are outside: 'I only have to think about a certain cat, and within a minute or so, the cat appears at the door. I just take their telepathy for granted.' Rona Hart, while living in Jerusalem, used to leave her cat Tiger to roam outside in the fields and gardens near her flat when she went to work. When she came home, Tiger often came to meet her, but otherwise she went outside to call her home in the evenings. 'I began to notice that, sometimes, when I was thinking of calling her home, Tiger would appear without my having to go outside. I found the "thinking" was slightly *more* effective than the actual calling.'

Here is another example, from Pauline Bamsay of Port Talbot in Wales, who is convinced that her cat has telepathic powers.

> When he is not around, I only have to think 'Come on home, Leo', if I feel he's been gone a long time, and within minutes, sometimes under a minute, he will appear, depending on how far away he is. He visits neighbours' gardens and also an old, disused allotment area just to the rear of our garden. It is his hunting ground. If I am in the garden and thinking 'Where are you Leo?' he calls to me verbally as he approaches the garden. If I am in the house, he comes bounding in through the cat-flap in the back door with a loud meow and even comes upstairs to find me. As I write this letter, I can see him on our garage roof, lying curled up asleep. I thought to myself, 'There you are, Leo.' Almost immediately he woke up, stood up and looked directly at me through the window, which is about 15 feet away from the garage. Then after a moment he turned and headed towards the allotment across the garage roof!

Some people find that telepathic calls seem to work the other way round. Their cats seem to call them, as I discuss later in this chapter.

Dogs

In the training of dogs, whether as working dogs, for agility and obedience trials, or simply as pets, the owners are generally near the dog, so it is difficult to separate the effects of direct mental influence from the normal senses and training. Most trainers and handlers simply concentrate on performance, without reflecting much on the means of communication between person and dog.

Some working dogs still know what to do when they are at a distance. But even then it is hard to know exactly what is going on. Raymond McPherson of Brampton, Cumbria, is a successful competitor in sheepdog trials, and the winner of the International Supreme Championship. He is convinced that his border collies are extremely intelligent. But is their skill at anticipating his intentions due more to their intelligence and working routine than it is to telepathy?

> If you have a dog with a brain and a natural instinct to herd sheep they can do an awful lot on their own without any commands at all. If you go to a sheepdog trial you just see a little of what they can do. It is when you go out on the hills in the day-to-day working with sheep that you find out how intelligent they really are. They will work out of sight, some will go three miles away and one dog can work with anything from three or four sheep to 500, and sometimes even more. You can build a tremendous connection with them and they anticipate what you want them to do before you ask them to do it. Kindness is the best way to build a good connection with a dog.

As usual, the best way of teasing apart the influence of sensory clues from direct mental influence is in situations where neither routine nor normal sensory communication can provide a plausible explanation. Some dogs, like cats, respond to silent calls and come to their owners when summoned. Most spectacular are calls when dogs are outdoors and far away from their owners.

Eric LeBourdais trained his golden retriever to respond to a dog whistle so that she can range quite far. One day, when she was about a year old, he suddenly remembered that he needed to do something at home. She was about a quarter of a mile away. He was about to reach into his pocket for the whistle, but the moment he had the thought she lifted her head as if he had blown the whistle, and headed straight for him. He was surprised, but put it down to coincidence. 'However, as the years passed this happened several dozen times – sufficiently often that I am absolutely convinced there was nothing coincidental about it at all. There was never any sort of action on my part - nothing "normal" which could have accounted for it. Sometimes she would be completely out of sight when I would begin to have thoughts of heading home. Each time she came to me directly, exactly as if summoned.'

In the case of working dogs and dogs that respond to calls, the command is usually one with which the dog is already familiar. The telepathy is in the timing. But the most striking instances of silent commands are those in which the person wills the animal to carry out a non-routine task; the influence in these cases is more detailed and specific. Here is an example of a pet dog responding to the silent commands of his owner, Janet Penney, who lives in Cornwall:

One day when my dog was sound asleep I deliberately thought to myself – 'Wake up and bring me your big blue ball and we'll go and play in the garden.' Maggers woke up, went over to his toy bowl and rooted around for the big blue ball (which he didn't like very much!), brought it to me and went to the back door (no, he didn't need to pee!). One day, towards the end of his life, he'd left all his toys all over the place and I was falling over them (I'm a bit unsteady – very arthritic). I didn't say a word (the poor dog was asleep) but thought how nice it would be if he could put his toys away. When I came downstairs he was lying with his toy bowl in the middle of the lounge floor, with *all* the toys in the bowl!

This kind of telepathic communication was explored by means of experiments by the late Vladimir Bekhterev, an eminent Russian neuro-physiologist.[5] Although his investigation was carried out many years ago, as far as I know it is still the only experimental study of this subject reported in the scientific literature.

The experiments of Vladimir Bekhterev

Bekhterev, an admirably curious and open-minded investigator, was intrigued by a dog act he saw in a circus in St Petersburg, in which the dog, a fox terrier called Pikki, seemed to respond to the mental commands of his trainer, W. Durov. Durov told Bekhterev that his method was to visualize the task he wanted the dog to do, for example fetching a book from a table, and then hold the dog's head between his hands looking into his eyes.

I fix into his brain what I just before fixed in my own. I mentally put before him the part of the floor leading to the table, then the legs of the table, then the tablecloth and finally the book. Then I give him the command, or rather the mental push: 'Go!' He tears himself away like an automaton, approaches the table, and seizes the book with his teeth. The task is done.

Bekhterev and several of his colleagues found they too could command Pikki in this way, even in the absence of Durov. They carried out a series of trials to find out if they were giving the dog subtle cues by means of eye, head or other body movements. Bekhterev also carried out tests with his own dog, and found that he too could respond to mental commands. He concluded:

1 The behaviour of animals, especially that of dogs trained to obey, may be directly influenced by thought suggestion.

2 This influence may be effective without any direct contact between the sender and the dog who is receiving, as when they are separated by a wood or metal screen, blindfolds, etc.

3 From this it follows that the dog may be directly influenced without the presence of any signs by which he could be guided.[6]

Bekhterev regarded these investigations as preliminary, and pointed out how desirable it would be to carry out further experiments with dogs. 'It would be important to study, not only the conditions governing the transfer of the mental influence from the agent to the percipient, but also the circumstances involved in both the inhibition and the execution of such suggestions. This would necessarily be of theoretical as well as of practical interest.' Unfortunately the pioneering work of Bekhterev has not been followed up, and these words remain as relevant today as when he wrote them more than 75 years ago.[7]

Guide dogs

Some of those who work most closely with dogs are blind people with guide dogs. I wanted to find out if any blind people had noticed that their dog seemed to pick up their intentions without their giving commands either verbally or through body movements. With the help of the British Guide Dogs for the Blind Association, Jane Turney and I asked more than 20 guide dog owners about their experience. We also received much valuable information through letters in response to an appeal for information in *Forward*, a British magazine for guide dog owners, published in Braille.

Some people with guide dogs had not noticed anything of this kind, but most had. Several commented on the fact that it depended on the closeness of their relationship with the dog, and that some dogs were much more responsive than others. Even responsive dogs may not pick up their owners' intentions every time:

Paxton, a black Labrador, is my second dog. It took me two years to get used to him. Now there are many times that I have felt that he can pick up signals that I do not give consciously, that I don't speak to him. I will think 'We've got to go right here' and we will go right even though I haven't said anything. He picks up very much on things I think and things I feel. There have been times where I have tried to test him, where I have deliberately tried to think about directions in my mind but I have

tried to keep as straight as possible, and he has still done it. He doesn't
do it all the time, though. Sometimes he is more in tune than others.
There are times when he is distracted or I am not thinking clearly
enough and not giving him precise directions. (Sarah Craig, Bridgend)

The most striking instances involve the dog responding to thoughts
the owners are not planning to put into action straight away. For example, Mike Mitchinson was walking from his home in Bath to a particular
shop some 20 minutes away. The route took him past his dentist's
surgery. 'I can remember thinking at the start of the relevant road "I must
not forget my dental appointment at 10 am on Thursday," (this was
Monday). I then walked on confidently and only half taking note of
where I was. Imagine my surprise when I found myself swinging to the
left and entering a gravel driveway! Yes, it was the dentist.' Likewise, John
Collen, of Southend-on-Sea, was walking past some shops one morning
and thinking that he would call in to the greengrocer's that afternoon to
get some apples when the dog led him into that shop. 'I told the owner I
was only *thinking* of coming in because I didn't want to carry the apples
about, and that I would come back later this afternoon, but the very fact
that I thought about it casually was enough for Pedro to pick up on it.'

Could it be that the guide dogs are responding to changes in the way
the owners walk or hold the harness? Several of our informants had
thought about this possibility, including Pedro's owner. 'I am totally
blind so I cannot see the dog, and I wouldn't be sure about direction of
travel. Under those conditions I wouldn't be making any indication as to
direction or stopping or starting, I am just walking along thinking, and
that is why I started to believe he is picking up something other than
visual cues or other physical indications.' Peter Neely of Kumnock, in
Scotland, has come to similar conclusions:

> When I am working with Sam, the black Labrador I have now had as a
> guide dog for two years, I would definitely say there is a telepathic link
> there because he seems to know which way I want to go. He seems to
> anticipate if I am changing my mind on the route. I believe that if you
> are a guide dog owner, plus a guide dog lover, there is a connection, a
> sort of invisible umbilical cord between you and the dog because
> what you are feeling and what he is feeling is travelling up through the
> harness. Some people might say your subconscious means you do a
> different tension on to the handle which the dog picks up, but I hon-
> estly don't feel that I am doing that.

Of course these are only opinions, but the opinions of people with
years of experience with guide dogs are of more value than the opinions

of people with no experience. However, given the physical contact through the harness, it is difficult to separate telepathic influences from subtle sensory clues, and I have not been able to think of a straightforward experiment with guide dogs that could conclusively eliminate the possibility of unconscious movements by the owner.

Horses

Many horse riders experience a close connection, physical, emotional and mental, with their horse. They find that the horse seems to respond to their thoughts. For example: 'I can be riding my horse at a walking pace and I think to myself "When I get to that tree I'll put her into a trot," and, as if my horse has read my thoughts, and I have at the moment given no (conscious!) body signal, it will start to trot. My husband and daughter have had exactly the same experiences with their horses.' (Andrea Künzli, Starrkirch, Switzerland) Experienced riders often take this responsiveness for granted. Here is how a less experienced rider found it out for herself:

> Riding Kazan became somewhat nerve-racking, since I never knew when he was going to spook. Until, that is, I tried communicating with him telepathically. I first tried it when I wanted him to cross a white wooden bridge. He wouldn't even place a hoof on it the first few times I tried, so the next time I came out to ride, I held in my mind a sharp and clear picture of him walking calmly across the bridge with me on his back. It worked! We approached the bridge, stepped on to it, and crossed it without a moment's hesitation or misstep. Hooray! I was so impressed by the success of my experiment, that I started using telepathy in my daily horse routines. When I want Kazan to step into a horse trailer, I picture it happening and in he goes. (Lisa Chambers, Chico, California)

With horses, as with guide dogs, it is difficult to disentangle mental influences from unconscious body signals, such as slight changes in muscular tension. 'It is tempting when one is riding a very well schooled horse, or a horse that knows one very well indeed, to think the horse is receiving telepathic messages. However, it may just be slight movements of the rider which are interpreted by the horse and acted upon.'[8] It remains an open question as to how such impressions of experienced riders can be explained.

One of the few people to carry out experiments on mental communication with horses was Harry Blake, a British horse trainer famous for his method of 'gentling' horses. He worked by establishing an empathy with the horse, as opposed to conventional 'breaking', and was often able to train horses remarkably quickly and effectively. (His method had something in common with 'horse whispering' and the procedures of the American horse trainer Monty Roberts.[9]) He summarized his research in a book called *Talking with Horses: A Study of Communication Between Man and Horse.*[10]

In one series of experiments, carried out with a horse called Cork Beg, he first trained him to go to one of two food buckets, placed ten yards apart, directing him 'merely by using telepathy' to the one that contained his breakfast, rather than the other, which was empty. 'Within a few days he was going straight to the bucket I directed him to, and I persevered with this for a fortnight.' In the tests themselves, the horse was offered two buckets, each containing equal quantities of food. For the first five mornings he directed him alternately to the left and the right, then for four mornings to the container on the left.

> The ninth morning brought the most difficult experiment of all. For four mornings running he had taken his breakfast from the container on the left, and on the ninth I wanted to change him to the container on the right. Much to my relief he went straight to it. Having come out of that successfully, he had to take it again from the right-hand container on the tenth morning, from the left on the eleventh and on the twelfth morning from the right. Each morning he went directly to the correct container.[11]

Since the horse could see Harry Blake, it is impossible to rule out subtle visual cues, of the kind picked up by Clever Hans (p.xvi). But Harry Blake did other experiments on telepathy from horse to horse, kept in separate buildings out of sight of each other, which seem to rule out such clues from Blake himself or from the other horse. These experiments are discussed in Chapter 9.

Two-way communication

If invisible bonds exist between animals and people, it would be surprising if they did not permit communications to take place in both directions rather than in just one.

I have collected over 1,500 accounts of seemingly telepathic or psychic influences of owners on their pets, and 73 cases where the influence seems to flow the other way. People seem much less sensitive to these influences than their animals, or pay little attention to them. But 73 is still a large number of cases, and presumably many people who have not written to me have had similar experiences.

Out of these 73 cases, ten concern deaths or accidents in distant places. I discussed these in Chapter 6. Most of the 63 other cases involve silent calls for help. The majority concern cats.

Cats calling people

Cats seem especially talented at getting what they want from their owners by subtle means. Some people are convinced that cats can influence them telepathically. The commonest situation in which this occurs is when the cat is outdoors and wants to be let in.

> My husband David soon found that he could tell when Suzie was outside in the garden, wanting to come in. The first time this happened was one Sunday morning when we were in bed, reading the papers. David suddenly said 'Suzie wants to come in,' got out of bed and opened the bedroom curtains to find Suzie sitting on the gatepost, staring intently at the bedroom window. After that, I got quite used to David's going to the front or back door to let in Suzie, even though I never heard her cry or scratch the door. David just said she 'fluenced' him. (Sonya Porter, Woking, Surrey)

Some cat owners know not only when cats want to come in, but also which of several cats is silently calling them. Laura Meursing owned six cats and lived on a large estate in Belgium: 'The cats were often outside on the grounds, but I felt every time when one of the cats wanted to get in and also which one'. And a French cat named Minet calls his owner telepathically even when she is asleep. 'I suddenly know that he is behind the door because his image, in the posture in which I will find him, imposes itself onto me, even waking me up if need be. There is no call, no meowing or other sign. Everything takes place in silence.' (Mme G. Woutisseth, Vanves, France)

Some dog owners have had very similar experiences, like Lydia Arndt, of Riverside, California: 'One of my Great Danes can be outside and when she wants in, she "wills" me to come to the back door. I can be at the other end of my home and she thinks so hard I have to stop everything and go let her in. We do this several times a day.'

Calls by lost cats

Cats that roam freely have a tendency to get lost, often because they are unintentionally shut into sheds or garages by neighbours. Some cat owners have found that they can somehow tell where the lost cat is. For example, Solomon, a Siamese cat in Whittlesey, Cambridgeshire, was very inquisitive and tended to get shut up. When he did not come home at night, his owner, Celia Johns, had to go and look for him. 'I never knew where he was, but I found that if I stood outside the back door and thought hard, I invariably turned in the right direction to find him.'

Some stories about the rescue of lost cats are quite dramatic and seem to show that the cat in some way draws the owner towards it. But often this happens only after a frustrating period of searching using the trial and error approach. For example:

> In June, Solitaire, the younger of our cats, disappeared. We searched for her without success. The third day, all of a sudden I felt that I had to go out right away and hurried up the street and turned into Fir Close. I went up to the second house on the right and rang the bell. A gentleman opened the door, I apologized for disturbing him and told him about my missing cat. He assured me that he had not seen it. I asked him if he would mind me having a look around his back garden as it would make me feel better. He took me through the back and I called 'Solitaire, Solitaire' and immediately a cat started to meow very loudly. I followed the sound to a large mound of garden rubbish. There was a hole at the top and on looking into it I saw my cat's face looking up at me from about three feet down. She was stuck and her neck was bent at an angle . . . I carried her home joyfully. (Martha Lees, Fleetwood, Lancashire)

In some cases the owners are not travelling on foot, but driving a car when they seem to know where to go. In the following example, as in the previous one, this knowing did not happen straight away, but only after exhausting the obvious possibilities. The cat, Whisky, had escaped from a cattery in a Yorkshire village while her family was on holiday. When they returned two weeks later, they learned that she had been missing for almost the whole time they had been away. Her owner searched the village for her, calling at every house and at the pub. Several people had seen a stray cat, but no one knew where it was.

> By the time that I had done this it was dark so that it seemed that I must go home and return the next morning. Having gone about a mile I felt compelled – no dithering – to turn around and go back to the village. This I did and turned down a dead-end road which leads only to a reservoir. Half a mile or so down I stopped the car, got out and called 'Whisky'. Immediately there was a meow and she jumped over the wall from a field. (Catherine Forrester)

How do the cats somehow manage to draw their owners towards them? This phenomenon is related to the ability of animals to find their owners, and is discussed further in Chapter 13.

Dogs in distress

Most of the stories I have received about dogs influencing their owners from a distance have occurred when the dogs were in great distress. For example:

> One day while at work it started to thunder and rain. As I worked I became increasingly edgy. Then very agitated. I couldn't take it any more. Something was wrong. At this point I will add that I never took time off work. I asked my employer if I could take the afternoon off, I didn't feel quite right. On my way home I knew Eric, my German shepherd, was in trouble, I knew he was bleeding. When I arrived home I rushed to the back patio. The window was broken. Frightened, Eric had hit the glass with his paw and had sliced off the front pads on the broken glass. He was bleeding very badly. I feel he needed me and called out the only way he could – telepathically – knowing I would come to him. (Dolores Katz, Deming, New Mexico)

Sometimes a feeling of distress is picked up without the dog being identified as the source. For example, one day when Jill Andrews was at work in her office in Exeter, she had a 'strange physical feeling' that she could not account for and knew that something was wrong. She felt the urgent need to return home, one and a half miles away, fearing that her elderly mother might be ill. When she reached the house, her mother greeted her with 'How did you know?' Their ten-year-old boxer had had a stroke and was paralyzed. 'I'm quite sure that he was making contact with me somehow. He was in a very distressed state and sadly had to be put down soon afterwards.'

In some cases the distress that people pick up comes from a pet that is actually dying, and I have discussed such cases in Chapter 6.

Horses, cows and other animals in distress

The picking up of distress signals from animals is not confined to dogs and cats. For example, a Swiss woman who kept sheep told me that one night she woke up and felt she had to go to the barn. When she arrived there she found that one of her sheep had just given birth. She was convinced that the sheep had 'called' her because she never normally woke up in this way or went to the barn in the middle of the night.

The horse trainer Harry Blake had a similar experience with a cow. Normally, he said, he slept like a log, but one particular night he woke up with a powerful feeling that something was amiss and went out to his animals. The cow was calving but it was a breech delivery and she was in difficulties. On thinking about it afterwards he worked out that he'd been awakened by the feeling that something was wrong and had been drawn subconsciously to where the cow was. He had similar experiences with horses. On one occasion, a horse to which he was very attached woke him up at three in the morning. 'I simply knew there was something wrong, and when I went out to have a look at him I found that he was having a violent attack of colic.'[12]

Other people have had experiences with horses in which they not only pick up their distress, but somehow seem to receive more specific information. Charles Craig, for example, woke up one night feeling uneasy and apprehensive, got dressed and went downstairs. He picked up his wire cutters and a torch, put on his boots and went out into a very dark night directly to the very spot, about half a mile from his house, where his favourite mare was caught up in barbed wire in a bog. He said that as he went downstairs he 'knew exactly where the mare was and exactly what had happened' because he could 'see it in his mind's eye'.[13]

Sometimes people respond to the distress of animals that they do not even know. For example, Lucy Crisp was asked to feed a neighbour's cats while the neighbour was on holiday. The first day she felt uneasy when she was leaving the house. The second day her uneasiness became more intense and she went round to the back of the house where she found a cage containing two desperate rabbits that had not been fed or watered for several days. 'I have no idea how these animals managed to send out their distress signals,' she said.

Animal communicators

In addition to these communications between domestic animals and their owners, there is a long tradition of communication with animals by shamans in tribal societies. One of the powers attained by yogis in India was said to be the understanding of the 'cries of all creatures'.[14] Some of the most appealing Christian saints, like St Francis of Assisi and St Cuthbert, were said to communicate with animals and to understand their language. And there have always been animal keepers and trainers who are extraordinarily 'in tune' with their animals and seem to know what they are feeling. In fiction, stories such as those of Dr Doolittle have a deep appeal to our imaginations.

There are also people who make a living as 'animal communicators' who claim to pick up telepathically what people's pets are thinking and feeling. Some give counselling and advice for a fee, either in person or over the telephone.

Given the background of shamanic communication with animals, the telepathic experiences of pet owners with their pets, and the remarkable sensitivity that some people have to animals, I am happy to accept that some animal communicators may indeed have extraordinary powers, even if these do not usually lend themselves to scientific testing. However, many of these so-called animal communications, especially when carried out for profit, may well be a projection of the communicator's own thoughts rather than genuine cases of telepathy.

Animal communicators themselves are well aware of the problems. Penelope Smith of Point Reyes, California, who has trained hundreds of people in 'inter-species telepathic communication' in her workshops, has seen people 'mixing their communication abilities with their own agendas or emotional shortcomings'. She has proposed a code of ethics for inter-species telepathic communicators which includes the following passage: 'We realize that telepathic communication can be clouded or overlaid by our own unfulfilled emotions, critical judgements, or lack of love for self and others.'[15]

Professional animal communicators are often ready to venture information about animals' feelings and even about their past lives, and they may well play a valuable role in counselling the animals' owners. But they are often reluctant to provide information that can be more immediately verified. In his book *Communicating with Animals*, the veteran reporter Arthur Myers[16] describes how he interviewed many communicators to find out how successful they had been at finding lost animals telepathically. Most told him that they try to avoid such jobs. However Myers did find some cases where communicators had been able to locate lost animals by describing where they were, and giving clues that enabled them to be found.

For me, the most interesting of these apparent communications from animals are those that can be tested empirically. I agree with Myers that the finding of lost animals seems the best place to begin.

Telepathic telephone calls

Before the invention of modern telecommunications, telepathy would have been the only way people could reach each other at a distance. In Chapter 4, I quoted a story of Laurens van der Post about the way the bushmen of the Kalahari desert knew what members of the group were doing many miles away, and when they were returning. The bushmen were under the impression that the white man's telegraph also involved a kind of telepathy.

Even in traditional long-distance communication by drumming, the message itself may not be transmitted simply through the sounds. Richard St Barbe Baker has suggested in his book *African Drums* that the drumming may primarily have served to tune in the senders' and receivers' attention to each other: 'May it not be that the drums create the atmosphere for the transmission of thought messages and vision which annihilate time and space? The more deeply I have delved into the problem of transmission, the more I have become convinced of the inseparable association between the transmission of a visual picture by telepathic means and the language of the drum'.[17]

Telepathic skills are not encouraged in modern societies. They are treated as superstition by rationalists, and ignored by institutional science and the educational system. In any case, modern technologies usually provide much easier and more effective means for communication at a distance. Television allows everyone to see images from far away, and telephones provide instant communication worldwide.

But ironically, telephones provide an excellent opportunity for studying telepathy, precisely because they fulfill the same function of communication at a distance. In order to make a telephone call to someone it is necessary to *intend* to call that person. The very act of calling someone focuses attention on that person at a distance. We have already seen that pets can respond to their owners' calls and intentions at a distance. Can some pets tell when their owners are calling, even before the telephone is answered?

Telephone-answering cats

I have received 17 reports of cats that respond to the telephone when a particular person is ringing, before the receiver is picked up. In all cases, the person calling is someone to whom the cat is very attached, usually the husband, wife, son or daughter of the person who notices the animal's responses. In Veronica Rowe's case it was her daughter Marian, whose cat Carlo would not allow any other member of the family to cuddle her.

> Seven years after she acquired Carlo, my daughter went to teacher training college and rang us infrequently. However, when the phone did ring and it was Marian, and not our son who was away at Kingston

Polytechnic, Carlo would bound up the stairs (the phone was on the half landing) before I had picked up the receiver!! There was no way that this cat could have known that my daughter was to ring us – it was a standing joke when he bounded up the stairs that Marian was on the other end of the phone. He never did this at any other time and was not allowed upstairs anyway.

Godzilla lived with David Waite (Figure 8.1), a public relations consultant who worked from his home in Watlington, near Oxford, England. When David went away several times every year his parents would come to mind the house, look after the cat and answer the many telephone calls. He used to ring home from North Africa, the Middle East and continental Europe to check that all was well and get any messages. 'Whenever I called, my cat would run and sit beside the telephone, as it

Figure 8.1 David Waite and his telephone-answering cat Godzilla, in Watlington, Oxfordshire (photograph: Phil Starling).

was ringing, whereas she ignored the other calls my parents took on my behalf. And the calls were made at random times.' Godzilla responded in this way before the telephone had been answered, so he could not have been reacting to David's voice.

Most of the cats said to respond to telephone calls from particular people reacted when the telephone began to ring, but five did so even before the ringing began. For example, Helena Zaugg describes how her family's cat at Bruegg in Switzerland responded to her father, to whom it was closely attached:

> After my father had retired he sometimes worked for an acquaintance in Aargau. Sometimes he called us from there in the evening. One minute before this happened the cat became restless and sat down next to the telephone. Sometimes my father took the train to Biel and then used a moped to get home from there. Then the cat sat down outside the front door 30 minutes before he arrived. At other times he arrived at Biel earlier than usual and then called us from the station, and the cat sat down near the telephone shortly before the call came. After it she went to the front door. All this happened very irregularly, but the cat seemed to know exactly where he was and what would happen afterwards.

Likewise, a Siamese cat belonging to Vicki Rodenberg 'perked up when a particular person called on the phone – only she did it moments before the phone rang! She would actually run to the phone and cry, and always that person.'

(I have also received reports of cats that come to the telephone immediately *after* it has been answered when a particular person is ringing, but in such cases it is impossible to know whether the cat was simply responding to the sound of the person's voice or to the reactions of the person answering the telephone. I have therefore excluded these cases from consideration.)

Dogs and telephones

Many dogs bark or react in some other way to the telephone when it is ringing, whoever is on the other end. But we have eight cases on our database where dogs respond to the telephone when a particular person is calling, before the telephone is answered. As in the case of cats, the people to whom the dogs reacted were their owners or other members of the family to whom the dogs were particularly attached. For example, Margaret Howard's dog Poppet was very attached to her mother and knew when she was telephoning or coming to visit:

I first noted Poppet showed restlessness, excitement, ears pricked up, tail wagging, wandering between front and back doors, and she developed a special type of bark which I always called 'a yipping' – and surely within minutes my mother arrived. No special times or routine to her visits, but Poppet's reaction was always the same – morning, noon or night. I gradually got to notice that I could tell whether my mother was coming via the front or back door, as Poppet would position herself at the right one. I also noted that when the telephone rang, although Poppet would look at it, she did not particularly bother, but I always knew when my mother was on the phone, as Poppet appeared all excited standing by the phone and using her special 'yipping' call.

As in the case of cats, this response of dogs does not seem to fall off with distance. Marie McCurrach of Ipswich had a Labrador dog, which joined the family when her son was ten. Four years later, her son went away to a naval school in North Wales and then went on to serve in the Merchant Navy, mainly sailing to and from South Africa.

Every time that he rang home the dog would run to the telephone before anyone could answer it. The dog never bothered about any other calls, only our son's, and we had to hold the phone to the dog's ear so that our son could speak to him and the dog would reply. Our son never gave us a time that he would phone and did not phone on the same day of the week or anything like that, so how did the dog know it would be our son on the phone before anyone had lifted the receiver?

Three dogs were said to react before the telephone actually rang. One was a dog called Jack, belonging to a family living near Gloucester, where the father worked for the Ministry of Defence. Some nights he could not return home owing to the urgency of the work or the lateness of the hour, and on these occasions rang to say so. 'Ten minutes or so prior to that call being received the dog would sit by the telephone until it rang. On the nights when no telephone call had to be made by my father the dog made no move whatsoever, and remained in his basket. Further, the dog would pay no attention to any other telephone calls at any other time.' (Mr S. Waller)

Dogs and cats are not the only pet species that seem to know in advance who is calling. Some parrots also appear to do so. Then there is the case of Sunday, a pet Capuchin monkey. Its owner, Richard Savage left the monkey with a friend in British Columbia, Canada, while he was away on film-making assignments. 'Several minutes before Richard would telephone to talk to me, Sunday would jump up and start chattering. After his call, she would settle down for days, ignoring the telephone – until just before Richard called again.'[18]

People who know when a particular person is calling

Once when I was discussing this research at a seminar, someone asked, 'If cats and dogs have the ability to know when particular people are calling, then why not people?' A good question. I then remembered that I myself had had the experience of thinking of particular people for no obvious reason, and then, shortly afterwards, they rang. I asked the participants in the seminar if anyone else had noticed this phenomenon, and to my surprise almost everybody had.

Many people have subsequently told me or written to me about it. For example, Lucinda Butler, who lives in London, often knows when a particular person is telephoning, especially her boyfriend:

> We have been going out on and off for five years, and I always know, and he does the same to me. He will pick up the phone and be so sure that it is going to be me he will say something stupid that I will find amusing. But he has got it wrong sometimes too. Also, I will think about someone and think 'Oh no, now I have thought about them, they will ring', and they do.

I have now carried out informal surveys of several thousand people at seminars, lectures and conferences in Europe and America, asking those who have had seemingly telepathic experiences with telephone calls to raise their hands. Usually 80 to 90 per cent of those present do so. I and my colleagues have also carried out formal surveys, using random sampling methods, in two very different parts of England: in Bury, an industrial town near Manchester; and in London. Both surveys confirm that a majority of people say they have experienced this phenomenon themselves.[19]

Most of the unexplained powers discussed in this book are better developed among non-human animals than people. Normally dogs seem to be the most sensitive, followed by cats, horses and parrots, with humans trailing far behind. Yet here, for a change, is an ability that seems better developed in people than in animals. But even if most people have had seemingly uncanny intuitions about who is telephoning, is a mysterious psychic power really at work, or can it all be explained as an illusion?

Research on telephonic telepathy

The standard sceptical view is that people are deluded by their selective memories: they remember only the times when they guessed correctly, and forget the hundreds or thousands of times they were wrong. Their correct hunches are just a matter of chance.

Sceptics have no experimental data to back up this suggestion; they are merely proposing a hypothesis that no one has yet tested, even parapsychologists. At present no one knows how many hunches about people calling are correct, and how many are wrong. The question is completely open. Maybe the sceptics are right. Maybe they are wrong. The only way to find out is by empirical research.

Those best qualified to conduct this pioneering research are people who have frequent telepathic, or seemingly telepathic, experiences with telephone calls. The first step is to keep a log. In Appendix A I suggest a simple, practical way to do this. Then if you are often right about particular people calling, the next stage is to carry out simple experiments in which they are asked to call at unexpected, randomly selected times.

This is a virgin field of enquiry. There are remarkable opportunities for original research. Although telephones have superseded telepathy for most practical purposes, they can help us rediscover it.

9
Animal-to-animal telepathy

If telepathy occurs between animals and people, and from people to people, what about telepathy from animals to animals?

Wild animals that live in social groups are often strongly bonded to each other, and practically incapable of leading an isolated existence. Complex social organization occurs even among the lowliest of animals, such as corals and sponges. What we recognize as a coral or sponge is in fact a colony of millions of tiny organisms, which together form a kind of superorganism, with its own characteristic form.

In this chapter I discuss the way that insect societies, schools, flocks, herds and other social groups are organized. The activities of the individual animals within a group are coordinated through the group's field. We have seen how this social field, called a morphic field, links humans and animals together and provides a means of telepathy between pets and their people. The same kind of bonding occurs between animals in the wild, and in this bonding lie the roots of animal-to-animal telepathy.

I begin by considering some of the most complex forms of social organization in the animal kingdom, achieved by creatures with brains smaller than the head of a pin.

Social insects as superorganisms

Societies of termites, ants, wasps and bees can contain millions of individual insects. They build large and elaborate nests, exhibit a complex division of labour, and reproduce themselves. They have often been compared to organisms or superorganisms.

The holistic conception of insect societies as organisms was taken for granted by practically everyone until the twentieth century, as was the idea of human societies as organisms. This organic way of thinking about our own societies is built into our language, as when we speak of the 'head of state', the 'arm of the law' and the 'body politic'. However, as mechanistic attitudes triumphed over such traditional ideas, by the 1950s, the superorganism concept was going out of fashion within institutional biology. The reductionist spirit took over. Edward O. Wilson, the founder of sociobiology, wrote of the superorganism concept in 1971 as a 'mirage that had dissolved'.[1]

However, this idea has proved indispensable, and it is now back in favour. Here is the same Edward O. Wilson writing with his colleague Bert Hölldobler in 1994:

> Consider the most organism-like insect societies, the great colonies of African driver-ants. Viewed from afar and slightly out of focus, the raiding column of the driver-ant colony seems a single living entity. It spreads like the pseudopodium of a giant amoeba across a hundred yards of ground . . . The swarm is leaderless . . . The frontal swarm, advancing at 20 metres an hour, engulfs all the ground and low vegetation in its path, gathering and killing almost all the insects and even snakes and other large animals unable to crawl away. After a few hours the direction of flow is reversed, and the column drains backward into the nest holes. To speak of a colony of driver-ants or other social insects as more than just a tight aggregation of individuals is to speak of a superorganism.[2]

As Wilson now points out, this concept invites us to look at the whole society as an organism. He compares the queen to the heart of this entity in both the hereditary and physiological sense. He compares the workers to the mouth, the gut, the eyes. This holistic approach allows Wilson to see an analogy between the way organisms develop from fertilized eggs and the way that societies are built up by the individuals within them.

Social insects and all social animals are bound together in their social groups by morphic fields, which carry the habitual patterns and 'programs' of social organization. In the case of social insects that build nests and other structures, these fields coordinate their architectural activity. They contain, as it were, an invisible blueprint for the nest. The morphic field of the colony is not merely inside the individual insects; rather they are within the morphic field of the group. The field is an extended pattern in space-time, just as the gravitational field of the solar system is not merely inside the sun and the planets, but contains them all and coordinates their movements.

Much has been discovered about communication among social insects by shared food, scent trails, touch and vision – as in the wiggle dance of honey bees through which they communicate the direction and distance of food. But the existence of all these forms of sensory communication works together with their connections through the morphic field of the group. It is this field, I suggest, that enables the insects to interpret these scent trails, dance patterns and so on, and to react appropriately.

Sensory communication by itself would be totally inadequate to explain how termites, for example, could build such prodigious structures, with nests up to ten feet high, filled with galleries, chambers and even equipped with ventilation shafts. These insect cities have an overall plan that far exceeds the experience of any individual insect.

Karl von Frisch, who discovered the wiggle dance of bees, has written an excellent book on animal architecture[3] in which he discusses the complex buildings of termites. The insects are blind and cannot see each other, but they mark trails with scent so that other termites can follow them, and they give knocking signals by striking a hard surface with their heads. But, as von Frisch points out: 'The information content of both modes of communication is small. The scent trail may lead to a goal, but it cannot explain what should be done there. Drumming is an alarm signal by which soldiers or workers induce other workers to flee into the interior of the nest . . . But it is just a general warning signal.' He concludes that the 'finished structures seem evidence of a master plan which controls the activities of the builders and is based on the requirements of the community. How this can come to pass within the enormous complex of millions of blind workers is something we do not know.'

Fortunately, a crucial experiment that sheds some light on this question has already been carried out by the pioneering South African naturalist, Eugene Marais. He started by observing the way in which workers of a *Eutermes* species repaired large breaches he made in their mounds. The workers started repairing the damage from every side, each carrying a grain of earth coated with its sticky saliva, and glueing it in place. The workers on different sides of the breach did not come into contact with each other and could not see each other, being blind. Nevertheless the structures built out from the different sides joined together correctly. The repair activities seemed to be coordinated by some overall organizing structure which Marais attributed to the 'group soul'. I think of it as a morphic field.

He then carried out an experiment to see what happened when the termites repairing the breach were separated from each other by a barrier. He took a steel plate and divided the termitary into two separate parts.

Now the builders on one side of the breach could know nothing of those on the other side by sensory means:

> In spite of this the termites build a similar arch or tower on each side of the plate. When eventually you withdraw the plate, the two halves match perfectly after the dividing cut has been repaired. We cannot escape the ultimate conclusion that somewhere there exists a pre-conceived plan which the termites merely execute.[5]

Unfortunately no one has ever repeated this experiment, or other experiments of Marais' which also seemed to show that the members of the colony were linked together by an 'invisible soul'. I believe that this is an area full of potential for fertile research.[6] If the behaviour of social insects is coordinated by a kind of field so far unrecognized by biology and physics, experiments with social insects could tell us something about the properties and nature of such fields, which may well be at work at all levels of social organization, including our own.

Schools of fish

At a distance, a school of fish resembles a large organism.[7] Its members swim in tight formations, wheeling and reversing in near unison. 'Either dominance systems do not exist or are so weak as to have little or no influence on the dynamics of the school as a whole. When the school turns to the right or the left, individuals formerly on the flank assume the lead.'[8] When under attack, a school may respond by leaving a gaping hole around a predator. More often it splits in half and the two halves turn outwards, eventually swimming back out around the predator and rejoining. This is known as the fountain effect and leaves the predator ahead of the school. Each time the predator turns, the same thing happens.

The most spectacular of the school's defences is the so-called flash expansion, which on film looks like a bomb bursting. Each fish simultaneously darts away from the centre of the school as a group is attacked, and the entire expansion may occur in as little as one fiftieth of a second. The fish may accelerate to a speed of ten to twenty body-lengths per second within that time. Yet the fish do not collide. 'Not only does each fish know in advance where it will swim if attacked, but it must also know where each of its neighbours will swim.'[9] This behaviour has no simple explanation in terms of sensory information from neighbouring fish because it happens far too fast for nerve impulses to move from the eye to the brain and then from the brain to the muscles.

Even in normal schooling behaviour, it is not clear how the movements are coordinated. Fish continue swimming in schools at night, so it does not seem to depend on vision. There have even been laboratory experiments in which fish were temporarily blinded by being fitted with opaque contact lenses. But they were still capable of joining and maintaining their position indefinitely within the school. Perhaps they could judge the position of their neighbours by their pressure sensitive organs, known as the lateral lines, which run along their length. But in other laboratory experiments by fish researchers, this idea has been tested by cutting the nerves from the lateral lines at the level of the gills. Such fish still school normally.[10]

Even if the means by which they are aware of each other's position through their normal senses were understood, this would still not account for their rapid responses. A fish cannot possibly sense in advance where its neighbours are going to move.

But if the behaviour of schools is coordinated by morphic fields, then these links and connections become easier to understand, in principle. The field helps shape the behaviour and activity of the school as a whole, and the individuals within it respond to their local field environment.[11] A simple physical analogy is provided by iron filings in a magnetic field. When the magnet is moved, the iron filings take up new positions and make new patterns of 'lines of force'. This is because each individual filing is responding to the field within and around it, and the field as a whole shapes the overall pattern.

It would be fascinating to know what happened if two parts of a school of fish were separated from each other by a barrier which blocked normal sensory contact. Would their activities still remain coordinated in any way? As far as I know, no one has yet attempted this kind of research.

Flocks of birds

Flocks of birds, like schools of fish, show such a remarkable coordination that they too have often been compared to an organism. The naturalist Edward Selous wrote as follows of the movement of a vast flock of starlings: 'Each mass of them turned, wheeled, reversed the order of their flight, changed in one shimmer from brown to grey, from dark to light, as though all the individuals composing them had been component parts of an individual organism.'[12]

Selous studied the behaviour of flocks of birds over a period of 30 years, and became convinced that it could not be explained in terms of normal sensory communication: 'I ask how, without some process of thought transference so rapid as to amount practically to simultaneous collective thinking, are these things to be explained?'[13]

There has been surprisingly little research into the behaviour of flocks, but in a landmark study in the 1980s by Wayne Potts, the banking movements of large flocks of dunlins were studied by taking films with very rapid exposures, so they could be slowed down to study the way in which the movements of the flocks occurred.[14] These analyses revealed that the movement was not exactly simultaneous, but rather started either from a single individual or from a few birds together. This initiation could occur anywhere within the flock, and the manoeuvres always propagated through the flock as a wave radiating from the site of initiation. These waves moved very rapidly, and took on average only 15 milliseconds (thousandths of a second) to pass from neighbour to neighbour.

In the laboratory, captive dunlins were tested to find out how rapidly they could react to a sudden stimulus. The average time they took to show a startle reaction after a sudden flash of light was 38 milliseconds. This means that it is impossible that they could bank in response to what their neighbours do, since this response occurs much quicker than their minimum reaction time.

Potts concluded that birds respond to a 'manoeuvre wave' that passes through the flock, adjusting their flight pattern to anticipate the arrival of the wave. He has proposed what he calls the 'chorus-line hypothesis' to explain this phenomenon, based on experiments carried out in the 1950s with human chorus lines. The dancers rehearsed particular manoeuvres, and in some experiments these manoeuvres were initiated by a particular person without warning, and the rate at which they propagated along the line was estimated from films. This was on average 107 milliseconds from person to person, nearly twice as fast as an average human visual reaction of 194 milliseconds. Potts suggests that this was due to the individual seeing the approaching manoeuvre wave and estimating its arrival time in advance.

In other words, Potts sees the birds or the chorus girls reacting to the manoeuvre wave as a whole. They reacted not to other individuals so much as the spreading pattern itself. This looks very like a field phenomenon, and I suggest that the manoeuvre wave is a pattern in the morphic field. This seems to me a more plausible explanation than the alternative, that the whole wave is coordinated through purely visual stimuli. This would require birds to be able to sense, notice and react to such waves almost immediately, even if they are coming from directly behind them. This would require them to have practically continuous, unblinking,

360° visual attention. The field hypothesis would make it easier to understand how the birds perceive and respond to the manoeuvre wave as a *Gestalt*, a German word conveying a combination of form and wholeness. Through it they could grasp the movement of the flock as a whole and respond to it in accordance with their position within it. The field underlies the continuum of the flock and the movement of patterns through it.[15]

If the flying of flocks of birds is coordinated through a morphic field, this field may well continue to link the birds together when they are engaged in other activities. For example, when a group of birds is foraging, if some members of the group find a good source of food, this discovery could propagate through the field of the scattered flock and alert other members of the group to it, and perhaps also set up attractions towards it, so that they can go in the right direction.

At least one naturalist, William Long, has observed that birds do indeed seem to respond in this way to the finding of food. He fed wild birds at irregular intervals, and noticed that when some found the food, others nearby soon appeared. There is no mystery in this, since they could have seen or heard the birds that were feeding. But he also found that relatively rare birds, widely dispersed over the countryside, would rapidly appear when food was available. After many observations, he came to the conclusion that the reasonable explanation was either that feeding birds can send forth a 'silent food call' or that their excitement spreads outwards. He suggested that it is 'felt by other starving birds, alert and sensitive, at a distance beyond all possible range of sight and hearing'.

To follow up such observations experimentally, it should be possible to work with flocks of domesticated birds such as chickens, ducks and geese. Two parts of a flock could be separated from each other so that no influence could pass along through the normal senses. If one part of the flock is frightened or disturbed, is an influence communicated to the other part? If one part of the flock is fed, does the other part become excited at the same time?

Telepathy within herds

Naturalists and hunters who have studied the behaviour of herds of wild animals, including caribou and elk, have often observed that a whole herd can get alarmed and flee after the sensing of danger by one or more of their number. In some cases this can be explained in terms of sensory signals, but in others observers are often at a loss to explain the sudden flight of animals that shortly before, under the same circumstances, were feeding or resting without suspicion. A sense of danger or alarm can spread silently and rapidly.

William Long studied the reactions of caribou on many occasions and in considerable detail. On one occasion after he had been tracking a herd for hours in New Brunswick, from the trail he read that one member of the herd was wounded, walking on three legs, his right fore-foot swinging helplessly as he hobbled along. Finally he came to a wooded slope from which he actually saw the herd about a mile away through his binoculars. He began to approach them, keeping well out of sight, when he came upon the solitary trail of the cripple, and shortly afterwards startled this animal in a thicket. It hobbled away into the woods. Long found an opening in the cover and turned his binoculars on the other caribou. Already they were in wild alarm and running off rapidly. He was convinced the rest of the herd could not hear, see, or smell him. He was still far away and yet they reacted immediately after the cripple was startled 'as if he had rung a bell for them'. Long followed the trail of the herd back to where they had been resting before taking alarm, and found there was no track of man or beast in the surrounding woods to account for their flight. He concluded that they had received some silent warning.

This does not always happen, because sometimes a member of the herd can be surprised without alarming the others. Long thought that in this case the solitary caribou was tremendously startled, and may have given a particularly intense warning to the rest of the herd. Similar observations of the behaviour of elk led him to conclude that whole herds could suddenly feel and understand the silent impulse to flee, and obey it without question, in a way that was essentially telepathic.[16]

Experiments with horses

The British horse trainer Harry Blake was convinced that horses were in communication with each other telepathically, and could also respond telepathically to people. He believed that this kind of communication was vital for their survival, since in the wild a herd of horses may well be scattered with some members out of sight and sound of each other. 'If one part of the herd should be frightened by the appearance of man, wolf, or some other predator, the rest of the herd, maybe among the trees, can be alerted by ESP even though they can neither see nor hear their fellows. Horses thus alerted will become first disturbed, then prick up their ears and snort, and start to move away from the area.'[17]

Blake carried out a number of experiments on telepathy between horses. To do this he chose pairs of horses that were brothers or sisters and living as close companions, in the habit of grazing together, walking together and acting together.

The pair were separated and kept out of sight and hearing of each other. Then one of each pair was fed and the other observed. For the purpose of this experiment the horses were not fed at the same time each day, nor fed at their regular feeding times. In 21 out of 24 such tests, Blake observed that when one horse was being fed, the second horse became excited and demanded food, though it could not see or hear the first one.

In a further series of experiments, when one of the pair of horses was taken out and exercised, on most occasions the other horse became excited. In another type of experiment Blake made a fuss of one of the pair, usually the one he liked least, and in most cases the other showed signs of disturbance suggesting it was jealous.

Overall, Blake carried out 119 experiments, and the results were positive in 68 per cent of them. He also ran control experiments with a pair of horses who were hostile to each other. In only one out of 15 experiments was there a positive result.

As far as I know, these pioneering experiments have never been repeated. They are significant in showing that the investigation of telepathic communication between horses, or other animals, can be investigated by means of simple, straightforward experiments.

Experiments with dogs and rabbits

The only experiments I know of to test for dog-to-dog telepathy were carried out with boxers by Aristide Esser, a psychiatrist at Rockland State Hospital in New York. His research was prompted by rumours that Soviet scientists were testing animals for ESP. One of these stories was that baby rabbits had been taken on board a submarine, while their mother was kept in a laboratory on land. When the vessel was submerged, the babies were killed one by one. The mother was said to have become agitated at the very moments they were killed.[18]

For his experiments, Esser used two soundproofed rooms in different parts of the hospital. A mother boxer was kept in one of these rooms and her son in the other. These dogs had been trained to cower at a raised, rolled newspaper. In the experiment, the son was 'threatened' by an experimenter with a rolled newspaper, and he duly cowered. The mother, in her isolated chamber, cowered at exactly the same moment.[19] In another experiment, a boxer was kept in one of the chambers, wired up to an electrocardiograph, while his mistress was in the other. The experimenters sent a man into her room without any warning, who shouted at her threateningly. Not surprisingly, she was scared. At the same time her dog's heartbeat accelerated violently.[20]

Probably few dog owners would enjoy taking part in experiments such as these, but it would be relatively easy to repeat this kind of experiment using isolated rooms and non-frightening stimuli. For example, in an experiment with two dogs one could be fed and the other observed to see if it showed any signs of excitement at the same time, as in Blake's experiments with horses.

Although the experiments with rabbits involving Russian submarines may just be rumours, some properly controlled experiments with rabbits have recently been carried out in France, with much the same results. In these tests rabbits were monitored for stress by measuring the blood flow through their ears. This was done painlessly by placing a small clip over a shaved part of one ear, on one side of which was a miniature light source, and the other side a photoelectric cell. In this way the amount of light that shone through the ear could be measured continuously. When rabbits feel stress, the blood vessels in their ears contract, the blood flow decreases, and more light passes through.

These experiments, conducted by René Peoc'h, involved pairs of rabbits taken from the same litter that had lived together in the same cages for months. They were compared with other pairs of rabbits that had been kept in isolation from each other in individual cages.

At the time of the experiment, each rabbit was placed in a soundproofed cage, which also isolated it from electromagnetic influences. During each experiment the stress experienced by both rabbits was measured by monitoring the blood flow through the ears. Peoc'h found that when one of the rabbits experienced a stress, the other tended to experience a stress within three seconds. By contrast, the control pairs of rabbits that did not know each other did not show the same kind of telepathic connection. The differences between the pairs of rabbits that knew each other and the control pairs was highly significant statistically.[21]

It would be surprising if rabbits and dogs could influence each other telepathically in experiments but not in real-life situations. And indeed several people who own two or more dogs have told me that they have noticed that the dogs seem to influence each other at a distance. For example, Margaret Simpson of Castle Douglas in Scotland has a whippet and a Labrador. When they are out walking, the whippet usually stays close to her while the Labrador ranges quite far and seems able to 'call' the whippet, especially when she finds a deer. 'For no sensory reason that I could discern, the whippet would get some sort of message and she would be off. It was exactly as if a thought had been transferred.'

Some dogs also react when another dog to which they are bonded has had an accident or died in a distant place. A sheepdog in France showed signs of great distress when her mother was killed on the island of La Réunion, over 6,000 miles away (p. 87). Another example, reported by Major Patrick Pirie, concerned a female golden Labrador and her daughter. When the daughter was about nine months old and living with Major Pirie in Somerset, 'for no reason at all and for the only time in her life she refused all food and remained quiet throughout the day. That evening we received a telephone call to tell us that her mother had been knocked down by a car and killed. I am convinced that she had some sort of perception and knew what had happened 100 miles away.'

Another of the examples on our database concerns some Burmese mountain dogs. 'One of my dogs was diagnosed as having cancer and was at Cambridge Vet Centre. Suddenly, just gone 12 midday, the other dog started howling and was very distressed for quite a while'. Later that afternoon, the vet from Cambridge rang to say that the sick dog had been put to sleep at midday. (Josephine Woods)

The examples of dogs, horses, caribou, and other species discussed in this chapter suggest that telepathy may be widespread within the animal kingdom.

The common features of animal telepathy

There are several characteristics of animal telepathy that recur in very different species. These point towards the following conclusions about the basic principles of telepathy within species:

1   Animal telepathy involves the influence of animals on other animals independently of the known senses.
2   Telepathy usually occurs between closely-related animals that are part of the same social group. In other words, it takes place between animals that are 'bonded' with each other.
3   In schools, flocks, herds, packs and other social groups, telepathic communication may play an important role in the coordination of the activity of the group as a whole.
4   At least in birds and mammals, telepathy has to do with emotions, needs and intentions. Feelings communicated telepathically include fear, alarm, excitement, calls for help, calls to go to a particular place, anticipations of arrivals or departures, and distress and dying.

In the case of domesticated animals, these same principles apply to telepathic communication between people and animals to which they are bonded.

These common features of animal telepathy seem to apply to much of human telepathy as well, especially to the most dramatic cases of spontaneous human telepathy concerning distant deaths or accidents.

One of the most important conclusions of the investigations described in this book is that telepathy is not specifically human. It is a natural faculty, part of our animal nature.

Does telepathy only work at a distance?

The fact that telepathic communication can occur when animals and people are *not* in sensory contact does not prove that telepathy still occurs when they *are* in sensory contact. Perhaps telepathy is a faculty switched on only when needed, as people switch on a radio intercom system when they are apart, and turn it off when they are together.

On the other hand, psychic links or emotional bonds connect animals and people both when they are together and when they are apart. Telepathic communication may well occur when communication is also taking place through the known senses.

We do not assume that animals cease to smell someone when they see or hear them. We are happy to accept that the senses are not mutually exclusive and generally work together. I think the same goes for the invisible communication that occurs through psychic bonds: it normally works together with the senses. The psychic link is not switched off when they are together, and switched on when they are apart; it is potentially there all the time, when together or apart.

Conclusion to Part IV

The scientific study of animal telepathy is still in its infancy. As research on this subject progresses, I expect that telepathy will seem increasingly normal, rather than being 'para' normal, 'beyond' the normal. It is an aspect of the biology of social groups and social communication. It enables members of the group to influence each other even when they are beyond the range of sensory communication, and may be of considerable survival value. If so, the capacity for telepathic communication must be subject to natural selection. Telepathy must have evolved. Its roots may lie deep down in evolutionary history, among the earliest social animals.

PART V

Senses of direction

10

Incredible journeys

Animals not only form bonds to the members of their social group, but also develop attachments to particular places. Many kinds of animals, both wild and domesticated, have the ability to find their way home from unfamiliar locations. This attachment to places depends on morphic fields, which underlie the sense of direction that enables animals to find their way home over unfamiliar terrain.

The sense of direction also plays a vital role in migration. Some species, like swallows, salmon and sea turtles, migrate from breeding grounds to feeding grounds, and back again, over thousands of miles. Their ability to navigate is one of the great unsolved mysteries of biology, as I discuss in the next chapter. Here too I think that morphic fields, and the ancestral memory inherent in them, could help provide an explanation.

Homing dogs, cats and horses

There are many stories of domesticated animals coming home after they have been left or lost far away. Some have achieved almost legendary status, like a collie called Bobby, lost in Indiana, who turned up at his home in Oregon the following year, having covered a distance of more than 2,000 miles. Such cases form the basis of the well-known animal adventure story *The Incredible Journey*,[1] made into a film by Walt Disney, in which a Siamese cat, an old bull terrier and a young Labrador find their way back home over 250 miles of wild country in northern Ontario.

Real-life incredible journeys happen over and over again, and remarkable cases are often reported in newspapers. In 1995 the London *Times* carried the following story:

A sheepdog who was abandoned by car thieves has been reunited with his owner after walking 60 miles home. Blake, a ten-year-old border collie, was stolen with his kennelmate, four-year-old Roy, while they were in the back of Tony Balderstone's Land Rover. The thieves, who took the vehicle from Cley, Norfolk, dumped the dogs at Downham Market, 60 miles from Mr Balderstone's home at Holt. Roy was caught in Downham Market two days later and returned to his master but Blake set off alone. Mr Balderstone, a shepherd, said yesterday: 'I knew he would make it home, as long as he did not get hit in a traffic accident or shot for worrying stock. I phoned farmers and gamekeepers along the route to alert them'. Blake took five days to make the journey to Letheringsett, a mile from Mr Balderstone's smallholding, where villagers recognized him.[2]

For every case like this that is reported in the newspapers, there must be dozens that remain unpublicized. On our database there are 60 unpublished stories of homing dogs and 29 of homing cats. Some, as in the case of Blake, concern animals that were abandoned or lost when they were away from home. But most are about animals that were taken to live in a new home returning to their old one.

In practically all these cases the animals were transported to the place from which they homed, rather than walking there by themselves. They would therefore have been unable to note the smells, landmarks or other details of the route. Usually their outward journeys were by car, but in some cases were by bus or train, and in one by boat along Lake Zurich. Sometimes they were taken by indirect routes. But in cases where they were spotted on the journey back, they were usually heading straight home, not following the route by which they had been taken. In any case, a dog or cat that tried to follow the roads or railway lines along which it had been carried on the outward journey would soon be squashed. Somehow the animals knew in what direction their home lay, even when they were in a place they had never been to before and had been taken there by an indirect route.

The clearest evidence that the animals' sense of direction does not depend on memorizing smells along the route, or other details of the outward journey, comes from cases where the animal was transported by air. During the Vietnam War, scout dogs were used by US troops and taken by helicopter to the war zones. One such dog, Troubles, was airlifted with his handler, William Richardson, into the jungle to support a patrol ten miles away. Richardson was wounded by enemy fire and was airlifted to hospital; the other members of the patrol simply abandoned the dog. Three weeks later, Troubles was found back at his home at the First Air Cavalry Division Headquarters in An Khe. Tired and emaciated, he would not let anyone near him. He searched the tents until he found Richardson's belongings, then curled up and went to sleep.[3]

Although most pet owners are astonished by the unsuspected homing powers of their animals, shepherds and other owners of working dogs are often well aware of these capacities. It is significant that Blake's owner, so confident of his return, was a shepherd. In the days of the droving of cattle down from the Scottish Highlands into England, it was the custom of the drovers to send their dogs back home on their own after they had delivered the cattle; the men stayed to work in the harvest. The dogs usually retraced the route they had taken on the way south, stopping at farms or inns where they had previously fed and rested. The innkeepers fed them and were paid by the dogs' owners when they stopped the next year.[4] Before the Second World War, Lincolnshire farmers used to drive their animals to markets over 100 miles away, in 20-mile stages. When the animals had been sold, the drivers would turn their dogs loose to find their own way home to save paying their rail fare. (Roger Dale)

Some horses also find their way home across miles of unfamiliar country, and their homing abilities would probably be expressed much more frequently if they were not shut up in fields and enclosures when taken to new places. The unwanted homing of horses is a nuisance, but sometimes a horse's ability to find its way back can be very useful.

One leisurely day, Jean Welsh was riding her horse in the Yorkshire countryside when she decided to explore an area that neither she nor the horse had ever been to before. After a while she realized she was lost. 'I have a dreadful sense of direction and was a bit panicky. I dropped the reins on the mare's neck and said "It's up to you now – get us home!"' The horse carried on purposefully, stopping at a gate they had never seen before. So confident did she seem that Jean opened it. 'Without any direction from me she continued on her way and appeared very much in control.' They followed unfamiliar tracks until they eventually came to a place Jean recognized, much to her relief, not far from home.

Other homing animals

The ability to home is widespread. As well as stories about dogs, cats and horses, on the database there is a tale of a flock of sheep that escaped from a farmer's field and travelled eight miles to their native pasture, a pet pig that homed from seven miles away, and several stories of homing birds. One of the most vivid is about Donald and Dora, Easter ducklings raised by the Erickson family in Minnesota.

We built a fine pen in the back yard of our home in the inner part of Minneapolis. We fed them and gave them baths in a big plastic pool. They became quite the focus of our summer. Months passed and they were full size. What would we do when winter came? Finally in mid August we decided to take them over to a pond in a large undeveloped park about two miles away. Mom said it was best if they joined their own kind and learned how to be wild before the snows came. We reluctantly agreed, and let them go. Dad had marked their wings with paint so we could watch them mix around with the wild ducks. We returned home sadly. Suddenly we heard neighbours out in the streets yelling and laughing. We ran out into the front yard and much to our amazement there on the top of the hill, in the center of the street waddled Donald and Dora, quack, quack, quacking. They had found their way back home through woods and busy city streets. (Leni Erickson)

In this case, the distance was modest, but some pet birds have found their way home over hundreds of miles, like a magpie that had been adopted by the children of the Beauzetier family in Drancy, near Paris, when it fell out of its nest as a baby. For the summer holidays of 1995 the children went to stay with their grandparents near Bordeaux, taking the bird with them. While they were there the magpie escaped. The children were upset, and at the end of the holidays they had to return home without her. Soon afterwards they saw her in a tree near their house. When they called her, she answered, and much to their delight came back to live with them. She had flown over 300 miles.

Even more spectacular was the return of a pigeon belonging to Ken Clark of Bakersfield, California, that he gave to some cousins visiting from Connecticut. He provided some feed and a cage for them to carry it in, and off they went. 'One month later the bird was back! Its tail feathers were mostly gone. It was dirty and a real mess.' His cousins had taken the bird all the way home, 3,000 miles away, but it escaped when they were trying to transfer it to a bigger cage.

The homing abilities of pigeons are no surprise, but they are by no means unique, and are shared by many other species.

Experiments with homing cats and dogs

Most pet owners are understandably reluctant to abandon their animals in unfamiliar places to study their homing behaviour. Apart from my research with the dog Pepsi, described later, I know of only two series of experiments of this type.

The first were carried out in Cleveland, Ohio, over 75 years ago by the zoologist F. H. Herrick, with his own cat. His research began unintentionally when he took the cat in a bag from his home to his office at Western Reserve University, five miles away, travelling by streetcar. But when he let the cat out of the bag, it escaped and was home the same night. He was puzzled by its direction-finding ability, and investigated it further by taking the cat in a closed container and releasing it at distances from one to three miles from his home. He established that the cat could home under a variety of conditions and from any point of the compass.[5]

The second series of experiments was carried out in Germany in 1931–2 by the naturalist Bastian Schmidt, who studied three sheepdogs. In each experiment, a dog was taken in a closed van by a roundabout route to a place it had never been to before. It was then released. Its behaviour was observed and recorded by a series of trained observers stationed along its probable homeward route. It was also followed by silent cyclists, who were instructed not to communicate with it in any way.[6]

The first experiments were in the Bavarian countryside with a farm dog called Max. When Max was released for the first time in an unfamiliar place, he scanned the landscape in various directions, as if taking his bearings. After several trials he began to concentrate on the direction of his home, looking resolutely homewards, and after half an hour he set off. He avoided going through woods, hid from passing cars and circumvented farmhouses and villages. After travelling for just over an hour, he came out on the familiar road into his village, and galloped home. The distance he covered was about six miles.

In the second trial he was released in the same place, and after hesitating for only five minutes set off along the same route as before, but this time took a short cut and reached home in 43 minutes. In a third trial he took longer, because he was forced by some heavy traffic to take a long diversion.

From the observations of Max's behaviour, Schmidt concluded that he 'made *no* use of the sense of smell, although this sense is so important to a dog'. He did not sniff at the trees, nor at the ground, nor try to pick up any trail. There was no reason for him to do so, Schmidt concluded: 'The picking up of a trail, human or canine, could mean nothing for a dog trying to return to his home.'[7] Nor could he have used his eyes to determine the homeward direction, because he could not see any familiar landmarks.

Schmidt then did some experiments with a city dog named Nora. She lived in Munich, and for the purpose of the experiment was taken in the early morning to a part of the city she had never been to before, more than three miles from her home. When she stepped out of the carrying basket, she found herself in a great square (Johannisplatz in Bogenhausen; she lived close to the Tierpark). When she was first released, she behaved very much as Max had done; she spent about 25 minutes taking her bearings, looking principally in the direction of her home, and then trotted off in the right direction. All went well until she encountered a frolicsome dog in the Tassiloplatz who led her astray. After some time she took her bearings again, and once more set off in a direct line towards her home. The journey took 93 minutes, including the time spent taking her bearings, playing and straying.

For the second experiment, nearly six weeks later, Nora was released in the same place as before. This time, again like Max, she took only five minutes to get her bearings, and set off along the route she had followed before, as far as the Tassiloplatz. This time there was no distraction, and she ran straight home, arriving 37 minutes after she was released.

Like Max, Nora was not sniffing, and seemed to be paying no attention to smells. She could not see any familiar sights, since there were many streets of houses between the release point and her home. Since neither smell nor sight seemed able to explain her behaviour, or that of Max, Schmidt concluded: 'Here we are confronted with an enigma, the mystery of an unknown sense, which one might perhaps describe simply as the sense of orientation.'[8]

Schmidt then tried out three similar experiments with another country dog, but they were all failures. The dog always went off in the wrong direction. This is a salutary reminder that dogs, like people, differ in their abilities; some have a better sense of direction than others.

Elizabeth Marshall Thomas, whose book *The Hidden Life of Dogs* chronicles her engaging observations of dogs left to their own devices, came to similar conclusions. One of her dogs, a husky called Misha, had excellent navigational skills and went on journeys that took him up to 20 miles away from home. (Misha's mate Maria did not get lost when she accompanied him so long as she followed his lead. But she almost always got lost when she went out on her own. Then she used her own way of getting back: she simply sat forlornly on someone's doorstep. Sooner or later, they looked on her collar for her telephone number and called Thomas, who collected her in a car.)

The first question Thomas asked when she started studying her dogs was about the nature of Misha's navigational skills. 'But this question, I was never able to answer.'[9] Misha did not seem to be navigating by landmarks, since once he had reached a destination he might easily take another route home. Did he use the stars or the position of the sun? The sound of the nearby Atlantic Ocean? Odours floating in the air? 'I didn't know, and could learn nothing by watching his sure trot, his confident demeanor.'[10]

Multiple destinations: experiments with Pepsi

As we have seen, many kinds of animals seem to have a sense of direction that enables them to home from strange places. But some are able to find more than one destination, and go to places other than their home across unfamiliar terrain. They seem to have a sense of direction for *several* places.

The most remarkable direction-finding dog I have met is Pepsi, a border collie-terrier cross who lives in Leicester. When her owner, Clive Rudkin, contacted me in 1995, Pepsi had already on 14 occasions made journeys all over the city of Leicester after escaping from Clive's own house or from his parents' or sister's houses, arriving within hours at the houses of friends or family. Most of these journeys covered distances of at least three miles, and took place in a variety of directions. Altogether, Pepsi found her way to six destinations, all of which she had been taken to previously by car, but to none of which she had ever been walked. During these car journeys she was usually on the floor and could not see out of the windows. On one occasion, for example, Pepsi escaped from Clive's parents' house, four miles northeast of his home, and turned up at a friend's house five miles north of there. She had not been taken to this house by car from the parents' house, but direct from Clive's own house.

Apart from these adventures, spaced over a period of four years, she was never left to roam the streets on her own and was always accompanied when walking.

Pepsi had never got lost nor suffered any injury, and Clive felt sufficiently confident of her abilities to agree to doing two experiments in which she was left to find her own way from unfamiliar places. These experiments were filmed for BBC television.[11]

In the first test, Pepsi was released in a park two miles southwest of her home, and followed by a BBC cameraman. She made her way home by a slightly indirect but scenic route, following the bank of a river for much of the way. The problem with this experiment was that she soon noticed the cameraman following her, and for some of the journey started following him. Since she insisted on interacting with him, he was unable to act as a detached observer, and it is hard to know how much Pepsi's journey was influenced by his presence.

For the second experiment, Pepsi was equipped with a Global Positioning System (GPS) monitor in a pouch attached to her back. This device, about the size of a portable telephone, recorded her position with an accuracy of about ten yards by means of signals from satellites. Our plan was to leave Pepsi on her own in an unfamiliar place very early in the morning, to minimize the danger from traffic, and to track her movements by satellite, her positions being recorded automatically at one-minute intervals.

On the summer solstice of 1996, as latter-day druids were celebrating the sunrise at ancient megaliths, Clive and I were in Ethel Road, Leicester, leaving Pepsi on a street corner two miles east of Clive's house. She had never been taken to this place before. We went there in a taxi; she travelled on the floor and was unable to look out of the windows. She looked at us quizzically as she sat on the kerbside and watched us disappear in the same taxi. We had taken the precaution of putting a message on her back explaining to anyone that found her that she was taking part in an experiment, and had informed the police in case she strayed.

We went back to Clive's house and waited. We had left her at 4.55 am, and expected her to turn up at Clive's house, or possibly at his parents', within two hours at most. By 9 am she had still not arrived, nor had she turned up at Clive's parents' house, and we were getting very worried. Finally, Clive thought of checking the house of his sister, who was away on holiday. And there we found Pepsi, lying calmly on the grass in the back garden. Pepsi had not been taken to this house for at least six months, and had never made her own way there. She had, however, escaped from this house on two occasions in previous years, and gone to a friend's house some four miles to the southwest.

In retrospect, we could see that this was the best choice for Pepsi, because it was the nearest house she knew, only a mile east of the place we left her. When we deciphered the record on the GPS device, we found that Pepsi had first gone about 500 yards north (the opposite direction from which we had departed in the taxi). She had then spent at least eight minutes going backwards and forwards in the surrounding streets, as if getting her bearings. She then headed due east for three quarters of a mile to the neighbourhood of Leicester General Hospital, and spent seven minutes moving around the hospital buildings. Then she went straight to Clive's sister's house about 500 yards south of there (Figure 10.1)

Pepsi could not have found the house by smelling it, because that morning there was a steady northwest wind, and at no point in her journey was she downwind of the house or its neighbourhood.

Since this experiment, Pepsi has escaped on a further four occasions, and has made more journeys across Leicester to houses she knows, and also to one that she had never made her own way to before, that of Clive's brother.

Figure 10.1 A map of part of Leicester showing where Pepsi was released (A), the succession of places she visited, as revealed by the Global Positioning System monitor carried on her back, and the house of her owner's sister (B) where she ended up.

Allot Gdns

10 15

Sch

11

14 17

12 HOSPITAL

13

Sch

16

Sch

Sch

EVING

PAR

B Evi H

Schs

| 0 | | 0.5 mile |
| 0 | | 0.8 km |

Pepsi's sense of direction somehow enables her to know where she is in relation to a variety of different houses, and to know where they are in relation to each other, even though she has been taken from one to the other by car, not looking out of the window.

One way of thinking about this would be to suppose she has a kind of mental map. But this is too abstract and too anthropomorphic a metaphor. And even if she did have a map, this would not enable her to know where she was when abandoned in an unknown place. Maps are useful if you know where you are, and where you want to go. But if you do not know where you are, a map is not much help. Rather than a map, Pepsi seems to have a sense of direction.

The sense of direction

How could a sense of direction work? Whatever the physical basis, I suppose that the animal somehow *feels* that a familiar place is in a certain direction, perhaps through some kind of 'pull' towards it. And it may also feel its nearness or distance.

In the simplest case, that of homing behaviour, the animal feels pulled towards its home, and if it drifts off course (as Nora did in Munich when she met the playful dog) it can take its bearings again, and reorient towards its home (Figure 10.2A). One metaphor would be that of magnetic attraction. Another would be of connection to its home by means of an invisible elastic band. Either way, there would be a kind of pull in the homeward direction, and a feeling of 'getting warm' on approaching the home. This feeling of 'getting warm' would also fit with the ability of animals transported in cars and other vehicles to know when they are nearing their home, as I shall discuss in Chapter 12.

I suggest that this pull towards the goal of home takes place within a field connecting the animal with its environment. The animal builds up a familiarity with its home environment. Its field of activity within its familiar environment involves the building up of memories.

I suggest that this field of activity, with its inherent memory, is a kind of morphic field. And if the animal is linked to its home environment by a morphic field, then this connection can stretch like an elastic band. It can continue to link the animal with its home even when it is miles away. And it can pull the animal in a homeward direction.

The animal's connection with its home may remain latent when the animal is busy foraging or exploring. Animals away from home are not being pulled back home all the time they are away, but they can usually find their home when the time comes to return. Their intention to go

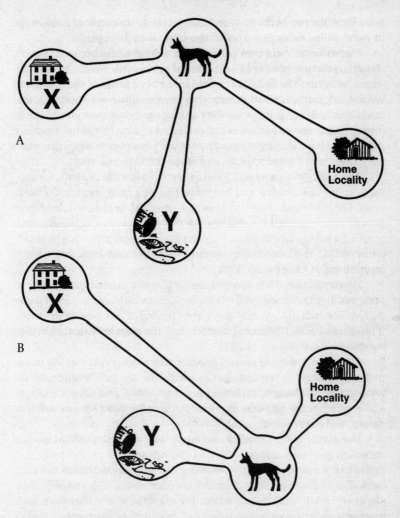

Figure 10.2 A: Connections through a morphic field between an animal and its home and other places of importance to it. B: The animal is in a different location, and hence the connections to its home and other places give it different directional information.

home gives a motivation to their behaviour, but finding the direction to their home or other place depends on the connections already established with particular places. Homing behaviour, like navigation in general, depends on a combination of motivation or intention on the one hand, and connections to significant places on the other. These connections were built up in the past, and I suggest that this memory is inherent in the morphic fields that connect the animals to these places.

The morphic field that connects an animal to its home is closely related to the morphic field of the social group with which the animal shares its home. The first kind of field underlies a sense of direction; the second, telepathic communication. But as we shall see in Chapter 13, the fields that connect animals to other animals not only provide channels for telepathic communication but can provide directional information as well. We have already encountered some examples of this phenomenon when cats or other animals in distress called their owners.

The analogy of the elastic band in itself implies directionality. Imagine you are blindfolded and hold one end of a long, stretched elastic band. The other end, many yards away, is attached to a place or held by a person. You not only feel a pull towards that place or person, but also feel a pull in a particular direction. This attraction or pull towards a goal can be modelled mathematically in terms of dynamical attractors within morphic fields (Appendix C).

When an animal has several familiar places to which it can travel, it presumably experiences pulls or attractions to different places (Figure 10.2A). For each place it may also have a feeling of nearness or distance. If the animal is in a different position, then the pulls are oriented in different directions (Figure 10.2B).

In the light of these ideas, I imagine that when Pepsi was left in an unfamiliar place, as she took her bearings, she sensed the direction of various familiar houses, including her own home, and Clive's parents' and sister's houses. She may also have felt that the sister's house was the closest, and hence set off in that direction.

The elastic band provides one metaphor for these pulls. Magnetic attraction provides another. One of the advantages of the magnetic metaphor is that it raises the possibility not only of attractions towards particular places, but also of repulsions from them. It is possible that places of which animals are afraid, for example where they have had traumatic experiences in the past, may repel rather than attract them, even at a distance. They may also have the feeling of 'getting warm' (perhaps 'getting cold' would be a better expression in this case) as they approach such places, and this feeling may be one of fear rather than excitement. This would fit with the fearful reactions of some dogs as they are driven in cars towards the vet (p. 98).

The direction-finding abilities of domesticated animals make good sense when we look at them in a larger biological and evolutionary context.

Home ranges of wild and feral animals

Any animal that has a home base, such as bees with their hive, robins with their nest, and wolves with their den, has a surrounding area of familiar terrain. The part of the familiar area they visit repeatedly is called the *home range*, the size of which may vary from day to day and from season to season. And within the home range they may have a *territory*, an area they protect. A domestic cat, for example, may have a territory about 100 yards in diameter that it knows intimately and which it protects, but it may also have a larger home range extending up to a mile or more from its home.

We too have our own familiar areas, and within them a home range covering our immediate neighbourhood, places we shop, work and play, places where we visit family and friends, areas we walk dogs, and so on. Within these home ranges are the territories we defend, usually our homes and gardens.

Generally speaking, finding our way around our home range depends on landmarks and other familiar features of the environment, and the same is true of animals. Familiar sights, sounds and smells enable animals to know where they are and find their way to familiar destinations. They do not need a special sense of direction when they are moving within the home range and following familiar routes.

But of course an animal's familiar area has not always been familiar to it. Every young animal has to get to know it for the first time, even if it is already well known to older members of the group. Each individual animal or group of animals when it settles in a new place needs to explore its surroundings. When it is exploring new terrain, it cannot rely on memory to find its way home, unless it retraces its footsteps.

Animals that have been out exploring may indeed find their way back by following landmarks or a scent trail. But another way to do so is by *navigation*. Biological navigation is defined as 'the capacity to orient towards a goal, regardless of its direction, without reference to landmarks'.[12] This way an animal can find its way back by taking short cuts, and without needing to memorize all the features of the outward journey. Navigation also enables it to find its way home from an unfamiliar place when it has not had an opportunity to learn the features of the outward route. For example, if an animal is being chased by a predator, it may escape by running into an unknown place without remembering all the details of its path. Likewise, hunting animals often move away from the familiar pathways of their home range as they follow and chase their prey. Birds may be blown off course by strong winds, and aquatic

animals be carried into unfamiliar waters by currents. In all these circumstances, the animals need to be able to navigate to find their way
back home.

As a general rule, the larger the home range, the more important
navigational skills will be for getting home or finding other important
places within it. For example, some packs of wolves possess and defend
enormous territories. In northern Minnesota, where deer are relatively
plentiful, territories are around 50 to 100 square miles. In Alaska, where
wolves mainly prey on moose, a territory may be 800 square miles. On
Arctic islands where prey populations are sparse, a pack's territory may
cover thousands of square miles. One pack on Ellesmere Island (to the
northwest of Greenland) was observed to range over 5,000 square miles
in a six-week period.[13]

Considering that wolves, the wild ancestors of dogs, possess navigational skills that enable them to find their way around in such vast areas,
the homing abilities of domestic dogs seem less astonishing.

Feral dogs have smaller home ranges than wolves, but they still display impressive abilities finding their way around. In central and southern Italy, for example, packs of free-ranging dogs are common, and
several have been studied by radiotracking and by visual observation. In
one of these studies, in a mountainous part of the Abruzzo region, the
overall home range was 22 square miles, and within this range, 'core'
areas were frequented much more than others, especially near the den
and the rubbish dumps where the dogs found food. The home range
shifted from season to season and from year to year, and the pack established new core areas as new food sources were found.[14]

On several occasions dogs went on major excursions outside the
home range, seemingly to explore. As a result of one of these expeditions,
a bitch established a new den ten miles away. Interestingly, the home
range of these feral dogs was in between the territories of two wolf packs,
with some overlap. The wolves' ranges were considerably larger than the
dogs'. One of them covered 110 square miles.

Cats generally have much smaller home ranges, though some farm
cats may cover areas of up to 50 acres (under a tenth of a square mile).[15]
Males generally have larger ranges than females, and some male feral cats
in the Australian bush range over two square miles.[16]

When animals such as cats, dogs and wolves find their own way
around, it is hard to know how much of their navigational skill depends
on keeping track of the route they have followed, using memory and
their normal senses, and how much it depends on a more mysterious
sense of direction. Maybe these factors all work together most of the
time.

Although domestic dogs and cats normally have less scope for moving around on their own than their wild and feral relatives, they can tell us more about this sense of direction precisely because they are less free. To study the sense of direction in free-living animals, it is necessary to capture them first, and then take them to an unfamiliar place before releasing them. Relatively few studies of this kind have been carried out. But large numbers of dogs and cats are moved around in cars and other vehicles. The fact they are transported passively, and often go to sleep on the journey, means they cannot study and remember the details of their route. Yet, as we shall see in Chapter 12, they often know when they are nearing their destination.

But the most impressive homing performances are by birds, and the best studied of these are pigeons.

Homing pigeons

The distance records for homing by birds are held by a range of wild species. Adélie penguins, Leach's petrels, Manx shearwaters, albatrosses, storks, terns, swallows and starlings have all been known to home from more than a thousand miles away.[17] When two Laysian albatrosses were taken from Midway Island in the central Pacific and released 3,200 miles away in Washington State, on the West Coast of America, one returned in ten days, the other in twelve. A third came back from the Philippines, more than 4,000 miles away, in just over a month.[18] In an experiment with Manx shearwaters, birds were kidnapped from their nesting burrows on the island of Skokholm, off the coast of Wales. One was released in Venice, Italy, and was back within fourteen days. Another returned in twelve and a half days from Boston, Massachusetts, a journey across the Atlantic of 3,000 miles.[19]

Although their range is more limited than that of such sea birds, racing pigeons are the obvious choice for detailed research. They have been bred and selected for their homing ability over many generations. Racing pigeons can fly home in a single day from a place they have never been to before, hundreds of miles away. The techniques for keeping and training them are well known. And they are relatively inexpensive.

Numerous experiments on homing have already been carried out with pigeons. Nevertheless, after nearly a century of dedicated but frustrating research, no one knows how they do it. All attempts to explain their navigational ability in terms of known senses and physical forces have proved unsuccessful. The best-informed researchers in this field readily admit the problem: 'The amazing flexibility of homing and migrating birds has been a puzzle for years. Remove cue after cue, and yet animals still retain some backup strategy for establishing flight direction.[20] 'The problem of navigation remains essentially unsolved.' [21]

To appreciate why this problem is still unsolved, it is necessary to consider the various theories of pigeon navigation that have been put forward over the years and see why all have proved inadequate.

The theory that they remember the twists and turns of the outward journey, first proposed by Charles Darwin, has been refuted by taking pigeons to an unfamiliar point of release in dark vans, within rotating containers, by devious routes. Some have even been anaesthetized throughout the journey. When they are released, they fly straight home.[22]

The theory that they rely on familiar landmarks has also been ruled out. Pigeons can find their way home by following landmarks in familiar territory, but they can also return from unfamiliar places hundreds of miles away where they cannot see any recognizable landmarks. And in experiments carried out in the 1970s, pigeons were even blinded temporarily by being fitted with frosted-glass contact lenses. They still found their way home over great distances, although they tended to crash into trees or wires very near their loft. They had to be able to see in order to land properly, but they found their way from many miles away to within a few hundred yards of the loft without being able to use their eyes.[23]

The sun navigation theory postulated that they use the position of the sun to work out their latitude and longitude, comparing its angle and motion at the point of release with those at home. This theory has been refuted in two ways. First, pigeons can home on overcast days, and can even be trained to home at night. This means that being able to see the sun is not essential for homing. Secondly, navigating by the sun is only possible with the help of a very accurate clock.[24] When pigeons have their internal clock shifted by six or twelve hours (by keeping them in artificial light for part of the night and in darkness for part of the day), and are released on sunny days, they are at first confused and set off in the wrong direction, but they soon correct their course and fly home. On cloudy days they set off in the right direction straight away. These results show that pigeons may use the sun as a kind of compass, but the sun is not essential for their knowing the direction of their home.[25]

The theory that pigeons smell their home from hundreds of miles away, even when the wind is blowing in the wrong direction, seems extremely implausible. Nevertheless, it has been tested in a variety of ways. In most of these experiments, the pigeons could still find their way home even if their nostrils were blocked up with wax, their olfactory nerves severed, or their olfactory mucosa anaesthetized. They may use smell in familiar regions where they can recognize the odours carried on the wind, but their ability to home from unfamiliar places cannot be explained in terms of this sense.[26]

Finally, there is the magnetic theory. Could it be that the pigeons have a magnetic sense, a biological compass? The problem is that even if pigeons do have a compass sense, it would not tell them where their home was. If you are taken to an unfamiliar place and given a compass, you know where north is, but not where your home is. The compass would be useful for keeping your bearings, but you would need to know where home was by some other means.

But what if the compass sense were so sensitive that it could give information on latitude? It could do this in two ways: firstly by detecting the small changes in Earth's magnetic field strength at different latitudes, and secondly by detecting the dip of the magnetic field. At the magnetic North Pole the needle points downwards; at the equator it is horizontal, and in between the angle varies according to the latitude. However, to detect changes in latitude, the pigeons' magnetic sense would have to be very accurate indeed. In the north-eastern United States, for example, over a distance of 100 miles in a north-south direction, the average field strength changes by less than 1 per cent, and the angle of the field by less than 1°. And even if pigeons had such an accurate compass sense, this would give no information on longitude, on how far east or west they were from home. Pigeons can home from all points of the compass.

In any case, the magnetic hypothesis has been tested directly by attaching magnets to pigeons. These should confuse their magnetic sense, if they have one, and yet birds with magnets attached to them get home as well as control birds with non-magnetic attachments of similar size and weight.[27]

The failure of all these theories leaves pigeon homing essentially unexplained. I myself think that pigeons' feats of navigation can only be explained in terms of a sense of direction, as I have already discussed in relation to the navigation of dogs, cats and other animals. No doubt pigeons' navigation can be aided by using the sun's position, and perhaps even a magnetic sense, to help keep their bearings, to stay on course. But without the directional pull through the morphic field connecting them to their home, they would be lost.

The human sense of direction

Our hunting and gathering ancestors were subject to the same selection pressures as other animals. Groups or individuals who travelled away from their home base and failed to find their way back probably perished, unless they were fortunate enough to find another human group that allowed them to join.

Until very recently, traditional peoples such as Australian Aborigines, the bushmen of the Kalahari and the navigators of Polynesia were famed for their sense of direction. Here were human beings whose abilities far exceeded those expressed or acknowledged in modern industrial societies. For example, Laurens van der Post, travelling in the Kalahari desert with some bushmen, after many miles of following a twisting trail had no idea where they were or in which direction their camp lay. But his companions had no doubt. 'They were always centred. They knew, without conscious effort, where their home was.' [28]

One of the most spectacular demonstrations of this ability was given by Tupaia, a dispossessed high chief and navigator from Raiatea, near Tahiti. Captain James Cook met him in 1769 on his first great voyage of exploration, and invited him to travel on board the *Endeavour*. During a journey of over 6,000 miles, via the Society Islands, around New Zealand, along the Australian coast and ending in Java, Tupaia was able to point towards Tahiti at any time, despite the distance involved and the ship's circuitous route between latitudes $48°S$ and $4°N$.[29]

By contrast, civilized peoples, and especially modern urban people, have so many artificial aids to navigation, such as signposts, maps and compasses – and now satellite global positioning systems – that a sense of direction is no longer essential to survival. It is neglected during our education, and very little attention has been paid to the subject by institutional science.

Nevertheless, the sense of direction has not atrophied altogether in modern people.[30] Most of us are vaguely aware of this sense, if only by comparison with other people who tend to get lost more easily, or who are much better at finding their way. Nevertheless, in the absence of artificial aids, most modern people are poor navigators compared with many non-human animals. And this is no doubt why we find the abilities of dogs and cats so fascinating, and why homing pigeons are especially intriguing. They can do something we can't. They have sensitivities that we have lost.

11

Migrations and memory

Homing and migration are closely related. Cycles of migration can be thought of as a double-homing system. For example, English swallows migrate 6,000 miles in the autumn to their winter feeding grounds in South Africa, crossing the Sahara desert on the way. They return to their English breeding grounds in the spring, often to the very same place they nested the previous year. They 'home' to Africa and then they 'home' to England again.

More amazing still is the instinctive ability of young birds to home to their ancestral winter quarters without being guided by birds that have done it before. European cuckoos, raised by birds of other species, do not know their parents. In any case, the older cuckoos leave for southern Africa in July or August before the new generation is ready to go. About four weeks later, the young cuckoos find their own way to their ancestral feeding grounds in Africa, unaided and unaccompanied.

Even insects can migrate enormous distances to places they have never been before. The most famous is the monarch butterfly. Monarchs born near the Great Lakes in the northeastern United States travel some 2,000 miles south, overwintering in millions on particular 'butterfly trees' in the Mexican highlands. They then migrate north in the spring. This first generation of migrants dies after breeding in the southern part of their range, from Texas to Florida. Their offspring continue the northwards migration to the Great Lakes region and southern Canada, where they breed for several generations. In the autumn, the new generation of migrants heads south towards Mexico to overwinter on the ancestral trees; but these are three to five generations away from their ancestors that overwintered in the same spot last year. The migratory cycle is continued through successive generations, and no individual butterfly experiences more than a part of it.[1]

How do these insects manage to find their way to these ancestral destinations? Are they navigating towards a goal, like homing pigeons do, using a sense of direction? Or are they merely following a series of genetically programmed instructions that tell them to go in particular directions, orienting by means of the sun, stars, and a magnetic sense?

In this chapter, I argue that the genetic programming theory is inadequate to account for most migratory behaviour. Instead, I suggest that migrating animals often rely on a sense of direction that enables them to navigate towards their goal, to which they are connected through morphic fields. I propose that their migratory pathways involve an ancestral memory inherent in these fields. But just as homing birds navigating towards a goal with a sense of its direction may also make use of a compass sense and the sun's position to help them keep their bearings, so migrating animals may also make use of magnetic and celestial clues.

The sun, stars and compasses

Migratory birds are usually imagined by biologists to have an inborn program that directs the migratory process on the basis of compass orientations derived from the sun, the stars and a magnetic sense. In the scientific literature this is called an 'inherited spatiotemporal vector-navigation program'.[2] But this impressive-sounding technical term merely restates the problem instead of solving it.

The main evidence for the role of stars is that when migratory birds are kept in cages in a planetarium at the beginning of the migration season, they tend to hop in the appropriate direction of migration according to the rotating pattern of 'stars'. In the northern hemisphere, the point around which the stars rotate is the celestial North Pole, and hence the movement of the stars can serve as a kind of compass.

However, in the real world, migrants can still find their way in the daytime or when the sky is heavily overcast.[3] For example, in a radar tracking experiment based in Albany County, New York, it was found that uninterrupted overcast skies lasting several days did not disorient nocturnal migrant birds of various species. There were 'not even subtle changes in flight behavior'.[4] Thus a star compass does not seem to be essential for their orientation.

Then what about a magnetic compass sense? Some species do indeed seem to be sensitive to the Earth's magnetic field, and captive migratory birds kept in cages change the direction in which they hop if the magnetic field around them is changed.[5]

Although a compass sense and the rotation of the stars can help birds in their orientation, knowing the compass directions cannot tell them where they are, and where their goal is.

The genetic programming theory proposes not that they know where they are going, but that they fly in a pre-programmed direction. There is a big difference between navigating to a goal and following a series of directions, if only that goal-directed navigation is more flexible. If you are trying to reach a city by road and you get lost, you can find your way there by a new route if you know where you are trying to get to. But if you do not know where your destination is but simply follow a series of directions, such as 'drive 75 miles northeast and then 20 miles north', you will not be able to adapt to any emergencies that cause you to lose your way.

A programmed migratory pathway would have to be very finely adjusted if the animals are to find their way to the wintering area from different starting points, and then to return to the same places the next spring. For example, swallows from western Ireland, eastern England and northern Germany set off in different directions and fly by different routes before they converge on the Straits of Gibraltar, where they cross over to Africa. On the return journey, they would have to be programmed to diverge at particular points after crossing back into Europe, and then to follow distinctive routes to their destinations. Such a rigid system would be inflexible, and any birds that were blown off course would have little chance of finding their way back to their breeding grounds.

Second, these hypothetical programs would have to be built up on the basis of chance mutations and natural selection over many generations, which would make it difficult for new migratory patterns to evolve, and would prevent the animals from adapting rapidly to changing circumstances.

And third, the only remotely plausible mechanism for programmed migratory behaviour is in terms of a magnetic sense, combined with information from the sun and stars. The problem is that not only does the Earth's magnetic field vary throughout the day and with the seasons of the year, but the magnetic poles themselves wander. The north magnetic pole is not at the geographical North Pole; it is currently in northern Canada, in the Queen Elizabeth Islands, around 103°W and 77°N. This means that compass needles do not point to true North, but rather deviate from it. The angle of deviation, called the declination, varies from place to place, being greatest in northern latitudes. Human navigators using compasses have to correct for this magnetic declination depending on their latitude and longitude, using correction factors that are continually updated as the magnetic poles wander. No animal could be genetically programmed to make such corrections.

As well as the wandering of the poles, the general pattern of the Earth's magnetic field itself changes considerably over the years, with quite large changes over timescales of a couple of centuries (Figure 11.1). Any genetically programmed magnetic navigational system that depended in detail on the Earth's magnetic field would be disrupted by these changes. A genetically programmed system would have to be reprogrammed continually, but the timescales of the changes in the Earth's magnetic field are too short for natural selection to be able to adjust the frequencies of the supposed 'migration genes'.

Natural selection would probably work strongly against any rigidly programmed system. We already know that dogs, cats, pigeons and other animals can home from places they have never been before. They show true goal-directed navigation (Chapter 10). This behaviour seems to depend on a link with their homes that gives them a sense of direction, enabling them to locate their home from wherever they are. The use of this more flexible sense of direction would probably be favoured by natural selection over rigid genetic programming, even if such programming were possible.

Finally, any kind of programmed migration that depended on a magnetic sense would have to be extremely adaptable in periods of revolutionary change in the Earth's magnetic field. At varying intervals, the magnetic poles reverse, so that the magnetic North Pole is near the geographical South Pole, and the magnetic South Pole near the geographical North. In the last twenty million years, the magnetic North Pole has flipped to the South Pole 41 times, and 41 times flipped back again.[6] (The history of these polar reversals has been reconstructed from the direction of magnetization in magnetic rocks, which provide a fossil record of the magnetic polarity prevailing at the time they were formed. A reversal of polarity is shown by the reversed magnetization of successive deposits of rock.)

Under these circumstances, natural selection would eliminate animals following a rigid magnetic-navigation program. Since all migratory animals today are the descendants of ancestors that have survived some 80 magnetic reversals in the last 20 million years, all must have had ancestors capable of reaching their goals in spite of reversals in the Earth's magnetic polarity.

Figure 11.1 The changing magnetic field of the Earth over the last few centuries. The contours indicate the strength of the field at the boundary between the molten core and the mantle. The lines of force come out of the southern and flow back into the northern hemisphere. The solid contours represent the intensity of magnetic flux into the core; the dotted lines flux out of the core (after Bloxham and Gubbins, 1985).

1715

1777

1842

1905

1969

1980

What if animals can calibrate their magnetic compass sense on the basis of clues from the sky, such as the direction of the sunset and the rotation of stars around the celestial North Pole? Research on migrating Savannah sparrows in America has shown that their compass sense can indeed be calibrated through observation of the stars, and can also be recalibrated throughout the lifetime of individual birds.[7] Species capable of such calibration could preserve a simple compass sense in spite of variations in the Earth's magnetic field.

But although some migratory species may well use the Earth's magnetic field to help keep them on course, this is very different from a navigation system that can tell them where they are and where their goal is.

Even if animals could somehow inherit a mental map and know where their goal is, it is very unlikely that they could navigate simply on the basis of a compass sense and the observation of the sun and stars. After all, until the eighteenth century, not even the most sophisticated sailors could navigate with any accuracy on the basis of maps, compasses and celestial observations. They used the sun's elevation at noon to determine their latitude, their north-south position. Magnetic compasses helped them keep their bearings. But they were incapable of working out their longitude, their east-west position. It was not until the invention of the chronometer by John Harrison, less than 250 years ago, that a precise determination of longitude became possible at sea, permitting accurate marine navigation.[8]

Oceanic migrants

Fish, such as salmon and eels, can migrate over thousands of miles, and the movements of the sun and stars cannot explain their orientation: they could hardly observe the heavens with any precision from under the surface of the sea. They must have other means of finding their way. Smell probably plays an important part when they are near their destination, and in the case of salmon, there is good evidence that they 'smell' their home river when they approach its estuary.[9] But smell cannot explain how they get near enough to the right stretch of coastline from oceanic feeding grounds hundreds or thousands of miles away. Similar problems arise when trying to understand the migrations of marine turtles.

Baby green turtles that have hatched on the beaches of Ascension Island, in the middle of the Atlantic, find their way across the ocean to their ancestral feeding grounds off the Brazilian coast. Years later, when the time comes for them to lay their eggs, they then make their way back to Ascension Island, only six miles across and over 1,400 miles away, with no land in between. The tracking of tagged turtles by satellite has shown that they can maintain straight courses over hundreds of miles, and that they 'have a surprising capacity to pinpoint specific targets during a long-distance journey in open seas, without movements indicating a random or systematic search'. They continue on their bearing at night, even when the moon is not visible, and they compensate for drift due to currents.[10]

If sea turtles are captured and released far away from their normal range, they can still find their own way back. An early unplanned experiment, reported in 1865, involved a green turtle caught at Ascension Island and taken by ship as far as the English Channel, at which point the animal looked unhealthy and was thrown overboard. Two years later it was caught again at Ascension Island, and recognized because it had been branded.[11] Turtles seem to have a magnetic sense,[12] but even the most sophisticated compass could not explain navigational feats such as this.

Most seasonal migrants move between breeding grounds and feeding grounds in a repetitive cycle, but some animals have no fixed routes at all. Albatrosses, for example, wander over the oceans for vast distances in search of food, with unpredictable routes, and yet they can still find their way back to their nesting places on mid-oceanic islands. Wandering albatrosses that nest on the Crozet Islands (in the southern Indian Ocean) have been tagged and tracked by satellite, and these studies have revealed that they can go foraging in any direction, and the outbound and inbound trips may be widely separated[13] (Figure 11.2). On their return trips, like the green turtles, they can approach their home island on a straight course as if they know exactly where it is, rather than searching for it. They cannot be locating their home by means of smell because they often return when there are crosswinds, or on routes that are upwind of the Crozet Islands.[14] Like the displaced turtles, they must be navigating towards their goal in a way that cannot be explained in terms of inherited programs and normal senses.

The sense of direction, morphic fields and ancestral memory

Just as a sense of direction in domestic pets and pigeons arises from their close links to familiar places, especially their homes, I propose a similar kind of connection links turtles to their native beaches and feeding grounds, albatrosses to their nesting islands and swallows to their breeding places and winter homes. These invisible connections take place through morphic fields and enable animals to navigate towards their goals. Such fields play an essential role in migration, just as they do in homing.

One of the features of morphic fields is that they have an inherent memory (Appendix C). This memory is transmitted by a process called morphic resonance, which causes a given organism, such as a migrating bird, to resonate with previous migrating birds of the same kind.[15] Thus when a young cuckoo sets off from England towards Africa, it draws upon a collective memory of its ancestors. This memory, inherent in the morphic field of its migratory path, guides it as it goes, giving it a memory of directions in which to fly, and an instinctive recognition of landmarks, feeding grounds and resting places. This collective memory also enables it to recognize when it has arrived at its destination, the ancestral winter home.

Natural selection would strongly favour birds that were sensitive to this ancestral migratory field and migrated in accordance with it. Those that were not in tune with it would probably not survive.

Migrations usually follow habitual routes, repeated over many generations. The migrating animals' sense of direction has a habitual

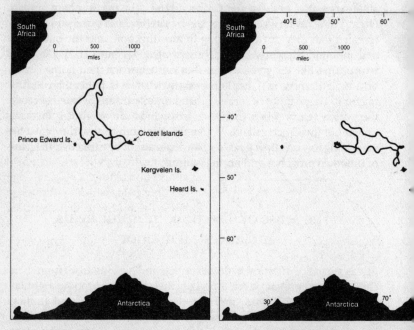

Route of male albatross 1   Route of male albatross 2

sequence of stages. For example, many North American migratory species are funnelled in 'flyways' towards Central America or the Gulf of Mexico, and then diverge again into South America. On their return migration they are again funnelled through Central America and the Gulf, and follow one of several major routes northwards: along the west coast, for example, or up the Mississippi basin.

Likewise some migratory species breeding in western Europe, like swallows, are funnelled towards the Straits of Gibraltar, the shortest sea crossing to Africa, and then fly across the Sahara desert. Populations of the same species breeding in eastern Europe are funnelled through the Bosphorus, where they cross the narrow strait between Europe and Asia.

In all these cases, the birds' sense of direction depends on the stage they are at in their journey. They do not set off in a straight line directed towards their winter or summer home, but rather follow flight paths towards traditional sea crossings, and often fly along coastlines and rivers.

Young birds that make the journey for the first time with no guidance from birds that have flown the journey before, like young cuckoos, have to rely entirely on this inherited sequence of directions and have no experience of the winter home, or of the intermediate stages on the way.

After having spent some time in a wintering or breeding area, some migratory birds are able to navigate towards this place not only along the usual route, but also from an unknown starting point. This establishment of a connection with the place is called 'site imprinting' in the scientific literature, but practically nothing is known about how it actually works.[16] I suggest that this imprinting involves the establishment of connections with the place through a morphic field, which continues to connect the bird with that particular place even when it is far away.

Figure 11.2 Tracks of three wandering albatrosses in the southern Indian Ocean (after Jouventin and Weimerskirch, 1990).

Route of male albatross 3

Experiments with migrating birds

In some classical experiments in the 1950s, conducted on a larger scale than any before or since, the Dutch biologist A.C. Perdeck investigated what migrating birds did when they were taken away from their traditional route. He displaced thousands of starlings and chaffinches by capturing them when they had actually started on their journey. These birds were ringed, taken hundreds of miles away and released from a place they had never been to before. An international network of ornithologists sent in data on the recovery of ringed birds. The purpose of his experiments was to find out whether experienced birds could navigate in a goal-directed way, like homing birds do, or whether they simply flew in a programmed direction. Perdeck explained the thinking behind his experiments as follows:

> The faculty of birds to orient themselves not merely in a particular compass direction, but to a certain geographical position has been called 'homing orientation', 'complete navigation' or 'true goal orientation'. Its existence is doubtlessly proved by homing experiments in many species during the breeding period. Therefore it seems unlikely that this highly developed mechanism of orientation is not used during migration when it has so many advantages compared with one-direction orientation . . . The homing experiments suggest that this faculty is developed especially in older birds, which have been already one or more seasons in the area of destination.[17]

In a series of experiments, repeated over several years, starlings migrating from the Baltic region to their usual overwintering areas in England and northern France were captured at their autumn stopover sites in Holland. Eleven thousand captured birds were ringed and taken by plane to Switzerland, about 375 miles to the southeast, where they were released. Juvenile and mature birds were released separately. Normally starlings fly in flocks of mixed ages, the juveniles travelling with more experienced birds, but in this experiment, they were forced to make their own way.

The juvenile birds continued to fly southwest, the direction they would have taken from the place they were captured towards their wintering grounds in England. In other words, they followed a path parallel to the normal one. Some of them ended up in southern France and Spain. But the adults reoriented (Figure 11.3) and found their way to the traditional wintering areas in England and northern France. In other words, the adults were showing navigational behaviour similar to that of

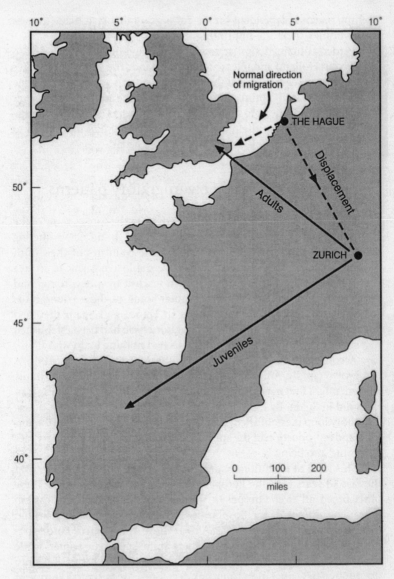

Figure 11.3 The directions of migration of adult and juvenile starlings after their displacement from Holland to Switzerland. The adults flew to their usual wintering grounds in England, but the juveniles flew in the direction that would have taken them from Holland to England if they has not been displaced. Consequently they ended up in France or Spain (after Perdeck, 1958).

homing pigeons, dependent on the connection they had made to their winter homes, their 'site-imprinting'.[18]

Perdeck obtained similar results with migrating chaffinches, also captured in Holland and released in Switzerland. The young chaffinches flew southwest, continuing in the same direction they would have done if they had not been captured and displaced. But the adults, like the adult starlings, flew northwest to their usual winter quarters in Britain,[19] showing an ability to reach their goal from a place they had never been to before, and flying in a different direction from usual.

The evolution of new migratory patterns

Perdeck's experiment had a fascinating ending. In the spring, some of the young starlings that had been displaced and had found new wintering grounds in France and Spain returned to the countries of their birth around the Baltic. This showed that they were able to navigate to an area they already knew, although they had to reach it by a new route. And remarkably enough, the following winter some of these young birds returned to the new feeding grounds in France and Spain they had adopted the previous year.[20] A new migratory cycle had been established in a single generation. Genetic mutations had nothing to do with it.

According to the morphic field hypothesis, new migratory pathways can evolve rapidly. Animals that have been blown off course, or simply strayed, might find new feeding grounds for the winter, as the young starlings did in Spain. By homing to their native lands in the spring, a new migratory loop is established. And if this new pathway promotes the survival and reproduction of the animals that follow it, a new migratory race will come into being.

This kind of evolutionary process has actually been observed over the last 30 years with the European blackcap, a kind of warbler. These birds breed all over Europe. In the autumn blackcaps from eastern Europe head towards the Bosphorus, and then make their way around the eastern Mediterranean to East Africa. Those from western Europe traditionally migrate towards Spain, where some spend the winter, while others cross into Africa and winter in Morocco or West Africa. But since the 1960s a new migration route has developed: from central Europe to Britain, where many thousands of blackcaps currently spend the winter. About ten per cent of the breeding population in parts of Belgium and Germany now overwinters in Britain instead of Africa.

This new pattern of migration has become possible because of the progressively milder winters in Britain in recent decades, and also because so many British people feed birds during the winter, providing a new source of food unavailable in previous centuries. This migration is much shorter and less hazardous than the usual journey to Spain or West Africa. Moreover, the birds that winter in Britain tend to return to the breeding grounds sooner than those that have to travel further, enabling them to pair with each other earlier, occupy the best territories and produce more offspring.[21] Thus natural selection favours this new migratory habit, and a new race of blackcaps is emerging.

According to the conventional genetic programming theory, the evolution of a new migratory pathway would depend on chance mutations that affect the genetic programming. Then these mutant genes would have to be favoured by natural selection over many generations for a new race to emerge.

By contrast, if migratory routes are more like habits that depend on an inherited memory, new races can emerge rapidly, as the example of blackcaps shows. To start with, this process need not require any genetic mutations at all. Blackcaps might originally have come to Britain because they were blown off course from their normal migratory route towards Spain, rather than because of mutations in hypothetical migration-programming genes. Likewise, the new migratory pathway of starlings from the Baltic to Spain rather than Britain happened because a Dutch scientist kidnapped them and took them to Switzerland in an aeroplane, not because of mutant genes.

Under natural conditions, new patterns of migration could arise whenever animals are carried away from their habitual route and are lucky enough to find themselves in a new feeding ground. If favoured by natural selection, this pattern could be repeated over the generations, as in the case of blackcaps. Neither the new destinations nor the migratory pathways themselves would be coded in the genes, but rather remembered through their morphic fields.[22]

This conclusion is supported by recent genetic research on green turtles. Although there are some genetic differences between races that breed far away from each other and follow widely different migratory routes, these differences are so small that researchers on this subject have concluded that 'migratory routes to specific destinations such as Ascension Island may not be genetically fixed or "instinctual" . . . Early learning, rather than "hard-wired" genetic behavior, would allow a more flexible response to altered nesting conditions, so that new migrational pathways could be established in a single generation'.[23]

12
Animals that know when they are nearing home

Many pet owners who travel with their animals have surely noticed a puzzling kind of behaviour shown by many dogs, cats, horses and other species. Their animals often seem to know when they are nearing their destination, even when they cannot see out of the vehicle in which they are travelling.

As we saw in Chapters 10 and 11, homing and migration depend on morphic fields that pull or attract the animals towards their destinations, and underlie their sense of direction. In this chapter, I suggest that this morphic field hypothesis can also shed light on the way that pets know when they are nearing their destination. In some cases, this behaviour depends on the morphic fields that connect animals to particular places. In other cases, it seems to depend on the people the animal is travelling with, and may well involve telepathy.

Animals travelling in cars

Our cat Remedy, unlike most cats, enjoyed travelling by car. For most of the journey she would sleep on a rug in her carrying basket. We left the door of the carrier open so that she could come out whenever she liked.

A mile or two before we arrived home, whether travelling by day or night, Remedy would wake up, come out of her basket, pace around the car and show obvious signs of excitement. My wife was the first to notice this. I am sorry to say that I was at first dismissive of this phenomenon, arguing that it must just be a matter of chance. I was afflicted by a closed-minded scepticism that led me to ignore or deny behaviour that seemed to have no immediate explanation. But in the end, the evidence became overwhelming. The cat did seem to know when we were nearing home. But how?

Was it because she smelled the home area? Possible, but unlikely, because it seemed to happen just as much in cold weather when the windows were closed as in hot weather when they were open. Did she recognize familiar bumps, twists and turns? Possibly, but then how could she be so familiar with the details of different routes through London, with variable patterns of movement, depending on traffic lights and road congestion? Was there some other quality of the home environment that she was responding to? Perhaps, but what could it be? Did she somehow pick up our own anticipation, even when we were not aware of any change in our behaviour? If so, how?

I still do not know the answers to all these questions, but I have found that many other people have noticed similar behaviour in their animals. There are over 60 such accounts on our database, and taken together they enable the possibilities to be narrowed down, as I discuss in this chapter.

No doubt when wild animals are making their own way home, they recognize familiar landmarks, smell familiar odours and hear familiar sounds. This information from the environment is necessary for finding their home, and without it they would be lost. But an animal finding its own way home is in a very different situation from a dog or cat asleep in a car, or a horse in a horse trailer. These animals are being transported whether they like it or not, and with no choice over the way they are going. This must be a very unusual situation for animals to be in. Wild animals are rarely carried around, although sometimes victims are carried off alive by predators, and young animals are sometimes moved by their elders, as when mother cats move their kittens by the scruff of their necks. But I can think of no parallel in the natural world for the transportation of domestic animals in vehicles, except perhaps for fish being carried along by currents, or birds by winds.

Arriving at familiar destinations

The most common situation in which animals react is when they are nearing home, just as Remedy did. Many dogs show similar signs of anticipation, and in most cases it seems unlikely that they know where they are by seeing landmarks. On car journeys they usually lie down, below the level of the windows, and go to sleep. Looking out of the windows is a result of their waking in anticipation, not a cause of it. And many dogs and cats react even when they are travelling at night.

Likewise, some horses when transported in vehicles seem to know when they are nearing home, and several miles beforehand start 'fidgeting', 'whinnying and getting excited', 'pawing and stamping' or showing other signs of restlessness.

It is rarer for bonobos to travel around by road, but those at Twycross Zoo in Warwickshire used to do so when they made a series of TV commercials for PG tea, in which they were dressed up as humans and acted out a sketch. Molly Badham, their trainer, found that on the return journeys after their filming work, they always seemed to know when they were nearing the zoo. 'Probably a mile away, they would wake up and know they were coming home. How they knew, I don't know – it was pitch black and they couldn't see out anyway – but they would wake up and start getting excited.'

Many animals show similar reactions when they visit familiar destinations other than their home, like Tasha, a poodle belonging to Alice Palmer, of Chicago, Illinois. 'When we went to visit my son, 120 miles away, and were within five to eight miles of his house, Tasha would jump up from her sleeping position in the back seat, sniff at the window in the back seat and excitedly watch until we reached the house.' Perhaps Tasha was responding to familiar smells along the road. But what happens when animals are taken by unusual routes?

Travelling by unusual routes

Several people have deliberately tried taking a different route to find out how the animal reacts. For example, Jenny Mardell of Bath found that her dog Mandy would always get excited when they were nearing her parents' home in London. 'We could never work out how, and would try different routes to the house – she always knew and would get hysterical in the car.' Likewise, Geneviève Vergnes found that when visiting her parents in Paris, 'the dog would wake up at about seven kilometres from their house and scratch the dashboard while "singing". We deduced she knew the way and tried different routes – the peripheral *quais*, the Champs Elysées, or by way of the suburbs – the duration of the route being different. She slept, and always at about the same distance she would scratch the dashboard and sing!'

Sometimes people are strongly motivated to try to stop their dog waking up and showing its excitement. This was the case with some friends in London when their twin children were babies. When travelling home by car, their Labrador dog and the babies would go to sleep. As they neared home the dog would wake up and move around excitedly, waking the twins, who started crying. To try to avoid the dog waking the babies, they came home by a variety of devious routes, but they failed to deceive the dog. He got excited and woke the babies anyway.

Experiences like these show that at least some animals know when they are nearing their destination irrespective of the route they are taking. Does this depend on some quality of the place that they can detect, even when asleep, when they are still miles away? Or does it depend on some influence from the people in the car?

After studying dozens of cases, I have come to the conclusion that in some, the place itself plays the most important role, but in others the pets are picking up the expectation of the people in the car. And probably both kinds of influence can work together.

Familiar and unfamiliar places

In most cases, the reaction of animals occurs only before arriving home, or at another familiar place. They do not react before reaching unfamiliar places. This suggests that they detect something about the places themselves, and their reactions depend on memory. This is particularly clear from the observations of Joséa Raymer of Aldermaston, Berkshire, the owner-driver of a lorry. She always takes with her at least one German shepherd for protection:

> I can drive for up to four and a half hours on all sorts of road conditions (stopping for traffic lights, etc., crawling through slow traffic or on fast motorways) and the dog/s will stay asleep, but as I near my delivery point or overnight stop the dog/s will react in direct relation to whether they have been there before, and how many times, and whether they were let out for a run. If I have never delivered there before, or if it was a place not suitable for letting them out, they will take no notice until I have stopped, or reversed into the loading bay or opened the door. If it is a place we visit often or especially a night stop where they can expect some fun, they will be up and getting excited whilst still on the public road, where you would not expect the motion of the truck to be any different from any other part of the road.

In cases such as this, memory of the places seems far more important than the behaviour or thoughts of the person. But what is it about the place that they respond to? We have already ruled out landmarks, since animals that are asleep, or at least lying down, cannot see them out of the window, and they still react when travelling in darkness.

So could it be smell? This is the most obvious possibility, and in some cases it may be the best explanation. But in most cases it does not fit the facts very well. The smell theory would predict that animals should react sooner in warm weather than in cold, since the vaporization of substances is greater at higher temperatures. They should also react sooner and more strongly when the windows are open than when they are closed. And their reactions should be dependent on the wind direction, occurring much further away when the destination is upwind than when it is downwind. There is no hint in any of the accounts that I have read or heard that this is the case, nor did I observe any such influence of wind direction, temperature or open windows on the reactions of our own cat.

These reactions may be related to the 'sense of direction' I discussed in the previous two chapters. This sense of direction is of primary importance when animals actively make their own way. It has evolved in the context of their finding the way home, or travelling to other familiar locations, and also plays an essential role in migration. I suggest this sense of direction depends on morphic fields, through which animals are attached to familiar places. These fields enable them to find these places, navigating over unfamiliar territory, and may also enable them to recognize when they are getting near to a familiar place when someone else is doing the navigating.

Reacting to people rather than places

When nearing their destination, the people in the car may feel relief or anticipation, and animals may pick up these changes and wake. If they are about to arrive at a familiar place, it is hard to separate the effects of the people from the effects of the place itself. But when they are travelling to a place with which the animal is *unfamiliar*, the animal can have no memory of the place, and the only possible clues could come from the people in the car.

In some cases, animals do indeed seem to react before arriving at a place they have never been to before. Jenny Vieyra of Leighton Buzzard, Bedfordshire, has a cat that has always known when she is nearing home, 'standing up in his basket, meowing frantically, trying to find a way to get out'. He also knows when they are about to arrive at the houses of friends or members of the family, or at catteries where he has stayed before. All this could be a matter of memory. But she recently moved to a new house 50 miles away, and when she took the cat there for the first time in his life, he reacted with his usual excitement before they arrived. He must have been picking up the anticipation of his owner.

Some people who have seen this kind of reaction repeatedly are convinced that their animals are telepathic, like Michaela Dickinson-Butler of Burton-on-Humber. She thinks her border terrier can read her thoughts. 'He knows exactly when we will stop the car and starts barking and whining before arrival at the destination, even if he's never been before and he doesn't look out of the window and we are silent.'

Peter Edwards, who lives in Essex, breeds Irish setters and often attends dog shows. When he is going home with his dogs in the car, they usually wake up and get excited some 15 minutes or more before arriving home. They do the same before arriving at a showground. Sometimes he takes the dogs to shows in new places, and they still react some 15–20 minutes in advance. Smelling other dogs already at the showground seems an unlikely explanation, because the response occurs many miles away, and it does not seem to depend on the wind direction. Moreover, Peter Edwards has found that they still do this when he arrives at a showground early, when very few other dogs have arrived. 'I think they are picking it up from me,' he says. He has enquired about other owners' experience of taking their dogs to shows, and has found this response is quite common. He concludes: 'It's almost as if they can read minds.'

This kind of reaction is illustrated particularly clearly by Morag, a Yorkshire terrier who travels on long car journeys between her home on the Isle of Skye, off the west coast of Scotland, and a village in Norfolk, in the easternmost part of England. Doris Ausden, the owner's mother, kindly kept notes for me on Morag's behaviour. On one occasion in summer she was accompanying her son from Norfolk to Skye. As they neared his home, the car was climbing a hill north of Uig:

> When we reach this point I always think, 'not much further now' (about seven miles). I have never actually said this aloud, but sure enough at that point Morag began to get agitated. It could not have been the sensation of going uphill (there are many hills on the way). On the way back to Norfolk we travelled all night with several stops for rest and refreshment. We made a detour to get some breakfast, and somehow took a wrong turning. For some time we were travelling in country unknown to us, but eventually I recognized a road sign I knew. I remember thinking, 'We are not far from home now.' Immediately, Morag, who had been fast asleep in her basket on the seat beside me, began to show her usual agitation.

This phenomenon has also been studied by Elizabeth Marshall Thomas, who describes in her book *The Hidden Life of Dogs* how her dingo Viva knew when they were about to reach their destination even if she had never been there before. Thomas tried to find out how she did it.

The bumpiness of the road when the car went off highways on to country byways was a clue, but not the only clue, because the destination was often reached over many miles of unimproved surface, and Viva still knew. Likewise the repeated turns on to smaller roads and driveways before the end of a trip were a clue, 'but often Viva brightened for arrival before the car began turning.' When Thomas realized that Viva was accurately predicting most arrivals, she tried to make sure she herself was not giving a clue by speaking or doing something different. 'I believe I succeeded in hiding my feelings. She still knew, though, and by the end of her life I was no closer to figuring out how she did it than I had been at the beginning. Dog ESP? Perhaps.'[1] The ability of an animal to pick up a person's anticipation of the end of a journey is not very different from picking up other kinds of thoughts and intentions, as discussed in the previous chapters of this book. Whether this depends on unconscious behavioural cues or on telepathy is another question. To find out, it would be necessary to do special experiments.

A simple experiment to test for telepathy

In cases where animals seem to be reacting to clues from people in the car, one possibility is that they are reacting to subtle behavioural changes, body language, verbal clues or other signs detectable by the normal senses. One way of testing this possibility is for the animals to be carried in the back of a van, while their owner rides in the front. The animals could either be observed by a person riding with them in the back of the van, who does not know the destination of the journey, or their behaviour could be recorded automatically by a video camera mounted in the back of the van.

In some preliminary experiments, conducted with the kind cooperation of the Manchester Police Dog Unit, we have established that it is quite feasible to videotape the behaviour of dogs in vans. But police dogs are accustomed to travelling in vans, and animals not familiar with this form of transport may take some time to get used to it.

With the animal in the back of the van, and the recording system in operation, the animal's owner then drives to destinations with which the animal is unfamiliar. Does the animal still show signs of anticipation? If so, the reaction could not be explained in terms of a memory of the place, or through seeing its owner's body language, or through other sensory clues. By a process of elimination, telepathic communication would be the most probable explanation.

13

Pets finding their people far away

In 1582, Leonhard Zollikofer left his native St Gallen in Switzerland to go to Paris as ambassador to the court of the French King Henri III. He left behind his faithful dog, aptly named Fidelis. Two weeks later, the dog disappeared from St Gallen. Three weeks after that he rejoined his master at the court in Paris, exactly at the time when the Swiss ambassadors were being led into an audience with the King. The dog had never been to Paris before.[1] How did he find his master so far away from home?

It would be easy to dismiss this as a fanciful tale but for the fact that there are many such stories, and even more heroic examples of canine devotion. One of these dates back to the First World War: Prince, an Irish terrier, was devoted to his master, Private James Brown of the North Staffordshire Regiment, and was inconsolable when this young man was posted to France in September 1914. One day he disappeared from his home in Hammersmith, London, then to everyone's amazement turned up at Armentières a few weeks later, and tracked down his master in the trenches in a frenzy of delight. Because no one could believe the story, the Commanding Officer had man and dog paraded in front of him the next morning. Evidently Prince had attached himself to some troops who were crossing the English Channel, and had then found his way to his owner. He became the hero of the regiment and fought beside his owner for the rest of the war.[2]

In both these cases the dogs were not homing or going to another familiar place. Such behaviour, if it really happens, cannot be explained in terms of a sense of direction, or at least not a sense of direction that depends on any quality of the destination itself. Rather, the animals somehow knew where to find the people to whom they were so attached.

In Parts II, III and IV of this book, we have seen how bonds between animals and people can enable intentions and calls to be picked up at a distance. Some animals seem to know when their owners have died, even if they are far apart, or when they have had an accident. These various phenomena can be described as telepathic. But can these bonds connect the person and the animal in a *directional* way, as if they are joined by an invisible cord?

We have in fact already encountered evidence for directional information in the bonds between animals and people. Some cat owners have found themselves drawn towards their lost cat in a way they cannot explain. They somehow know in which direction to look (Chapter 8). Then there is the fact that some animals not only know when their owners are coming home, but also seem to know which direction they are coming from. They may wait at one or another side of the house depending on the direction from which a person is approaching.

In this chapter I look at cases of animals finding their people in unfamiliar places. If some animals do this in a way that cannot be explained by chance, sight, hearing or smell, then there must be two different kinds of sense of direction: a sense of direction for places; and a sense of direction for people or animals. My own hypothesis is that both kinds of bonds depend on morphic fields. I suggest that the morphic fields linking animals to places and also to people are indeed directional. But whereas a sense of direction for places is a familiar idea, a sense of direction for people or other animals is much less familiar. Finding people or animals at a distance is much rarer than finding places. Nevertheless, there are 42 such cases on our database, 32 concerning dogs, and ten cats.

I begin by looking at these spontaneous cases to see if there are any common patterns, and to examine how convincing the evidence seems to be. There is generally no possibility of doing experiments on this phenomenon, because pet owners are rightly reluctant to risk losing their animals. Practically the only source of evidence is from unplanned, real-life events.

The most important alternative explanations to account for these cases are: First, chance – the animal simply searched at random, and the cases we hear about are merely the few that had a happy ending. Second, smell – the animal tracked the person using its sense of smell. These are important arguments, for if chance or smell can explain the evidence, we have no need to postulate the existence of a mysterious, invisible bond that could somehow pull the animals towards the person.

Could the animals have found
their people by smell?

Some of the cases on our database involve dogs or cats finding people in new homes less than a mile or two away from their previous home. Because the journeys of removal were made by car or van, tracking the person by following an odour trail along the road does not seem very likely. Nevertheless, smell and chance remain possible explanations, especially as the people may have left odour trails in the vicinity of the new home that an animal exploring at random could have picked up.

Sometimes dogs find their owners at their place of work, several miles away, never having been taken there. When the owners travel to work by car, tracking by scent seems a very unlikely explanation. Even if a dog or cat could follow the scent trail of a car's wheels, distinguishing these wheel tracks from those of many other vehicles, to put this ability into practice would involve the hazardous procedure of sniffing along roads. Even if traffic was sparse, in order to avoid these animals drivers would have to notice them, and might well remember seeing them. I know of no reports from motorists of such road-sniffing animals.

Patricia Burke lived on a farm on the Isle of Skye, Scotland, and went to work six miles away in Portree, leaving her terrier at the farm when she did so. She did not drive directly to work, but first went three miles in a different direction to pick up a workmate. One morning, to her surprise, she found the dog sitting outside her workplace in Portree. 'How did he know I worked there? He'd never been to Portree.'

A sceptic could argue that the dog detected the smell of the workplace, having become familiar with it from smells on the owner's clothing. But this would not explain how the dog found its way to Portree to start with, unless the sense of smell is imagined to extend far beyond the ranges for which there is any evidence.

In any case, the smell theory cannot apply to dogs that find their owners in places that the owners themselves have never been to before. The dogs could never have smelled the odour of that place on their owners' clothing or hair. Nevertheless, there are several cases of dogs finding their people in a house they are visiting for the first time, or in a hospital to which they have been rushed, or in an unfamiliar pub.

For example, when Victor Shackleton was a teenager he kept a greyhound, Jonny, to whom he became very attached. Unfortunately the dog was unwelcome in his family home owing to lack of space, and much to his dismay, his father arranged to sell Jonny to a nephew who lived in a mining community in Yorkshire. They travelled there by train from their

home in Cheshire and handed the dog over to its new owner. Having tied
the dog up in his back yard, the nephew insisted on a farewell drink
before they began the long journey home. They squeezed into a battered
van and drove to a pub frequented by greyhound enthusiasts:

> I sat mournfully as they talked. I thought of Jonny locked in that
> strange back yard, lonely, abandoned. The pub filled up and then sud-
> denly the door was flung wide open, I was smothered with body and
> paws. It was Jonny, a piece of broken rope dangling from his collar.
> Everyone who saw Jonny arrive at the pub could not believe it. When
> my dad and his nephew explained the sequence of events that
> evening, it hit us all – how the hell did the dog find us at this pub,
> three miles away and in a place he had never been before? At once,
> expert dog handlers in the pub insisted that greyhounds cannot hunt
> by smell, they rely on sight entirely.

There seems no possible explanation for Jonny's behaviour in terms of
sight or hearing, and the smell theory is very improbable, as the experts
pointed out.

Sometimes the ability of dogs to find their owners has actually saved
the person's life, as in the case of Uri Geller, the celebrated spoon bender.
Around the age of 14, Geller was living in Cyprus and loved to go exploring the hillside caves above his school near Nicosia. Usually he went with
friends and stuck to tested paths. This time he did neither.

> I got lost. Deep in the caves, cold, wet and terrified, I spent two hours
> hunting with a failing flashlight for a way out. Finally I curled into a
> ball and prayed to God that someone would find me before I starved
> to death, as two of my school mates had. I'll never know how my dog,
> Joker, reached me. I'd left him miles away at my stepfather's hotel. But
> huddled in the darkness I heard him barking – and suddenly his paws
> were on my chest and he was licking my face. Joker knew the way out,
> of course. It was as if my prayers had summoned him.[3]

Even if the dog was able to locate Geller within the cave by following a
scent trail, this would not explain why he went to the cave in the first
place, and did so at exactly the time he was needed.

In most cases, we have no information about the way the dog
behaved on its journey. What route did it follow? Was it sniffing as if following a scent trail? Fortunately, I have received one account in which
two dogs were accompanied all the way on their journey. Dr Alfred Koref
and his wife kept two dachshunds at their home in Vienna, Austria.
When they went out for the evening they left them at the house of their

maid. In the morning, Dr Koref picked them up from the maid's house and set off to walk them home while his wife drove on to visit some friends who lived two miles away.

> Instead of going home, though, they pulled me through little streets that were unknown to them, until we came to the big street that my wife had driven along. Then they raced along this street and arrived at the block of buildings where our friends lived. The dogs had never visited them. Still, they went into the right entrance, climbed upstairs straight to the door where my wife could be found. She was quite surprised at our appearance.

Although in this case the finding of the right entrance and right apartment could perhaps be explained by smell, the journey through unknown streets and the racing along the pavement to the right buildings cannot be accounted for in this way. The smell theory becomes even more implausible when animals find their people over tens or hundreds of miles.

Finding people over great distances

The longer the distance over which the animals finds its person, the less plausible the random search and smell theories become. None of the cases on my database involve animals finding people at distances over 50 miles. Luckily, this subject has already been researched by one of the pioneers of parapsychology, J.B. Rhine, of Duke University, North Carolina. In the 1950s, he identified this phenomenon and named it 'psi-trailing', the term 'psi' referring to the psychical nature of this ability.[4] Rhine and his colleagues built up a collection of cases through appeals in newspapers and magazines and from reports in local newspapers, through which some of the most remarkable cases first came to light. Wherever possible, they followed up these accounts with interviews and visits to obtain more details.

In 1962, Rhine and Sara Feather published a summary of their investigations. From their initial collection of data, they first screened out cases for which too little detail was given, or where the people involved could not be identified and located. That left 54 cases of what appeared to be psi-trailing in animals, 28 with dogs, 22 with cats and 4 with birds.[5]

They then excluded all those cases in which the animals that found their people could not be conclusively identified as the former pet, as opposed to a stray resembling it that had found them by chance. Some were excluded because no further enquiries were possible, either because the events happened too long ago, or because the people were unable or unwilling to cooperate. And all those involving distances under 30 miles were ruled out, to reduce to a very low level the probability of the animal making a merely random search. After all these exclusions there remained a number of quite impressive cases that they described in detail.

In one of these, Tony, a mongrel dog belonging to the Doolen family of Aurora, Illinois, was left behind when the family moved over 200 miles to East Lansing, Michigan, around the southern tip of Lake Michigan. Six weeks later Tony appeared in East Lansing, and excitedly approached Mr Doolen on the street. The rest of the family recognized Tony, and he them. His identity was confirmed by the collar, on which Mr Doolen had cut a notch when they were in Aurora.[6]

The most remarkable cat story is about Sugar, a cream-coloured Persian belonging to a family that lived in California. When they were leaving California for a new home in Oklahoma, Sugar jumped out of the car, stayed for a few days with neighbours and then disappeared. A year later, the cat turned up at the family's new home in Oklahoma, having travelled over 1,000 miles through unfamiliar territory. Sugar was not only recognizable by her appearance and familiar behaviour, but also through a characteristic bone deformity on the left hip, which Rhine himself examined.[7]

In the case of Pigeon 167, the identification was made certain by the number on its leg-ring. The owner of the pigeon was a 12-year-old boy, in the eighth grade at school in Summersville, West Virginia, where his father was sheriff. This racing pigeon had stopped in his back yard; the boy had fed it, and it stayed and became his pet. Some time later, the boy was taken for an operation to the Myers Memorial Hospital at Phillippi, 105 miles away by road (70 by air) and the pigeon was left behind at Summersville.

> One dark, snowy night about a week later, the boy heard a fluttering at the window of his hospital room. Calling the nurse, he asked her to raise the window because there was a pigeon outside, and just to humor the lad, she did so. The pigeon came in. The boy recognized his pet bird and asked her to look for the number 167 on its leg, and when she did so she found the number as stated.[8]

As well as this collection of cases by Rhine and Feather, similar stories have been reported from many different countries. In France, for example, a two-year-old sheepdog was left by his owner with a cousin in Bethune, in northeastern France, while he set off on a career as a travelling building worker. One day when he was working in Avignon, 500 miles away, he was told of a stray dog behaving strangely in the vicinity. He went to investigate and was almost bowled over by his dog, overjoyed at being reunited with his master.[9]

There is even a story about a pet magpie, reported by Mrs M. Johnson, a schoolteacher in Lund, Sweden. One day in her school a magpie flew in through the open window of a corridor and perched on the shoulder of a boy in a group of about 40 children. He exclaimed: 'It's our summer bird!', and explained that his family had spent the summer in a cottage about 50 miles away, where they had acquired a magpie they kept as a pet. When they moved back to the city, they left the bird behind. It was so clear that the bird knew the boy that his teacher excused him from school so that he could take it home.[10]

There are so many stories of this kind that I am convinced that animals can indeed sometimes find their people, just as people can sometimes find their animals (Chapter 8) in a way that cannot plausibly be ascribed to smell or to chance.

Dogs finding their owners' graves

Stories about pets finding their owners are not confined to living owners. Over and over again, there are tales of dogs finding their owner's grave. I find these stories very baffling. At first I assumed that the bond between pet and owner would be dissolved when the person died. I took it for granted that it would not connect the animal to the person's dead body. But this assumption seems ill-founded. It simply cannot account for most of the stories of grave-finding dogs. Consider this one from Austria:

My father-in-law had a small farm and on it he kept a watchdog, Sultan. One day my father-in-law became ill and was taken to hospital by ambulance. A few days later he died and then he was buried in the local graveyard, five kilometres from the farm. Several weeks after the burial the dog was not seen for days. This seemed strange to us, as Sultan never used to stray. But we did not make much of it, until one Sunday a former employee came along, who lived near the graveyard. She told us: 'Imagine, when I went across the graveyard the other day, Sultan lay at your family grave.' I cannot fathom how he could have found the way all these five kilometres. There were no footprints of his former master that he could follow. And he had never been taken to the graveyard, not even to the fields, since he had to keep watch at the house. How is it possible that he found his master's grave? (Joseph Duller, Graz, Austria)

Presumably members of the family had been to visit the grave, and could perhaps have left scent trails leading there. But they would presumably have left scent trails to many other places, so if Sultan followed them, why did he go specifically to the cemetery, and how could he have known about bodies being buried in graves?

Why should mourning dogs be attracted to their owners' graves at all? The only possible reason seems to be that their attachment to their person persists after his or her death, and continues to be focused on the owner's body. In Chapter 5, we have already seen several striking examples of faithful dogs that stayed by their dead owners' bodies, or kept vigil by their graves. The bonds that attach animals to their owners are not necessarily dissolved by the owner's death. I would expect this connection to be much weakened or dissolved by cremation, when nothing remains of the body except ashes. Indeed all the cases I know of concern burials; I have never heard of animals being drawn to crematoriums or places where ashes are scattered.

This attachment of dogs to the dead bodies of their much-loved people may seem strange. But many people, after all, retain a remarkably strong connection to the bodies of their loved ones. These continuing connections have given rise to tombs and gravestones, and simple acts of devotion like the placing of flowers on graves. After all, cemeteries are not just visited by the occasional mourning dog, but by human beings. And the burial places of particularly important people, such as saints or national heroes, become places of pilgrimage for thousands, even millions. If we understood better why we visit graves ourselves, we might gain more insight into the bonds that continue to link some dogs to the dead bodies of their owners.

Animals finding other animals

Occasionally reports appear in newspapers about farm animals separated from their young that succeed in finding them again. Here is one example:

> Blackie, a two-year-old heifer, broke away from the new farm she had been sold to and, walking seven miles through strange country, 'homed in' on the new farm that her calf had been taken to. The story started when the heifer and her calf were sold separately in Hatherleigh market in Devon. The mother was sent to Bob Woolacott's farm near Okehampton where she was bedded down for the night with a supply of hay and water. But her maternal instinct led her to break out of the farmyard, and over a hedge into a country lane. Next morning

she was found seven miles away reunited and suckling her calf at
Arthur Sleeman's farm at Sampford Courtenay. Mr Sleeman was able
to identify Blackie as the mother by the auction-labels still stuck on
their rumps.[11]

We have checked the details of this story by interviewing the people
involved. Mrs Mavis Sleeman told us that her husband put the newly
purchased unweaned calf with the other calves. 'The next morning my
sister-in-law saw a cow coming down the lane. It came straight round to
our building, where the calf was, this was at eight in the morning. It obviously wanted to get in there so she opened the door and let it in and the
cow walked immediately over to her calf to suckle her.'

Here is a similar report from Russia: 'Caucasian farmer Magomed
Ramazhanov was a little surprised when one of his cows went in search
of her calf, sold earlier to a farmer in a neighbouring district. Originally
fearing that the creature had been killed by wild predators, Magomed
eventually found his mild-mannered milker – reunited with her offspring – 30 miles from home.'[12]

As far as I know there has been practically no research on the way
that animals can find each other at a distance. One of the few investigators who has looked into this question is the American naturalist
William Long. In his pioneering studies on the behaviour of wolves in
Canada, he paid particular attention to the way the members of the pack
were linked together, even when they were far apart. He found that
wolves that were separated from the pack seemed to know where the
others were.

> In the winter time, when timber wolves commonly run in small packs,
> a solitary or separated wolf always seems to know where his mates are
> hunting or idly roving or resting in their day-bed. The pack is made up
> of his family relatives, younger or older, all mothered by the same she-
> wolf; and by some bond or attraction or silent communication he can
> go straight to them at any hour of the day or night, though he may not
> have seen them for a week, and they have wandered over countless
> miles of wilderness in the interim.[13]

Through long periods of observation and tracking, Long concluded that
this behaviour could not be explained by following habitual paths, tracking scent trails, or by hearing howling or other sounds. For example, he
once found a wounded wolf separated from the pack that lay in a shel-
tered den for several days while the others ranged widely. He picked up
the tracks of the pack in the snow, followed them while they were hunting and was near them when they killed a deer. They fed in silence, as

wolves commonly do, and there was no howling. The wounded wolf was then far away, with miles of densely wooded hills and valleys between him and the pack.

> When I returned to the deer, to read how the wolves had surprised and killed their game, I noticed the fresh trail of a solitary wolf coming in at right angles to the trail of the hunting pack . . . I picked up his incoming trail and ran it clear back to the den from which he had come as straight as if he knew where he was heading. His trail was from eastward; what little air that was stirring was from the south; so that it was impossible for his nose to guide him to the meat even if he had been within smelling distance, as he certainly was not. The record in the snow was as plain as any other print, and from it one might reasonably conclude that either the wolves can send forth a silent food-call, or else that a solitary wolf might be so in touch with his pack mates that he knows not only where they are but also, in a general way, what they are doing.[14]

These connections may be a normal feature of animal societies, even though we have hardly begun to understand how they work. The bonds between the members of a social group such as a wolf pack may not only enable them to know of the others' activities and intentions at a distance, but also provide directional information. And if wolves and other wild species have such abilities, then the ability of pets to find their owners and owners to find their pets can be seen in a much wider biological context.

Bonds to members of the social group and bonds to places

If some animals have the ability to find other animals or their human companions, it seems unlikely that non-human animals alone would be possessed of this power. We might expect to find the same kind of phenomena in people, though probably to a lesser degree.

I would expect, therefore, that there might be stories about people who have found other people in a remarkable way, without knowing how. I would expect that these stories would principally be about people who were strongly attached to each other, such as parents and children or husbands and wives. I would also expect that in traditional hunting and gathering cultures, where finding both places and people was necessary for survival, these abilities may have been cultivated and encouraged, and may have been far better developed than in modern industrial societies.

Just as a sense of direction must depend on a connection between the animal and a *place*, so finding a person who has moved away must depend on a connection between the animal and a *person*. And just as the animal-place connection can be compared to a magnetic attraction or to a stretched elastic band, so can the animal-person connection. Both animal-person and animal-place fields, like magnetic fields, contain directional information.

The magnetic field of the Earth contains directional information, which is why you can use a compass to find out where north is. In the technical language of science, magnetic attractions and repulsions are *vector* phenomena, ones which have a direction as well as a magnitude. (By contrast, a *scalar* quantity has magnitude but not direction, for example temperature.)

These animal-person connections and animal-place connections are vectors, with both direction and magnitude. Only if the pull is strong enough does the animal set off on its journey and keep going in spite of all distractions and adversities. And only if the pull has a direction does the animal know which way to go.

The idea of morphic fields linking animals to other members of their social group provides a basis for understanding both telepathic communication and a directional pull towards animals or people. The idea of morphic fields linking animals to particular places provides a basis for understanding the sense of direction as expressed in homing and migration. Thus the morphic field hypothesis may be able to account for a wide range of unexplained powers of animals, both telepathic and directional.

But there is one major category of unexplained perceptiveness where this hypothesis may not prove so helpful, namely premonition. This is the subject of the following two chapters.

PART VI

Animal premonitions

14

Premonitions of fits, comas and sudden deaths

Premonition literally means a warning in advance, a forewarning. Some premonitions seem to depend on telepathy, as when animals know in advance when their people are coming home (Chapters 2 to 4). Some may be explicable in terms of the detection of odours, sounds, electrical changes or other physical stimuli. But others may involve precognition, which literally means 'knowing in advance', or presentiment, 'feeling in advance'.

Precognitions and presentiments are more mysterious than other forms of premonition because they imply that influences can travel backwards through time, from the future to the present, and from the present to the past. Such a notion confuses all our usual ideas of causation, in which the cause precedes the effect. Or else it confuses our ideas of the present, suggesting there are no sharp divisions between future, present and past.

Can we avoid these problems and paradoxes? Can premonitions be explained without precognitions or presentiments? Some kinds can; perhaps others cannot.

In the following chapter I examine the ability of companion animals to forewarn us of external dangers, such as earthquakes. In this chapter I also discuss their warnings of internal dangers, such as impending epileptic fits. But first it is important to consider the biological context of warnings and alarms.

Danger, fear and alarm

Fear is related to danger. Even the word itself comes from a root that means danger, as in the German for danger, *Gefahr*.

We all know fear from our own experience. We feel something bad is imminent. We become more alert. Our hearts beat faster. A surge of the hormone adrenaline prepares us to react. Our faces become pale; our hair stands on end; in extreme cases we may tremble with terror, and our sphincters relax. Fear is an emotion we share with non-human animals, and which we can easily recognize in them. And it is of obvious survival value, especially in relation to potential predators.

Fear triggers defensive behaviour in any animal capable of defence. It can set animals running, diving, hiding, freezing, screaming for help, slamming shells shut, baring teeth or bristling quills.[1] But in many animals, including ourselves, fear is not merely an individual feeling, but a collective one. In social animals the giving of alarms and the communication of fear are of obvious survival value. Many animals respond to signs of danger by alerting others. They give alarms. In an extreme form, the spreading of fear through the group results in panic.

Some alarms are visual. A pigeon that takes off suddenly causes the rest of its group to take alarm and fly off too. The white tails of rabbits and of white-tailed deer are especially conspicuous when they are running, and serve as alarm signals to other members of the group.

Some alarms are smells of danger, like a fright-inducing substance under the skin of minnows that is released when they are injured, causing other members of the school, and even fish of other species, to avoid going near. Ants alert other members of their group to danger by releasing alarm substances.[2] Some go further: aggressive slave-making species such as *Formica subintegra* employ these smells not only in defence of their own colonies but also to terrorize their victims. A massive discharge of alarm substances sends the ants they are attacking into a panic, enabling the aggressors to take over their nest with little need to fight.[3]

Many species, for example blackbirds, have special alarm calls that alert other members of their group to danger. They often alert members of other species too.

Barking is the canine alarm call. Dogs have made themselves useful for tens of thousands of years by giving warnings of people approaching, and alerting their human companions to other potential sources of danger. This may well have been their primary function in the early stages of domestication.

This warning role of dogs is played out in many ways, not just in alerting people to the approach of strangers. Some of these warnings depend on smelling, hearing or seeing potential sources of danger. Some depend on picking up intentions, as in the case of dogs that warn their owners of a hostile person's threatening intent. And some depend on picking up intentions at a distance, as in the case of dogs that know when their owners are coming home. Here, of course, their signalling their anticipation of a person's arrival is not a warning of danger, but more in the nature of an announcement.

Dogs and other domesticated animals can help us by warning us of danger in a variety of ways. Sometimes they do it by alarm calls; sometimes by obvious signs of fear and distress; sometimes by taking practical steps to help or defend us.

What is epilepsy?

In Leesburg, Virginia, two or three times a week Christine Murray's dog, a pit bull and beagle mix named Annie, leaps on to her lap and begins licking her face furiously. Christine stops what she is doing and lies down, and a few minutes later is racked by an epileptic fit. 'It's amazing,' she said, 'I can't explain it, I don't know why. But Annie can tell when I'm going to have a seizure.'[4]

Annie is not unique. Many other dogs give warnings of epileptic seizures. How do they do it? No one knows. But they make a big difference in the lives of people with epilepsy.

Epileptic seizures, fits, turns, attacks or blackouts happen when normal brain activity is suddenly disrupted. In the most dramatic type, the so-called 'grand mal' seizure, sufferers first become rigid, and may fall if standing. They then undergo convulsions, suffer from laboured breathing and may also become incontinent. At the beginning of the fit, they may cry out and stop breathing and then their face may turn blue.

Such seizures can be very alarming to watch, but the person having the seizure is not in pain and usually remembers little of what has happened. After a few minutes, the fit comes to an end spontaneously and the person recovers. He or she may at first be confused and, if the fit has occurred in public, may be embarrassed, especially if he or she has been incontinent. Some sufferers then pass into a trance-like state and behave very unpredictably.

Not all kinds of epilepsy involve convulsions, and some seizures affect only part of the body. The mildest form of epilepsy, traditionally called 'petit mal', involves a brief interruption of consciousness without any other signs, except perhaps for a fluttering of the eyelids. Such fits occur most commonly in children, and are usually known as 'absences'.

Epilepsy is the most common of the serious neurological disorders and affects people of all ages. About one person in 200 suffers from it, and in many cases the fits begin in childhood. Although it can often be controlled by drugs, and by avoiding situations that bring it on, some people continue to have seizures despite taking appropriate precautions.

In classical times, epilepsy was known as 'the sacred disease'. No other disease arouses so much folk belief as epilepsy, probably because none is so suggestive of possession. One of the problems that epileptics have to face is the social stigma attached to the disorder, or at least the uneasiness that many people feel in their presence.

Most people with epilepsy are able to lead reasonably normal lives, although for obvious reasons they are not allowed to drive. For those whose attacks cannot be completely controlled by drugs, one of the greatest difficulties is their unpredictability. In some cases preliminary symptoms, known as the 'aura', which can include uncontrolled twitching in parts of the body, certain sensations, or bizarre behaviour, come on before the fit begins. But in many cases the disturbance spreads so rapidly that the patient is unconscious before he or she has time to notice anything.

No one wants to be walking along the street, shopping or climbing stairs when an attack begins. Even within the safety of home there is danger of injury if blackouts occur when people are on their feet. They fall over. This is why dogs that know when an attack is about to occur can change the lives of epileptics.

The predictive behaviour of dogs

For many years there have been stories of dogs that anticipate epileptic fits, but almost no research has been done on the subject until very recently. Most dogs that give warning to their owners do so spontaneously, and not as a result of any special training. Here is a typical account from someone who noticed this behaviour for herself:

> When I am at home, Penny, my Dobermann, seems to predict my epileptic fits and in doing so every time she pushes me into my chair. I mentioned this to a doctor but he just smiled. I have warnings myself, but Penny always beats me to it. She has never failed me in my home. Outside she stays by me until help arrives. (Hilary Spate, Little Sutton, South Wirral)

Ruth Beale, whose golden retriever Chad won the British PAT Dog of the Year award in 1997 (see p. 78), has a son who suffers from both petit mal and grand mal fits. Chad alerts Ruth several minutes before her son has grand mal seizures, but usually ignores the lesser attacks. 'He will come up and start pawing at my lap to get attention and sometimes he will bark as well.' This often occurs when Ruth is in a different room from her son. She is able to go to him in time and prevent accidents caused by his falling over.

In some cases the dogs give warnings only a few minutes in advance; in others they can alert their owners half an hour or more before an attack. Antonia Brown-Griffin suffers from up to twelve major seizures a week and was housebound until she took on a rescue dog named Rupert, who has become her lifeline to the outside world.

> He can sense, up to 50 minutes before, that I am going to have an attack and taps me twice with his paw, giving me time to get some-where safe. He can also press a button on my phone and bark when it is answered, to get help, and, if he thinks I'm going to have an attack while I am in the bath, he'll pull the plug out. I just can't imagine life without him.[5]

No one knows how many people with epilepsy are fortunate enough to have dogs that warn them, but there are probably many thousands worldwide.

The pioneering research of Andrew Edney

In the early 1990s a British veterinarian, Andrew Edney, carried out the first systematic survey of the warning behaviour of dogs prior to epileptic seizures. He contacted epileptic dog owners through an appeal in *Epilepsy Today*, the newsletter of the British Epilepsy Association, and through journals and newspapers. He studied in detail 21 dogs that seemed able to predict attacks. There was no particular breed that predominated in this sample; the seizure-alert dogs included working dogs, gun dogs, ter-riers, toy dogs and mongrels. Both male and female, and young and old dogs did it.

On the basis of questionnaires, Edney was able to compile a profile of the dogs' behaviour before the seizure began. Typically, they were described as looking anxious, apprehensive or restless. They alerted people in the vicinity or went away to seek help. Barking and whining were frequent, as were jumping up and nuzzling the person, and licking the hands or face. The dogs sat by or 'herded' the person to safety, and encouraged him or her to lie down. While the seizure was taking place, they either stayed beside the person, some licking the face or hands, or went to seek assistance. And they were remarkably reliable. As Edney commented: 'No dog seemed to get it wrong – one even ignored "fake" seizure attempts.'

None of the animals in Edney's sample had been trained – they had all shown their warning behaviour spontaneously. And most of the epileptics had to discover their animals' behaviour for themselves. Some of them commented that it took some time before they realized the significance of their dog's signals.

Edney concluded: 'The behaviours observed before seizures are largely attention-getting and seem to be designed to stop subjects in their tracks so action can be taken. Action during the seizure is fairly consistent. It appears to be directed towards protection and resuscitation, as well as some degree of alerting others in the proximity.'[6]

Cats and rabbits

With two exceptions, all the reports of warning behaviour prior to seizures of which I am aware concern dogs. The first exception is a rabbit belonging to Karen Cottenham of East Grinstead, Sussex.

Karen used to sustain terrible injuries when she collapsed during epileptic fits, including broken ribs, fractured ankles and cuts on her face. She and her husband bought a rabbit, Blackie, and because she did not like to keep him in a hutch outdoors in the cold, she house-trained him and kept him indoors. Soon afterwards, she realized that he 'flitted' around her legs before she had a seizure, enabling her to get to safety. When Blackie died, she bought another rabbit, Smokie, who soon took on Blackie's role. 'I don't know how or why, but several minutes before I have a fit, Smokie darts around my legs in a frenzy. I know I have to get to bed or lie on the floor so I won't fall over. When I come round, Smokie is usually nestled by my face, as if willing me back to consciousness.'[7]

The second exception is a cat. Kate Fallaize, who lives in Staffordshire, has a five-year-old tortoiseshell that warns her of impending fits up to an hour in advance. 'Before I have a fit she starts to act strangely – she keeps coming right up to my face and staring at me, and she sits next to me and touches me with her paws every few seconds. She will not leave me or let me out of her sight. I now go and lie down if she starts doing this'. The cat stays with her throughout the fit and is still there when Kate wakes up. This cat has not been trained to give warnings, and Kate's previous cat did not do so, although he did stand guard over her after the fit had come on.

The training of seizure-alert dogs

The training of dogs to give warnings of seizures is being pioneered in Britain by a small charity in Sheffield, called Support Dogs.[8] The Training Manager, Val Strong, trains dogs to recognize the signs of a seizure. "It is important that dogs are specially selected for this work," she says. However, the dog has to develop a close bond with the owner to be able to signal so that their owner recognises the warning.

The first successful training of this kind was with Molly, a rescued collie-German shepherd cross. To start with, Molly was not being taught to be a seizure-alert dog, but simply to help her epileptic owner, Lise Margaret. First she was trained to a good level of general obedience. She then learned specialized tasks such as fetching Lise a blanket after a seizure to prevent her getting too cold, and bringing the telephone. 'It can be difficult to talk, so now I just press a programmed number and Molly will bark down the phone. Friends know that I need assistance.'

Molly would already have been a big help to Lise if this had been the limit of her talents, but Val Strong had a hunch that she could go further. She began videotaping Lise and Molly, and after examining many hours of tape noticed a definite but subtle change in Molly's behaviour about 30 minutes before Lise had a fit. Molly began staring at Lise. 'We just needed to encourage her to be more demonstrative. She's very dramatic now – she barks and licks, no matter where she is.' Building on this experience, Support Dogs has subsequently trained a series of other dogs to help alert their owners to oncoming seizures.

In the United States the training of seizure-alert dogs is being coordinated by the National Service Dog Center of the Delta Society.[9] The Delta Society is also helping to raise awareness among the public of Service Dogs in general. Whereas guide dogs for blind people are widely recognized and admitted to places such as shops and restaurants where pets are normally not allowed, there is less recognition of hearing dogs for deaf people, assistance dogs for disabled people and seizure-alert dogs. For example, Christine Murray has had her dog Annie barred from some restaurants and stores in Virginia. 'I try to tell them that it's a seizure dog, but they don't believe me.'[10] As seizure-alert dogs become better known, this problem should diminish.

How do they know?

So far there has been almost no research on the ability of dogs to predict epileptic fits,[11] and no one knows how they do it. The three most common speculations are:

1   The animal notices subtle changes in behaviour or muscular tremors of which the person is unaware.
2   It senses electrical disturbances within the nervous system associated with an impending seizure.

3   It smells distinctive odours that might be given off by the person before an attack.

All three possibilities would require the dog to be quite close to the person. Indeed, the detection of electrical changes in the nervous system, if possible at all, would require them to be very close indeed. Dogs would not be expected to react if they are out of range of sight or smell.

However, some dogs seem to react to their owners' thought and intentions at a distance (Parts II and IV), and some also seem to know when their owners have had an accident or are dying, even hundreds of miles away (Chapter 6). It may therefore be worth considering the additional possibility that the dogs are not simply reacting to subtle sensory cues, but may be picking up signals of a nature as yet unknown to science. Can dogs still give warnings of seizures if their owner is out of sight, and some distance away from them?

Normally, epileptics like to have their dog nearby, so that it can warn them if a fit is coming on. But I know of three cases in which the dog still seems to know when it is in another room. Steven Beasant of Grimsby, Lincolnshire is regularly warned of impending fits by his dog Jip, a mongrel. Normally Jip follows him around and stays very close prior to an attack, and when Steven is sitting down, the dog jumps up on him. But Steven says that Jip sometimes 'comes bounding through from the kitchen and then he will pin me to the chair'. So whatever signals Jip is reacting to can be felt in a different room. The same seemed to be true of Sadie, a Dobermann that belonged to Barbara Powell of Wolverhampton. Until she died at the age of 13, Sadie gave warnings of her owner's impending seizures by whining. She usually did this when she was in the same room, but sometimes she still did it in a different room.

Dr Peter Halama, a neurologist in Hamburg, Germany, has an epileptic patient whose dogs also react when they are in a different room:

> Before an attack her dogs (two mongrels, one male, one female) stay close to her and as soon as the attack strikes they try to help her. One of them even tries to get between her and the floor when she falls. When she lies on the floor they lick her face and hands until she recovers full consciousness. They do not permit any other person to get close to her when she is in this condition. When she is in a different room from the dogs, shortly before an attack they come running to her room and stay with her, ready to help her in the same way. Her husband has often seen it and can testify to this behaviour.

Interestingly these dogs also respond to this woman's homecomings. Her husband has found that they 'get restless and go to the front door before she comes back from shopping (at irregular times). They show this behaviour 20–30 minutes before her arrival.' If these dogs can react telepathically to the woman's intention to return, then perhaps their reactions to impending epileptic attacks when in a different room could also involve telepathy. But there is a major difference between these two situations: her coming home involves a conscious intention; but the onset of a fit is neither conscious nor intentional.

Pets and diabetics

Some dogs belonging to diabetics give warnings when their owner's blood sugar levels are dangerously low. Such hypoglycaemic attacks can lead to comas, epileptic fits, and even death.

For example, Alan Harberd of Chatham, Kent, has a collie called Sam who warns him when he is hypoglycaemic. If this happens when Alan is asleep, Sam wakes him before he slips into a coma. 'My blood sugar level is low, but not so low I can't get up and do something about it. It is touch and go sometimes, but it is uncanny the way he does it.'

A pioneering survey was published in the journal *Diabetic Medicine* in 1992 by a group of clinicians at the Bristol and Berkley Health Centre in Gloucestershire, who interviewed 43 pet-owning patients who had suffered from hypoglycaemia. Fifteen of them said they had noticed reactions on the part of their animals. Fourteen of these animals were dogs. They helped their owners by barking, fetching neighbours or other appropriate responses.[12]

Some cats give warnings too, and wake their owners in the night when their blood sugar levels are dangerously low.

The most likely explanation for this kind of behaviour is in terms of smell, since diabetics can give off characteristic odours when they are hypoglycaemic. But this is no more than a guess.

Diagnosing cancer

Several pet owners say that their animals have helped to diagnose cancer and other ailments, and some cases have been reported in medical literature. For example, in 1989 an article in the *Lancet* by Hywel Williams and Andrew Pembroke of the Dermatology Department of King's College Hospital, London, described the way in which a woman had been referred to their clinic with a lesion on her left thigh, which turned out to be a malignant melanoma.

The patient first became aware of the lesion because her dog (a cross between a border collie and a Dobermann) would constantly sniff at it. The dog (a bitch) showed no interest in other moles on the patient's body but frequently spent several minutes a day sniffing intently at the lesion, even through the patient's trousers. As a consequence, the patient became increasingly suspicious. This ritual continued for several months and culminated in the dog trying to bite off the lesion when the patient wore shorts. This prompted the patient to seek further medical advice. This dog may have saved her owner's life by prompting her to seek treatment while the lesion was still at a thin and curable stage.[13]

There are several similar cases on our database. For example, Joan Hart, of Preston, Lancashire, found that when she sat down with her slippers on, Lady, her Sheltie bitch, would take off one particular slipper and lick her instep. Joan had a cyst there, and she eventually went to her doctor about it. He thought it was a wart but sent her to the hospital for some tests, to make sure. It turned out that Joan had a rare type of malignant cancer. She said, 'I wish I had taken more notice of Lady, who was trying to tell me about it.'

As far as I know, the possibility of using sniffer dogs in cancer clinics has not yet been seriously considered. It is not the type of medical research in vogue at present; the emphasis is on high technology.

Animals that warn of other kinds of illness

Epileptics have seizures repeatedly and therefore have time to recognize signals their animals may be giving them, and pay attention to them. But some animals also seem to anticipate other kinds of illness before any symptoms have been noticed by the people themselves, or members of their family. Their reactions may well be misunderstood at first. For example, an Alsatian belonging to the Albrecht family of Limbach, Germany, started to follow the woman of the family, Hilde, for no apparent reason, looking at her in a strange way and whining. 'I told my husband to go to the vet with her because something must be wrong. A few weeks later it was I who was ill, not the dog, and I had to have an operation.' Several years later, the dog behaved in the same way with her daughter, who later turned out to have appendicitis, and the same thing happened with this girl's younger sister.

Similarly, Christine Espeluque of Nissan-les-Enserune, France, has a dwarf golden cocker spaniel which seems to know in advance when her young children are going to fall ill. For example, with her five-year-old son, 'Before the illness breaks out she begins to follow him everywhere. She gets on the chair he is sitting in, sleeps on his bed with him the whole night, she cries all day long when he is in school until he comes home. Now that I've got used to it I always know ahead when my children will be ill.' But the dog only reacts to the children in this way, and does not seem to predict their mother's illnesses.

Sometimes the dog's warning is so unmistakeable that it is effective the first time it happens, as in the case of Esther Allen of Bushbury, in the West Midlands:

> I was decorating the lounge room ceiling, and to reach it I had to stand on a chair on the table. I only had about another square foot to finish, when Fara, my miniature longhaired dachshund, got up on a chair, then on to the table and started tugging at my skirt. I said, 'Just a minute, I won't be long,' but she wouldn't let up, so I got down. As I reached the floor I blacked out for a few seconds. When I came to she was licking my face. If Fara had not made me get down off the table and chair, I certainly would have had a serious injury.

Here the dog's behaviour resembles that of the seizure-warning dogs of epileptics. But how did it anticipate her collapse? In a similarly puzzling way, some dogs anticipate heart attacks, and take action that minimizes the damage caused by falling down. For example: 'My partner suffered from heart attacks several times, so that she simply collapsed. Rolf, our Alsatian, normally quite a rough fellow, always anticipated these attacks and placed himself in front of his mistress in such a way that she never fell on her head but always on her back.' (Hans Schauenburg, Roelbach, Germany)

Obviously, the first possibility that needs to be considered is that the animal picks up some subtle change in the person's behaviour, or movements, or even unusual smells. But sometimes animals react when the person is in a different room or further away. In this case, a cat reacted even while his person was out on a walk:

> One afternoon in July my husband went for his usual walk before supper. Ten minutes later our cat displayed unusual behaviour. He ran through the flat restlessly, growled to himself and had his back-hair standing on end. After one hour my husband came back and said, 'I don't feel well. I'll lie down a little before the meal.' He went into the bedroom, and I continued my work in the kitchen. Suddenly Aimo became even more restless and pushed his muzzle against my legs. Then he ran away from the kitchen, looking behind to see whether I was following him. Like a dog he led me to the bedroom, where I

found my husband writhing with kidney pains. We called an emergency doctor and he relieved my husband's pain. Soon afterwards Aimo was our good old quiet cat again. (Erni Weber, Grosskut, Austria)

If this were an isolated case, it would be tempting to suppose either that it was 'just coincidence', or that the cat had noticed some signs before Herr Weber set out on his walk and that it took Frau Weber some time to notice the cat's unusual behaviour. But as we saw in Chapter 6, there are many cases in which animals reacted when their owners died unexpectedly in distant places, or when they were in distress. In that context it is not so surprising that a cat should pick up when its owner was not well when he was out on a walk.

Forebodings of sudden death

The reactions of pets before the onset of illnesses are easily misunderstood, and their meaning only becomes clear in retrospect. The same is true of unusual behaviour prior to sudden deaths.

In 1995, Christine Vickery and her husband were living in Sacramento, California. She describes him as a 'fitness fanatic, 52 years old and very fit.' He started each day with vitamin pills, had a low-fat diet and in addition to working out on his 'cardioglide' exercise machine, he used to walk part of the way to work.

On the evening of 1 December , he arrived home at 6.30 pm as usual. Instead of running to greet him, my dogs Smokie and Popsie stayed in their baskets in another room. He called them. They refused to move. At 9 pm the dogs came to the lounge and sat at my husband's feet, staring up at him. My husband was upset and wondered what (as he said) they knew, that he did not. They kept up this odd ritual for the next five days. On the night of 6 December, the older dog, Smokie, caressed my husband's leg with his nose. Popsie offered him a paw. At 1.30 am on 7 December my husband died in his sleep. I envied my dogs. They had known somehow and had said their goodbyes.

Cats can have similar forebodings. For example, Dorothy Doherty, who lives in Hertfordshire, says that the day before her husband collapsed and died, their cat continually rubbed round his legs. 'I remember him saying "What's wrong with her today?" As she had never been so persistent before I have often wondered if she knew what was going to happen.'

There are many other examples of forebodings by dogs and cats about medical emergencies and sudden deaths. But like all premonitions, their significance is only apparent in retrospect. Sceptics will say that there must be thousands of cases of unusual behaviour not followed by death or disaster and soon forgotten, so there is nothing more mysterious at work than chance coincidence and selective memory. But although this standard argument may sound scientific, it is no more than an untested hypothesis. Sceptics have not collected any statistics to support it. In fact practically no research has been done in this area.

The arguments of sceptics are of scientific value if they are treated as reasonable possibilities to be tested; but they are anti-scientific if they are used as a way of inhibiting enquiry. Unfortunately, this has all too often been the case. That is why we still know so little about these fascinating phenomena.

15

Forebodings of earthquakes and other disasters

Reactions of animals before earthquakes

On 26 September 1997, a major earthquake devastated the Basilica of St Francis in Assisi, Italy, and caused much damage in nearby towns and villages. Shortly before the earthquake many people noticed that animals were behaving strangely. The night before, some dogs barked much more than usual; others were strangely agitated and restless. Cats seemed nervous and disturbed, and some went into hiding. Pigeons flew 'strangely'. Wild birds fell silent a few minutes before the earthquake struck, and pheasants 'screamed in an unusual way'.[1] Some changes in the normal behaviour of animals were noticed several days beforehand:

> A friend told me, 'Don't go to eat at the taverns by the river in Foligno because there are rats along the river, big ones.' At least a week before the earthquake people started saying that Foligno was invaded by rats. I have been living here for a long time, and this never happened before. Rats were everywhere, but nobody connected it to the earthquake. (Silvana Cacciaruchi)

Foligno is 12 miles from Assisi and was badly damaged by the quake. Why did the rats leave the sewers? How did so many other animals seem to anticipate the coming catastrophe?

Sceptics explain away such stories in terms of chance coincidence and selective memory: people may recall such behaviour only if it is followed by an earthquake or other catastrophe, and forget about it otherwise. No doubt there is some truth in this argument. But it would be rash to dismiss all the evidence in this way. Many experienced observers of animals are convinced that animals have indeed behaved unusually prior to earthquakes. Within three weeks of the Assisi earthquake, while aftershocks were still occurring, Anna Rigano, my Italian research assistant, was on the spot in Assisi, Foligno and other earthquake-affected areas of Umbria, where she interviewed dozens of people, including pet owners, pet shop proprietors and veterinarians, while memories were still fresh. Most had noticed the unusual behaviour of animals prior to the earthquake and most were confident that this behaviour was indeed exceptional.

Similar patterns of animal behaviour prior to earthquakes have been reported independently by people all over the world. I cannot believe that they could all have made up such similar stories, or all suffered from tricks of memory.

The first detailed description from Europe concerns a cataclysmic earthquake in 373 BC at Helice in Greece, bordering the gulf of Corinth, in which the port city was swallowed up by the sea. Five days beforehand, according to the historian Diodorus Siculus, animals such as rats, snakes and weasels left the city in droves, to the puzzlement of the human inhabitants.

Other reports from classical times include the statement of the Roman writer Pliny the Elder that one of the signs of a coming earthquake is 'the excitation and terror of animals with no apparent reason'. There were similar accounts in the Middle Ages, for example from Württemberg in 1095: 'The fowl left human habitations to go and live wild in the woods and mountains.'[2] In recent centuries, the strongest earthquake to shake Europe happened in 1755 at Lisbon, Portugal, causing enormous devastation, and was so powerful that the earth's motion caused church bells to ring as far away as Sweden. This earthquake was discussed by many contemporary writers, including the philosopher Immanuel Kant, who summarized a sign of an impending earthquake as follows: 'Animals are taken with fright shortly before it. Birds flee into houses, rats and mice crawl out of their holes . . .' There were reports of a 'multitude of worms' coming out of the ground eight days before the Lisbon earthquake, and of cattle being 'highly excited' a day before.[3]

There are literally hundreds of other examples preserved by historians and chroniclers, and many more recent cases too; for example: 'Before the Agadir earthquake in Morocco in 1960, stray animals including dogs, were seen streaming from the port before the shock that killed 15,000 people. A similar phenomenon was observed three years later, before the earthquake which reduced the city of Skopje, Yugoslavia, to rubble. Most animals seemed to have left before the 'quake.'[4] Before the earthquake that destroyed much of Kobe, Japan, on 17 January 1995, unusual behaviour was observed in mammals, birds, reptiles, fish, insects and worms.[5]

Yet in spite of this wealth of evidence, most professional earthquake researchers ignore the stories of animal warnings, or dismiss them as a matter of superstition or selective memory. As far as I know, none of the hundreds of millions of dollars a year currently spent on seismological research in the West are devoted to investigating the reactions of animals. Here is yet another area where taboo and prejudice have closed the minds of professionals, and where scepticism serves to inhibit scientific enquiry rather than promote it. But in this case, it is not just our scientific understanding that is impoverished by this attitude. Animals could provide valuable warnings and help save lives.

Earthquake prediction

Many politicians and taxpayers believe that the large amounts of public money spent on seismological research will help to develop methods of earthquake prediction. But unknown to those who fund them, most professionals believe that detailed predictions are impossible, and no longer even try to make them. An article by four eminent experts published in the American journal *Science* in 1997 stated its thesis succinctly in the title: 'Earthquakes Cannot Be Predicted'. It quoted with approval the remarks made in 1977 by Richter, developer of the eponymous magnitude scale, in which he dismissed earthquake prediction as 'a happy hunting ground for amateurs, cranks, and outright publicity-seeking fakers'. Rather than predicting specific earthquakes, they see the role of seismology as contributing to 'earthquake hazard mitigation'.

> Statistical estimates of the seismicity expected in a general region on a timescale of 30 to 100 years and statistical estimates of the expected strong ground motion are important data for designing earthquake-resistant structures. Rapid determination of source parameters (such as location and magnitude) can facilitate relief efforts after large earthquakes.[6]

These are indeed useful roles for seismology to play. But while this cautious attitude protects seismologists against making public mistakes through issuing false alarms, it justifies the continued neglect of research on the warnings that animals can give.

By contrast, in China in the 1970s, earthquake researchers actually encouraged members of the public to watch out for and report possible portents that, according to age-old Chinese traditions, were supposed to herald the coming of catastrophic earthquakes.

In June 1974, the Chinese State Seismological Bureau issued a warning that a serious earthquake should be expected in Liaoning province in the next few years, on the basis of a historical analysis and geological measurements. As a consequence, the scientific observation network was expanded, and groups of amateur observers were organized in factories, schools and agricultural communes. Over 100,000 people were trained to watch out for unusual behaviour by animals and changes in the level and cloudiness of water in wells, as well as strange noises and unusual kinds of lightning.

In the middle of December 1974, snakes came out of hibernation, crawled from their burrows, and froze to death on the snow-covered surface. Rats appeared in the open in large groups and were often so confused that they could be caught by hand; cattle and fowl were strangely excited; and the water in the springs became cloudy. There was a minor earthquake on 22 December, but throughout January 1995 reports of unusual animal behaviour continued, with more than twenty species showing great signs of fear. Plans were made to evacuate Haicheng, a city of half a million people. At the beginning of February, the number of reports climbed steeply, as cattle, horses and pigs began panicking. 'Geese flew into trees, dogs barked as if mad, pigs bit each other or dug beneath the fences of their sties, chickens refused to go into their coops, cattle tore their halters and ran away, and rats appeared and acted as if drunk . . . Groundwater anomalies began spreading.'[7]

On the morning of 4 February the decision was made to evacuate Haicheng. The same day, at 7.36 pm the anticipated earthquake finally came, with an intensity of 7.3 on the Richter scale. Over half the buildings in the city were destroyed. Tens of thousands of people might have lost their lives had it not been for this timely warning. But there were still some victims. 'Most of those were people who had put too little faith in official earthquake predictions to put up with February temperatures outdoors.'[8]

For a while, some Western seismologists were impressed. The possibility of using anomalous animal behaviour for earthquake warnings was even discussed within the US Geological Service.[9] But within a few years the conventional scepticism predominated again, and the idea was dropped. Nevertheless, the Chinese have continued with their earthquake prediction programme. They have had some spectacular failures, most notably the unpredicted Tangshan earthquake of 1976, in which at least 240,000 people died. But they have continued to make successful predictions. For example, in 1995 they warned local authorities in

Yunnan province one day before a major earthquake struck.[10] On 5 April 1997, Xinjiang seismologists predicted an earthquake between magnitudes 5 and 6 would strike within a week. According to a report in *Science*,

> During the night, authorities evacuated 150,000 people to shacks and canvas shelters. Early the next morning, a magnitude-6.4 quake occurred, and at noon a magnitude 6.3 struck. Together, they destroyed 2,000 houses and damaged 1,500 more, but no one was killed. Similarly based predictions preceded a magnitude-6.6 quake on 11 April and magnitude 6.3 on 16 April.[11]

The Xinjiang scientists also cried wolf once during this period. Nevertheless, the Chinese have been remarkably successful, in striking contrast to their Western counterparts who do not even try. The Chinese continue to pursue a pragmatic approach, combining seismological and geological measurements with observations of wells and springs and other 'alternative methods' (a euphemism used in Western scientific publications for unusual animal behaviour). However, the Chinese seismologists are modest about their achievements, and themselves point out that their approach works best when applied to earthquakes with foreshocks, as in Haicheng; they have been much less successful with other kinds of quakes.[12]

Research with animals in California

Currently, no official research on the anticipation of earthquakes by animals is going on in the West, as far as I know. Animal behaviourists ignore the subject, and so do seismologists, who concentrate their attention on physical measurements with instruments. Given the successes of the Chinese, this seems a remarkable omission.

My colleague David Jay Brown and I have begun a program of research in California to find out more about unusual animal behaviour, with two ends in view.

First, we want to be able to characterize the kinds of behaviour that various animals show, so that we can produce a set of guidelines enabling pet owners and others to recognize this behaviour. Second, we want to know what animals are reacting to. How do they know when an earthquake is on the way?

We have started by asking people if they noticed any unusual behaviour by animals before two of the most destructive recent earthquakes, the Loma Prieta earthquake of 17 October 1989 which caused much damage in Santa Cruz, Silicon Valley and other parts of northern

California, and the Northridge quake of 17 January 1994, with its epi-
centre in the San Fernando valley, in the suburbs of Los Angeles.

In both areas, many people did in fact notice strange and seemingly
inexplicable behaviour in both domestic and wild animals. Here is just
one example: 'My cocker spaniel was really fearful. Her eyes were big,
and she ran around and around, like crazy, back and forth, and back and
forth. She would come to me, and go away, and come to me, and go away,
like she was trying to tell me "You have to get out too." I thought, "This
dog has gone crazy," and I was really angry. After about an hour the earthquake happened'. (Renata McKinstry, San Jose, California)

Most of the accounts we have received are about dogs and cats,
which may simply reflect the fact that these are the commonest pets.
Dogs were said to be barking for no apparent reason, snarling, howling,
whining, running around, hiding, or showing signs of nervousness, restlessness and agitation. Cats seemed nervous or disturbed, and many ran
outside or hid. But other animals reacted too. Caged birds became very
restless. Horses ran around in unusual ways, goats became agitated, and
some chickens stopped laying eggs. And some people noticed that soon
before the earthquakes struck, there was a strange silence as wild birds
and crickets stopped singing.

Even emus responded. These giant birds, related to ostriches, have a
habit of pacing along fences. In their native Australia they are often
called 'birds in search of a fence', because even when they have huge
open spaces to range in they will go to a fence and pace it. In Sandy
Scott's emu farm in Auburn, Washington, the birds normally walk beside
the fences, and bed down in their sheds about half an hour before dark.
But on two particular evenings their behaviour was different: 'They were
almost running up and down the fence. And when it started to get dark,
and they finally did bed down, they bedded down outside their sheds,
instead of inside them.' On both these occasions, there was an earthquake in the night, several hours after the emus began to show their
unusual behaviour.

Although many animals became agitated before the earthquakes
struck, there were also many that did not. For example, Susan Gray, who
lives in Reseda, near Northridge, commented: 'The cats were as shaken
by surprise as we were. It was early in the morning, and both cats were
in the bedroom with us. They were down the hall, and out the cat door
within seconds of the quake beginning.' These cats, like many other cats,
were terrified and would not come back into the house for days. After
they did come back, they both picked a spot they would run to where
they sat out every subsequent quake. 'Lessa, my tabby, is the one that follows me around, so she's the one I notice the most. She picked a chair in

my bedroom that has a skirt on it that goes all the way to the floor, and she'd run under there whenever there was an aftershock. But sometimes I'd get up in the morning, and Lessa would – for absolutely no reason – go running under that chair, and up to three hours later we'd have an aftershock.'

Susan Gray, like many other cat owners in the San Fernando Valley, noticed that after the big earthquake, they cats were very 'jumpy' and were easily startled. 'If you moved quickly they'd turn around startled, and race towards the door, or towards their hiding places.' The fright caused by the big earthquake seemed to have sensitized them. Perhaps a similar sensitization occurred with animals in China when major earthquakes were preceded by foreshocks, and it was in these situations that animal warnings were most effective. But even so, Susan Gray's cats were not always right: 'Sometimes they were jumpy for a few hours and nothing happened. But far more often than not, when they got that way we did have one.'

The reactions of fear and agitation shown by animals before the Loma Prieta and Northridge earthquakes in some cases began several days beforehand, in others a matter of hours, and in others only a few minutes. David Brown and I are building up a database of such accounts and hope to construct a profile of the kinds of reactions that animals show, the time-course of these reactions and the conditions that affect their responses. We are also interested in finding out whether they respond to some kinds of earthquake more than others.

Not only non-human animals react before tremors; some people do so too, describing symptoms such as agitation, headaches and nervousness for no apparent reason. Some say they wake up just before earthquakes, others suffer from unaccountable sleeplessness. Some have found themselves especially sensitive to aftershocks, like Barry Cane: 'I could often feel an aftershock coming. It was like there was a change in the atmosphere. I don't really know the words for it, but I'd say, uh oh, here we go. And anywhere from one to five minutes – boom – it would hit.'

An animal-based earthquake warning system

Imagine what could happen if instead of being ignored, the warnings given by animals – and by people – were taken seriously in California and other parts of the Western world.

Through the media, millions of pet owners could be informed about the kinds of behaviour their pets and other animals might show if an earthquake were imminent. If they noticed these signs, they would immediately call a telephone hotline with a memorable number – say 1-800-PET QUAKE. Or they could send a message on the internet. A computer system would then analyze the place of origin of the incoming calls. No doubt there would be a stream of false alarms from people who had misunderstood their pet's symptoms – the animal might simply have been sick, for example – and there might well also be some hoax calls. But if there was a sudden surge of calls from a particular region, this could indicate that an earthquake in that region was imminent. It would then be important to check that the surge of calls was not due to other factors known to affect the behaviour of animals, such as dramatic changes in the weather, firework displays, local fires or an influx of predators.

At first, this system would have to be used for research purposes only, to see if it worked reasonably reliably. It would not be appropriate to issue any warnings until this had been established. False alarms could cause panic and disruption, and could set back research on this subject for years. Ideally, the reports of unusual animal behaviour would be combined with the monitoring of other precursors of earthquakes, including seismological measurements, as in China.

There are already some indications from research in California that such a system could work. In the late 1970s, following the successful Chinese prediction of the Haicheng earthquake, the US Geological Service funded a pilot project based at the Stanford Research institute. The coordinators, Leon Otis and William Kautz, recruited 1,200 volunteer observers located in earthquake-prone parts of California who undertook to call a toll-free hotline whenever they observed 'unusual animal behavior whose cause was not immediately observable and obvious'.

This project ran from 1979 to 1981. During this period there were no earthquakes with magnitudes greater than 5 in the areas under observation. Altogether, 13 earthquakes of magnitudes between 4 and 5 were appropriate candidates for analysis, although none of them occurred within the areas where observers were concentrated. Seven of these earthquakes were preceded by a statistically significant increase in calls about unusual animal behaviour.[13] In some cases the statistics were very impressive indeed.[14] At this stage funding was discontinued and no further research was carried out.

If instead of a mere 1,200 observers, millions could be recruited, a much more detailed assessment of the potential of animal warnings could be made. Pet owners could play a vital role in this process, and especially senior citizens, who have more time and opportunity to observe their animals than people who are out at work all day.

How do they know?

As far as I am aware, there has been almost no research anywhere in the world on the means by which animals somehow sense an imminent earthquake, with the exception of some recent experiments in Japan. But there are several possible theories, as follows:

1   They somehow pick up subtle sounds, vibrations or movements of the earth.

    There are several problems with this theory. First, some of the kinds of animal that seem to respond in advance to earthquakes have no more sensitive hearing than our own.[15] Second, small earth tremors and minor earthquakes are common in seismically active areas. For example, in 1980 there were 350 earthquakes (excluding aftershocks) of magnitude 3 or less in California.[16] If animals were exquisitely sensitive to weak vibrations, they would be giving false alarms frequently. They should also respond to vibrations caused by passing trucks or other kinds of heavy machinery with fear and alarm. And third, if so many species of animals can pick up characteristic vibrations before major earthquakes, then seismologists should also be able to identify them with their very sensitive instruments. But they have so far failed to do so, despite years of intensive research.

2   Animals respond to gases released by the earth prior to earthquakes.

    Although some species, such as dogs, are far more sensitive to smells than we are, others, like songbirds, are less sensitive. There seems to be no correlation between animals' sense of smell and their sensitivity to earthquakes. Also there is no evidence that earthquakes are generally preceded by the leaking of characteristic gases out of the earth. And if such gases are released by tiny cracks in the earth's surface before earthquakes, then why do animals not respond with fear and panic when people dig holes or mines, or even when animals burrow?

3   Animals respond to electrical changes preceding earthquakes.

    This is far more plausible than the two preceding theories. There is evidence that some earthquakes are indeed preceded by changes in electrostatic fields, which probably arise from changes in seismic stress in rocks. It is well known that in some crystals and rocks, changes in pressure generate electrical charges (the piezoelectric effect), and such electrical effects preceding earthquakes could not only help to explain the reactions of animals, but also other electrical anomalies, like interference in radio and television broadcasts and strange auras and lights coming from the earth (technically known as seismo-atmospheric luminescence).[17]

Conventional seismologists are sceptical about these electrical precursors of earthquakes, but a maverick group in Greece, the so-called VAN group, led by P. Varotsos, claim to be able to predict earthquakes on the basis of geoelectrical signals.[18] And in California, the Time Research Institute, headed by Marsha Adams, issues a regular series of earthquake forecasts on the basis of a network of electromagnetic sensors, the input from which is analyzed by specialized computer software.[19] This programme is supported not by public funds, but by private subscription (slogan: 'Support Earthquake Forecasting Research – Be Generous to a Fault').

Meanwhile, Motoji Ikeya and his colleagues at Osaka University in Japan have recently carried out laboratory experiments in which they exposed a variety of animals, including minnows, catfish, eels and earthworms, to weak electrical currents. Fish showed panic reactions, and earthworms moved out of the soil and swarmed when the current was applied.[20] These preliminary findings could help to explain the anomalous behaviour of animals in water and in moist environments before earthquakes. But what about animals like dogs and cats inside buildings? Are they responding to electrically charged ions in the air? Many questions remained unanswered, but this is clearly a promising line of research.

4 Finally, animals may somehow 'sense' in advance what is about to happen in a way that lies beyond current scientific understanding. In other words they may be 'presentient', having a feeling that something is about to happen, or 'precognitive', knowing in advance what is going to happen.

This hypothesis would be unnecessary if all the facts could be explained satisfactorily by more conventional theories. Many scientists, including myself, would prefer not to have to consider the idea of influences working 'backwards' in time, from the future to the present. I confess that I would prefer to put this idea aside unless compelled to take it seriously. At present, the electrical theory seems sufficiently promising to justify ignoring this more radical possibility.

The trouble is that there are other kinds of animal premonitions that cannot be explained electrically, as we will shortly see.

Whether we like it or not, precognitive forebodings do seem to occur. And if they occur in other situations, perhaps they also play a part in premonitions about earthquakes. But first I turn to a kind of apprehension that seems to support the electrical theory.

Forebodings of storms

'It was a beautiful warm summer day, with a clear blue sky. I set off for a long walk with my Alsatian Rolly. After we had gone for about one hour he would not go any further. I tried to make him move on, but nothing helped. I wondered what was wrong. Finally he lay down in the ditch. What else could I do but turn around and go home? Half an hour later the sky darkened and the first thunder could be heard far away. We went on a little faster, and when we had entered the house there was torrential rainfall with hailstones. Then I realized that Rolly must have sensed this much earlier.' (Louise Forstinger, Graz, Austria)

Some animals are terrified of thunderstorms and show signs of distress long before their owners are aware of a storm approaching. Dogs and cats often hide. Many other kinds of animals become apprehensive before storms, including horses, parakeets and tortoises.

Most of the accounts I have received concern reactions half an hour to an hour before the storm breaks, but in some cases the animal's anticipation begins three hours or more in advance.

The reactions of some animals before storms and before earthquakes are similar, and any animal-based earthquake warning system would need to take this fact into account, otherwise impending storms could be mistaken for impending earthquakes, resulting in false alarms.

Lightning is of course an electrical phenomenon, and it could well be that some, if not all, of the anticipatory reactions of animals depend on their sensitivity to the electrical changes that precede thunderstorms. This would support the electrical theory of earthquake anticipation. And perhaps some animals with hearing more sensitive than our own hear the thunder when it is still far away. But other kinds of animal forebodings cannot be explained in these ways.

Warnings of air raids

'During the war, when the German bombing raids were going on, we had a black mongrel dog who used to go to our back door and bark to go out, and you could bet that around ten minutes later the sirens would sound for an air raid. We got so used to the dog doing it that I would run up and down both sides of the street and knock on all the doors to warn of an impending raid. She was never wrong once.' (Teddy Pugh, Birmingham)

I have collected 22 other accounts of dogs that gave warnings of air raids before the sirens sounded the official alarm. Some of them let their owners know by whining; some barked; some hid; and others led the way to the air raid shelter or cellar where the family took refuge. British dogs gave warnings of German air raids during the Second World War, and German dogs gave warnings of British air raids.

Some dogs were said to alert their owners a few minutes before the sirens went off; most reacted 10 to 30 minutes beforehand; and in three cases the warnings the dogs gave were said to be over an hour in advance.

One little dog called Dee sometimes stayed curled up in her basket when the siren went, and invariably no planes came over. Equally, sometimes she would become very agitated when there was no warning siren and would urge everyone to take cover, and sure enough an unexpected raid would take place.[21] As an added bonus, some families were able to get back to bed before the 'all clear' signal was sounded. 'The dog would suddenly get up, leave the shelter and settle into its basket with a contented sigh. Five minutes later the all clear would sound'.[22]

The most recent account I have received of air raid warnings by a dog is from a kibbutz in Israel. During the Gulf War in 1991, when the air raid alarm was sounded, members of the community took refuge in a sealed room that was supposed to serve as a gas-proof bomb shelter. 'The dog was the first one to feel it before the alarm went off, and it would rush to the sealed room a minute or two before. It never did this when there was not an alarm.' (Savyon Liebrecht)

During the Second World War, cats also anticipated bombing attacks, usually by showing obvious signs of agitation or by hiding. Some were said to give warnings more than an hour in advance. Birds too seemed to know when bombers were on their way: seagulls flew off; cock pheasants gave warning calls; and ducks and geese also raised the alarm. Here is how a German parrot did it:

During the wartime year of 1943 I stayed with acquaintances in Leipzig. They had an old parrot. Suddenly, about 9 pm, it was extremely upset in its cage, lifted its left wing and called, 'Da oben! Da oben!' ('Up there!') It even looked up and nobody could get it quiet. I was surprised and asked my hosts what all this meant. 'He always does this before an air alert,' the lady said, 'usually two hours in advance.' That same night the Tommies really came. They destroyed the Crystal Palace. (Dagmar Kessel)

Warnings given by German pigeons were a source of trouble to an unfortunate Austrian sculptor, Heinz Peteri, who was arrested during the war for his 'undiplomatic' words and deported to Bochum, in the Ruhr, to defuse unexploded bombs. He lived in a small room in the tower of the police administration building. From his window he used to watch the pigeons that lived on the remaining roofs of the city, and noticed that 'the birds often flew away suddenly, all of them, and half an hour later (at the most) the bombers came. Afterwards the birds came back. This was repeated many times.' He used this knowledge to warn his comrades and superiors of impending raids, and his predictions repeatedly proved to be accurate. When the Gestapo heard about it, he was arrested once again under suspicion of being a spy 'in contact with the enemy'.[23]

How did all these animals know when air raids were imminent? The most obvious possibility is that they heard the enemy planes when they were still too far away for humans to hear them. But a few moments' reflection shows that this is not a very plausible suggestion, for at least four reasons. First, as we have seen (p. 19-20), the sensitivity of hearing by dogs and other domestic animals is not much greater than our own, although dogs can hear more high-pitched sounds than we can. The bombers used in the Second World War flew at about 250 miles per hour when loaded; hence an animal that responded half an hour before an air raid would have had to hear them about 125 miles away. Some animals were said to respond even earlier, when the bombers would have been over 200 miles away. Even animals that responded only a few minutes before the sirens went off would have had to hear the planes more than 30 miles away, assuming that the siren gave about five minutes' warning. It is very implausible that they could have heard the enemy aircraft at such distances.

Second, hearing distant sounds depends on the wind direction, and there is no evidence that the regular warnings given by animals occurred only when the enemy aircraft were upwind. Rather, the evidence suggests that animal warnings were remarkably reliable, and not dependent on the wind direction. Moreover, since the prevailing winds in Britain are southwesterly and the German bombers approached from the east, in most raids they would not have been upwind, and hence their sounds would have been blown away from, rather than towards, the animals that sensed their approach.

Third, there were many other aircraft in the skies, including the country's own bombers heading towards enemy territory. Apparently the animals did not give warnings of the approach of 'friendly' bombers. The hearing theory would require the animals to distinguish between the sounds of different kinds of bomber at a great distance, irrespective of the wind direction. There is no evidence that this is possible.

Finally, during the last year of the Second World War, the Germans were firing supersonic V2 rockets at London. These missiles were launched from Holland and headed upwards at about 45°. Their engines cut out after a minute or so, and they followed a ballistic trajectory, reaching speeds of over 2,000 miles per hour as they plunged downwards, arriving unseen and unheard. They took only five minutes to reach their targets in England, some 200 miles away, carrying a ton of high explosive.[24] They were particularly terrifying because their explosion was preceded by no warning, and they could strike anywhere in southeast England at any time of day or night.

Dr Roy Willis, who was 17 at the time, was living in Essex, just to the east of London. 'I noticed that our dog, an Alsatian-elkhound cross, was seemingly able to sense the imminent arrival of a V2 rocket. The dog, called Smoke, would go to the window and stare out, hackles raised, as if in anger and fear. After about two minutes, during which time he remained in the same aggressive posture at the window, I would hear the ominous crump of an exploded rocket.' At least one other dog owner had a very similar experience, his animal reacting shortly before the explosions. Assuming that these accounts are reliable (which I have no reason to doubt), the dogs could not have heard these missiles coming, however acute their hearing, precisely because they were both silent and supersonic.

If animals were not anticipating air raids by hearing the approaching bombers or rockets, how did they know the attacks were coming?

No explanation is possible in terms of electrical charges in the earth and the atmosphere, such as those that precede thunderstorms, and which may serve as warning signs before earthquakes.

As far as I can see, only two possibilities remain:

1 Telepathy. The animals picked up influences telepathically from people or animals along the flight path of the bombers. As a wave of alertness and alarm spread through the human and animal populations as the bombers flew by, this alarm spread telepathically. The trouble is that this telepathic alerting might have taken place in all directions, and hence caused false alarms in places to which the planes were not flying.

   Alternatively, the animals might have picked up the hostile intentions of the German bomber crews as they moved towards their targets, with their attention focused on the places they were planning to attack.

Obviously, these possibilities are highly speculative, and there is no way of putting them to the test experimentally since, fortunately, air raids are no longer taking place. And although telepathy may be able to account for some of the available facts, it cannot account for all of them. In particular, no telepathy theory could explain how dogs could anticipate the arrival of the supersonic V2 missiles: no one was aware of their flight path, and they were unmanned. Even the Germans who launched them did not know exactly where they would land.

2   Precognitive forebodings. Perhaps the animals somehow intuited what was going to happen in the near future, or at least had an apprehension that *something* was going to happen without knowing what. This theory would be able to account for the dogs that anticipated the V2 attacks, as well as many other kinds of premonition. One trouble is that it is a very vague theory. Another is that it raises terrible logical problems and mind-twisting paradoxes, since it implies that something in the future can have an effect 'backwards' in time. There is a further logical problem with precognitions. It is not possible to know if a precognition is true until the foreseen event has actually happened. It is only in retrospect that a precognition can be identified as such.

I would prefer to avoid this theory, if possible. I find telepathy easier to accept than precognition. And the two V2 cases are the only evidence so far that seem to necessitate a theory of this kind. But there are many other examples of foreboding, to which I now turn, that make the idea of precognition or presentiment almost unavoidable.

Other kinds of premonition

As well as all these examples of warnings that animals gave before air raids and earthquakes, I have received 98 other accounts of apprehensive behaviour prior to accidents, catastrophes or dangers.

It is not uncommon for horses to refuse to go on when danger lies ahead, as Franziska Kabusch found one snowy winter in Austria when she was taking a horse and sleigh to a neighbouring village.

The horse and I set off, but after only ten metres she would not go any further. She could not be made to move on by any means. When I insisted she simply started to walk backwards, and we fell into the village brooklet. I was desperate: how could this otherwise good-natured horse be so stubborn? Suddenly there was a great thundering noise. A huge avalanche came down from the roof of the barn in front of us and dropped right on to the part of the road which we were about to use.

It is just possible that the horse heard some telltale sounds that alarmed it, in advance of the avalanche. We can avoid the idea of precognition by clutching at this straw of possibility.

I have received dozens of accounts of other animals that prevented their owners going ahead when unexpected danger was imminent. Some dogs refused to walk along paths when shortly afterwards branches or trees fell where the person, and the dog, would have been. Other dogs, horses and cats delayed or prevented their owners setting off on foot or by car when road accidents happened soon afterwards, in which they might well have been injured or killed. One dog adamantly refused to enter a pedestrian subway so the person with it had no option but to turn back. 'We had barely turned around when there was a great bang and the concrete ceiling came down!' Another dog prevented its owner from getting on to a boat that exploded shortly afterwards. Another dog pulled its owner away from the roadside just before a van hurtled round the corner and crashed into the place they would have been. And so on.

In some of these cases, it is just possible, though implausible, that the animals heard something unusual that caused their alarm. In others it is impossible, because the animal's apprehension began long before it could possibly have heard anything that might have given any clue. For example, a woman who was driving with her cat in the back of the car, where it normally slept, found the animal became more and more disturbed. She tried to calm it, but it eventually went so far as to touch her arm and then slightly bit into the hand that held the steering wheel. 'So I finally stopped. Right at that moment a big tree fell on to the road, a few metres in front of the car. Had I continued as before, it would have fallen on the car.' (Adele Holzer)

In any case, some of the dangers to which animals alert people are silent, and hearing could have played no part in arousing their apprehension. An Austrian couple were travelling towards their holiday destination on a steep mountain road with rocks on one side and an abyss on the other when their poodle Susi suddenly started to howl. 'She even put her paws on my husband's shoulders to stop him. My attempts to keep her quiet failed. Her behaviour became mad. Startled, my husband slowed down, and when we turned around the next bend we were shocked: the road was gone. Only a few metres in front of us there was a precipice. A landslip had taken the road with it. Susi saved our lives.' (Friedel Ehlenbeck)

In most cases I have heard of, the behaviour of the animals helped protect their people from danger. But not everyone heeded the warnings they tried to give:

> One morning my dog Toby tried to stop me going out of the front door. He barged against me, leant on the door, jumped up at me and pushed me. He is normally a quiet, loving dog and knows my routine; I would have been back within four hours. I had to lock him in the kitchen and left him howling, something he has never done before or since. I set off at 7.30 am and by 9.40 am I was involved in an horrific road traffic accident resulting in a fractured neck and right arm, and many other injuries. When I was in hospital an image of Toby kept appearing to me through the drugs and I could feel his anguish. I sent a mental 'OK, I'll be back soon' and the images disappeared. On speaking to my husband about it he said Toby was very agitated for 24 hours and then suddenly became quiet. I am slowly recovering. In the future I'll listen to Toby. (Elizabeth Powell, Powys, Wales)

Sometimes the animal's reactions are not specific warnings about which the person can do anything, but seem to be presentiments of something alarming about to happen. In 1992, Natalie Polinario was living in North London near Staples Corner, where IRA terrorists detonated a large bomb on 11 April. Her white German shepherd, Foxy, was outside in the garden.

> I was lying on the bed watching TV. About one minute or two minutes before the bomb went off she came in running and literally crying, in a really weird mood. She got on the bed and just lay there next to me, really stiff as if something had really scared her, but there was nothing out there. And then I heard this almighty bang which was the bomb at Staples Corner. The minute it went off she was fine again. She has never done anything like it since then, or before.

It is hard to avoid the conclusion that some of these forebodings must indeed have been precognitive. What other explanation could there be? And if forebodings of disasters, accidents and air raids can be precognitive, then so might some premonitions of storms and earthquakes, even though others might be explicable in terms of a sensitivity to electrical changes or other physical causes. Perhaps some of the forewarnings of epileptic fits, comas and sudden deaths discussed in the previous chapter might also include an element of precognition.

Human precognition

All around the world we find beliefs in the ability of some people to foresee the future. Shamans, seers, prophets, oracles or soothsayers are found in most, if not all, traditional societies, and even in modern industrial societies, fortune tellers and clairvoyants still flourish. No doubt some of them are fraudulent. But there are far too many convincing examples of human premonition to dismiss this entire area of experience out of hand.

Many people who are not professional fortune tellers have had premonitions that have turned out to be true, and there are many stories of people whose lives have been saved by dreams, presentiments or forebodings that led them not to take planes that later crashed, or to go to places that would have exposed them to grave but unexpected dangers. Sometimes they do not or cannot act on these premonitions, either because they are not specific enough, or because they do not take them seriously. But sometimes they do.

These different reactions were illustrated in a dramatic way prior to the assassination of President Abraham Lincoln in 1865. A week before he was shot in the Ford Theater in Washington, he told his wife and his friend Ward H. Lamon of a dream in which he heard sounds of mourning in the White House. Anxious to discover the cause, he went from room to room until in the East Room, with a 'sickening surprise' he saw a catafalque on which rested a corpse in funeral vestments, guarded by soldiers and surrounded by a throng of mournful people. As the face of the corpse was covered, he asked who it was. 'The President', he was told, who had been killed by an assassin.[25]

Less well known is the fact that General Ulysses S. Grant and his wife Julia were supposed to accompany the President to the Ford Theater and sit in his box. That morning Mrs Grant felt a great sense of urgency that she, her husband and their child should leave Washington and return to their home in New Jersey. The General could not leave because he had appointments throughout the day, but Mrs Grant's sense of urgency increased and she kept sending him messages begging him to leave. So great was her insistence that he finally agreed to do so, even though they were due to accompany the President to the theatre. When they reached Philadelphia, they heard the news about the assassination, and later learned that they were on the assassin's list of intended victims.[26]

Of course, not all precognitions are as dramatic as this, nor do they necessarily involve danger. And many pass unnoticed, especially when they occur in dreams. Precognitive dreams are surprisingly common. The classic book on this subject, *An Experiment With Time*, by the British engineer J.W. Dunne, contains simple instructions that enable readers to investigate their own dreams.[27]

There is also some impressive evidence for presentiment from laboratory experiments by parapsychologists, including some fascinating studies recently carried out at the University of Nevada by Dean Radin. In these experiments, people were shown a series of pictures on a computer screen, most of which were emotionally calming, such as photographs of landscapes, nature scenes and cheerful people. But some were emotionally arousing, including pornographic pictures and pictures of corpses. In each trial, the computer screen was blank to start with. Then one of these images, calm or emotional, appeared on the screen for three seconds. The screen then went blank again. The sequence in which the pictures were shown was randomly determined by the computer itself. While these tests were going on, the participants' blood pressure, skin resistance and blood volume in the fingertips were monitored. All these changed when people were emotionally aroused, providing an objective measurement of their reactions.

Not surprisingly, there were dramatic changes in all these measures of arousal after the 'emotional' images were shown, and these changes did not occur with the calm images. The remarkable feature of the results is that the arousal began *before* the 'emotional' images appeared on the screen, even though nobody could have known by any normal means which picture was coming next. This anticipation began about four seconds before the emotional pictures appeared. These results are highly significant statistically, and have been replicated independently at a laboratory in Holland.[28]

These remarkable experiments seem to show that even under laboratory conditions there can be presentiments that something emotionally arousing is about to happen, even though this could not have been known by any 'normal' means.

I believe that we stand on the threshold of a new phase of science, of which this kind of research is just one example. Open-minded enquiry into spontaneous human experience, complemented by laboratory research, can help deepen our understanding of human nature. Further research on the unexplained powers of non-human animals can help us to place this understanding in a wider biological and evolutionary context. And precognitions may be able to tell us something very important not only about the nature of life and mind, but also about the nature of time.

PART VII
Conclusions

16

Animal powers and human minds

Animal and human perceptiveness

Many dogs, cats and other pets can pick up people's intentions miles away. They can find their way home over unfamiliar terrain without maps and artificial aids. And they can have forebodings of earthquakes and provide warnings, even though most humans feel nothing and have no idea when an earthquake will strike.

Of course, not all animals are equally perceptive, and some species are more so than others. Just as species differ in their sense of smell and in other sensory abilities, so they differ in their telepathic perceptiveness, their sense of direction and their ability to feel impending danger.

Most kinds of perceptiveness found in animals also occur in modern people, but to a lesser degree. Why are we so insensitive? Is it because we are human? Perhaps our sensitivity diminished over tens of thousands of years as our brains evolved. Or perhaps the evolution of language has led to a decline in our abilities to communicate telepathically, or to experience forebodings, or to find our way around in unfamiliar places. If so, since all human cultures have language, we would expect human beings in all parts of the world to be less perceptive in these respects than animals such as dogs and wolves.

But perhaps this decline in sensitivity is not so much a feature of our being human or using language, but a more recent phenomenon, a result of civilization, literacy, mechanistic attitudes, or dependence on technology. There seems little doubt that people in traditional, non-industrial communities were often more perceptive than educated people in modern industrial societies.

Many explorers and travellers reported that telepathic communications and the sense of direction were well developed in societies such as those of aborigines in Australia, or the bushmen of the Kalahari.[1] In rural societies in Europe, unexplained forms of perceptiveness were generally recognized, like the 'second sight' of Scottish highlanders[2] and the ability of people in rural Norway to anticipate arrivals by hearing the *vardøger* of a person on the way to their home (p. 67-68). In non-Western civilizations, such as India, such forms of perceptiveness are still widely taken for granted.

Even in modern societies, there may be differences in perceptiveness between different kinds of people: on average, children may be more sensitive to telepathic influences than adults, and women more than men.[3] On the other hand, men may be more sensitive than women in their sense of direction.[4]

Whether or not people in traditional societies are less perceptive than animals, human and non-human perceptiveness do not exist in isolation from each other. People and domesticated animals have lived together for many thousands of years. People relied on dogs' warnings long before the invention of agriculture. And even before the domestication of dogs, countless generations of our hunter-gatherer ancestors survived by paying close attention to the behaviour of wild animals.

A symbiosis has developed between human and animal perceptiveness, and our ancestors may have made up for any deficiencies in their own sensitivity by relying on that of the animals around them. We can still do so today.

Animal perceptiveness and psychical research

Curiously enough, the unexplained perceptiveness of animals has been ignored not only by mainstream scientists, but also by most psychical researchers and parapsychologists.[5] Why?

The main reason seems to be historical. The scientific investigation of telepathy and other psychical phenomena began in the late nineteenth century, when the pioneers of psychical research hoped to investigate scientifically the question of the conscious survival of bodily death. Telepathy was of interest for the light it shed on the nature of the human soul. In this context, psychic phenomena were seen as peculiarly human, rather than as part of our biological heritage.

The Society for Psychical Research was founded in Britain in 1882 'to examine without prejudice or prepossession and in a scientific spirit those faculties of man, real or supposed, which appear to be inexplicable on any generally recognized hypothesis'. There is nothing here to deny the existence of such faculties in non-human animals. But the focus is explicitly on the 'faculties of man'. The same human-centredness characterizes parapsychology.

Psychical research and parapsychology are usually treated as of no importance, or at best of marginal significance, for the mainstream of science. The situation changes radically if telepathy and other unexplained faculties are seen as being not specifically human, but part of our biological nature. Then we can recognize that human telepathy is rooted in the bonds that coordinate members of animal societies. The human sense of direction is derived from the ability of animals to find their way home after foraging and exploring. And human premonitions are closely related to forebodings in many other species. Psychical research and parapsychology can at last be linked up with biology, and the phenomena they study can be seen in an evolutionary perspective.

The power of intention

Human intentions can bring about effects at a distance in a variety of ways: a dog can pick up its owner's intention to come home from many miles away; a cat can respond to its owner's silent call; and a person can feel the intention of someone to call by telephone. Likewise, animals' intentions can affect people to whom they are bonded, as when cats in distress call their owners to the rescue. And animals' intentions can also affect other animals. All these kinds of intention can work telepathically through morphic fields.

But what if an animal's intentions are directed towards an inanimate object, rather than a member of its social group? If its intentions could influence such an object at a distance, without any known forms of physical contact, then this would be an example of *psychokinesis*, the name given by parapsychologists to the action of mind on matter.

In some astonishing experiments with young chicks, the French researcher René Peoc'h has demonstrated just such an effect. His experiments involved young chicks bonding to a machine instead of their mother.

Newly hatched chicks, like newly hatched ducklings and goslings, 'imprint' on the first moving object they encounter and follow it around. Under normal circumstances, this imprinting instinct causes them to bond with their mother, but if the eggs are hatched in an incubator and young birds first meet a person, then they will follow that person around instead. In laboratory experiments they can even be induced to imprint on moving balloons or other inanimate objects.

In his experiments, Peoc'h used a small robot that moved around on wheels in a series of random directions. At the end of each movement, it stopped, rotated through a randomly selected angle, and moved in a straight line for a randomly determined period before stopping and rotating again, and so on. These random movements were determined by a random-number generator inside the robot. The path it traced out was recorded. In control experiments, its movements were indeed random.

Peoc'h exposed newly hatched chicks to this robot, and they imprinted on this machine as if it were their mother. Consequently they wanted to follow it around, but Peoc'h stopped them doing so by putting them in a cage from which they could see the robot. They could not move towards it; instead, the chicks made the robot move towards themselves (Figure 16.1). Their desire to be near the robot somehow influenced the random-number generator so that the robot stayed close to the cage.[6]

Chicks that were not imprinted on the robot had no such effect on its movement.

In other experiments, Peoc'h kept non-imprinted chicks in the dark. He put a lighted candle on the top of the robot, and put the chicks in the cage where they could see it. Chicks prefer being in the light during the daytime, and they 'pulled' the robot towards them, so that they received more light.[7]

Peoc'h also carried out experiments in which rabbits were put in a cage where they could see the robot. At first they were frightened of it, and the robot moved away from them; they repelled it. But rabbits exposed to the robot daily for several weeks were no longer afraid of it and tended to pull it towards themselves.[8]

Thus the desire or fear of these animals influenced 'random' events at a distance so as to attract or repel the robot. This would obviously not be possible if animals' desires and fears were confined to the inside of their brains. Instead, their intentions reached out to affect the behaviour of this machine.

I interpret this influence in terms of a morphic field that projects out to the focus of their attention, connecting them to it. Just as a field of intention can affect people or animals at a distance, so it can affect a physical system. In one case, intention has effects at a distance, mediated by fields, on brains. In the other case, intention has effects, mediated by fields, on random events within machines.

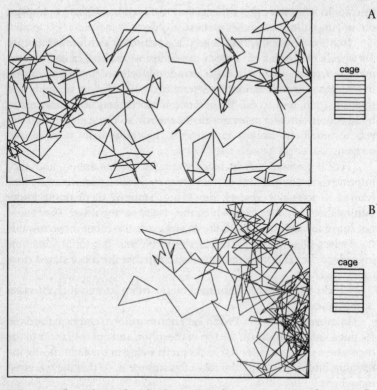

Figure 16.1 The path traced out by the moving robot in experiments of René Peoc'h. A: A control experiment in which the cage was empty. B: An experiment in which day-old chicks imprinted on the robot were kept in the cage (reproduced by courtesy of René Peoc'h).

As far as I know, no one has yet repeated Peoc'h's experiments. It is possible that they involve some technical flaw that no one has yet spotted. But if they are reliable and repeatable, then they are very important indeed. If I were an entrepreneur, I would propose to Peoc'h that his robots be mass produced and marketed through toy stores as well as scientific equipment companies. It would be fascinating to be able to do these experiments at home or in schools, as well as in research laboratories, testing out animals' and people's abilities to influence the activity of the robot, willing it to move one way or another. It would even be possible to stage psychokinetic contests in which one contestant or team wills the robot to move one way, and the other wills it to move in the opposite direction: a battle of wills in the form of a game.

There is already good evidence from experiments at Princeton and other universities that people can indeed bring about 'mind over matter' effects at a distance on random-event generators linked to computers. These devices produce the equivalent of electronic 'heads' and 'tails' in a random sequence, like tossing a coin. Participants are asked to try and influence the system so that, in a given period, there are more 'heads' than 'tails', or more 'tails' than 'heads'. These experiments have given highly significant and repeatable positive results. People really can influence chance events at a distance in accordance with their intention, and some people are better at it than others.[9]

Peoc'h's pioneering experiments imply that animals, both domesticated and wild, may well affect what happens around them through their fears and desires. But no one knows how great the power of animal intention may be. Nor do we know how great is the power of our own.[10]

The feeling of being stared at

Intentions reaching out beyond the brain may also give rise to the feeling of being looked at.

Many pet owners have told me that they can attract the attention of their animal by looking at it. If it is asleep they can even wake it up by their gaze. Some also say that they can feel when their animal is looking at them. A recent survey in the United States has shown that these experiences are quite common among both children and adults, with over a third claiming that they could feel the stare of an animal, and over half claiming that animals could feel their stare.[11]

But this phenomenon is not confined to gazes between humans and animals. Most people have, on occasion, felt other people looking at them from behind, and most have also looked at others from behind and found that they turn around. Surveys show that between 75 per cent and 97 per cent of Americans and Europeans say they have experienced the feeling of being looked at from behind.[12]

All around the world, there is much folklore about the power of looks. On the positive side, in India people will travel hundreds of miles for the blessings conferred by the look, the *darshan*, of a holy man or woman. On the negative side, there is the belief that a look of anger or envy can blight what it falls upon. In English this is called the 'evil eye', and there are equivalent terms in many other languages. Throughout the world, people take protective measures against the evil eye through prayers, charms, talismans and amulets.[13] The idea that a malign glance can do grievous harm to person and property is of great antiquity, and is mentioned in the Bible, as well as in Sumerian and other ancient near-eastern texts.[14]

Precisely because such beliefs are so common, most scientists treat them as superstitions, unworthy of serious consideration. They are denied or dismissed.

Nevertheless, it is possible to investigate the feeling of being stared at by means of simple, inexpensive experiments, as I showed in my book *Seven Experiments That Could Change the World*.[15]

In these experiments, people work in pairs, one person wearing a blindfold and sitting with their back to the other. The other person either looks at the back of the subject's neck or looks away. In a series of trials the sequence of 'looking' and 'not looking' periods is randomized. In each trial, the person wearing the blindfold has to guess whether he or she is being looked at or not. The guess is either right or wrong; and the scores are recorded. (Those interested in carrying out such experiments for themselves can find detailed instructions on my world wide web site: www.sheldrake.org)

To date, over 20,000 trials have been carried out to test for the reality of the feeling of being looked at. The results are overwhelmingly positive and highly significant statistically[16] (Figure 16.2). Far from being a superstition, this seems to be a real effect. These experiments confirm that most people are sensitive to gazes from behind.

Staring experiments have also been carried out through closed circuit television. In these tests the skin resistance of the subjects was monitored, as in a lie-detector test, in such a way that emotional changes could be measured electrically. People's skin resistance changed significantly when they were being looked at on a TV monitor by someone in another room, even though they had no conscious awareness of it.[17]

What these experiments show is that just looking at someone can have an effect. The mind seems capable of reaching out to influence what is at its focus of attention. Vision seems to involve a two-way process: the inward movement of light into the eye, and the outward projection of an influence that connects the looker to that which is looked at.

If something moves outwards during vision, then what could this be? I suggest that the perceiver is connected to the object of perception through a *perceptual field*. The perceptual field is linked to the activity of the brain, but it is not confined to the brain. It stretches out far beyond the body to embrace whatever is being perceived. This field is a kind of morphic field (see Appendix C).

Through perceptual fields, people and animals are connected to the objects of their attention. Indeed, the very word *attention* implies such a process. Its Latin roots have the meaning of stretching the mind towards

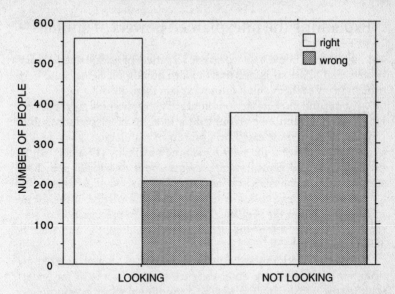

Figure 16.2 Results of experiments on the feeling of being stared at carried out with a total of 900 subjects. The figures shown represent the number of people whose guesses were more often right than wrong ('right') and those who were more often wrong than right ('wrong'). (The people with an equal number of right and wrong guesses are not included in this analysis.) The results shown are for 'looking' trials, when people were being looked at from behind and for control 'not looking' trials, when they were not. In the 'looking' trials many more people were right than wrong, and this effect was highly significant statistically ($p<10^{-37}$). In the 'not looking' trials there was no significant difference. These results show that the sense of being stared at works when people are in fact being stared at. In the control trials, when people are not being looked, they are being asked to detect the *absence* of an effect, and in this very artificial situation they were just guessing, with results no better than chance (Sheldrake, 1999).

something: *ad* = towards and *tendere* = to stretch. It is closely related to the world *intention*, which means to stretch the mind *into* something.

The feeling of being looked at is unlikely to be confined to humans and companion animals. Wild animals may well be able to feel the looks of other animals, both of their own kind and also the more dangerous looks of strangers and potential predators.

If prey animals can feel when a hidden predator is looking at them, this would probably be of great survival value. Natural selection, consequently, would favour the development of the feeling of being looked at. But nothing is yet known about the evolution of sensitivity to looks, nor about the natural history of this phenomenon in the wild.

Explaining the unexplained powers of animals

Throughout this book, I have discussed a variety of unexplained animal powers, and I have suggested that the idea of morphic fields could help explain many of them. But it cannot explain them all.[18]

For me, the most mysterious kinds of perceptiveness are those premonitions that cannot be accounted for in terms of telepathy or subtle physical clues. In these cases, by a process of elimination, precognition or presentiment seem the only remaining possibility (Chapter 15). In precognitions and presentiments, events about to happen somehow seem to influence animals now, and alert them to potential danger.

I do not pretend to know how animals' knowledge of the future might work. But at the very least, the existence of precognition or presentiment implies a blurring of what is happening now and what is about to happen.

There is a continuity between past, present and future, as we know from our own experience, and as science assumes as a basis for understanding the course of nature. But the conventional scientific assumption is that influences work only from the past. Causes precede effects. Energy and causation flow from past to present, and from present to future. There is supposed to be no flow of influence in the reverse direction.

The existence of precognition would imply that the conventional assumption is wrong, with huge implications for our understanding of mind, time and causation.[19]

One way of thinking about precognition is to suppose that there are time-reversed information flows. An alternative is to re-examine our normal concept of the present. Perhaps this is too limited. What we call 'now' is a moment that has a certain 'thickness' in the space-time continuum, some fraction of a second. But what we consciously experience as 'now' may be much shorter than what unconscious parts of ourselves experience as 'now'.[20] In the experiments of Dean Radin, people became physiologically aroused a few seconds *before* they saw an emotionally stimulating image (p. 223), suggesting that the present may indeed be thicker than our conscious awareness.

There are big issues at stake, and there is much we do not know. In order to understand more about the way forebodings and precognitions might work, I believe we need to start from a better documented natural history of animal and human premonitions. The research so far is only preliminary. In Appendix A, I suggest ways in which readers can contribute to this ongoing investigation.

Invisible interconnections

The development of science has involved the progressive recognition of invisible interconnections between things that are separated from each other in space or space-time. The concept of morphic fields takes this process further.

Modern science began in the seventeenth century with a grand vision of universal interrelationship. According to Isaac Newton's theory of gravitation, the Earth attracts the Moon through empty space, and the Moon attracts the Earth, as revealed by its influence on the tides. Likewise, the Sun attracts the Earth, and the Earth attracts the Sun. Indeed every material body in the universe attracts every other body: everything is interconnected.

Then there are the magnetic fields of the Earth, the Sun and all other magnetic bodies, stretching out far beyond the material bodies themselves. Look at a compass when you are flying in a plane at 30,000 feet and it will still point North. The magnetic field of the Earth pervades the space around it.

Radiation travels to Earth from distant galaxies through electromagnetic fields extending over billions of light years. On Earth, electromagnetic fields can connect us invisibly to events in distant places, as our experience of radio, television and mobile telephones continually reminds us. The room you are in is full of radiations from thousands of radio and television transmitters. You are surrounded by vast amounts of invisible information, whether you have a receiver that can tune into it or not.

All these kinds of interconnection are now beyond dispute. They are the basis of the modern technologies on which we all depend. We take them for granted. It is easy to forget that they would have been inconceivable only a few generations ago. Who could have imagined television in the eighteenth century, or the world wide web? But physics has already gone further.

According to quantum theory, there is an inevitable linkage between the observer and that which is observed, breaking down the sharp separation between subject and object. Scientists are no longer detached observers, seeing reality as it were through a plate-glass window. They participate in the reality they are studying. 'We can no longer maintain the old Cartesian view that we can observe Nature like a bird-watcher with a perfect hide. There is an unbreakable connection between the observer and the observed.' (John Barrow[21])

Even more surprisingly, according to quantum physics, particles that come from a common source, like two photons of light emitted from the same atom, retain a mysterious interconnection such that what happens to one is instantaneously reflected in the other. This is known as 'non-locality' or 'non-separability' or 'entanglement', and is also referred to as the Einstein-Podolsky-Rosen paradox, or as Bell's inequality. No one knows how far this process extends, or how extensive is this instantaneous interconnectedness. Some physicists speculate that everything in the Universe is interconnected through quantum non-locality:

> Once two particles have interacted with one another they remain linked in some way, effectively parts of the same indivisible system. This property of 'nonlocality' has sweeping implications. We can think of the Universe as a vast network of interacting particles, and each linkage binds the participating particles into a single quantum system. (Paul Davies and John Gribbin[22])

Morphic fields

Morphic fields also connect together parts of a system that are seemingly separated, although no one yet knows how they are related to quantum nonlocality. These fields are the basis of interconnections not only in space but in time.

A wide range of unexplained powers of animals might be explicable in terms of morphic fields:

- Morphic fields link together members of social groups and can continue to connect them even when they are far apart (Figure 1.5). These invisible bonds act as channels for telepathic communication between animals and animals, people and animals, and people and people (Chapters 2–4 and 7–9).
- These links, acting like invisible elastic bands, also underlie the sense of direction that enables animals and people to find each other (Chapter 13).
- Animals 'imprinted' on their home environment or on other significant places are linked to these places by morphic fields. Through these connections, they can be pulled or attracted back towards familiar places, enabling them to navigate across unfamiliar terrain. The sense of direction given by these morphic fields underlies both homing and migration (Chapters 10–12).
- Morphic fields link animals to the objects of their intentions, and could help to explain psychokinetic phenomena.

- Morphic fields link animals to the objects of their attention, and through these perceptual fields animals can influence what they are looking at. These fields underlie the sense of being stared at.

Thus the idea of morphic fields may be capable of giving a unified explanation to a wide range of seemingly disparate phenomena.

Other people may prefer to call these fields by different names, or to use words like 'system' or 'interrelationship' instead of the word field. But whatever such interconnections are called, I expect that they will have to have most of the properties I attribute to morphic fields, discussed in more detail in Appendix C.

Learning from our animals

Whatever explanations turn out to be the best, there is no doubt that we have much to learn from our dogs, cats, horses, parrots, pigeons and other domesticated animals. They have much to teach us about social bonds and animal perceptiveness, and much to teach us about ourselves.

The evidence I have been discussing in this book suggests that our own intentions, desires and fears are not just confined to our heads, or communicated only through words and behaviour. We can influence animals and affect other people at a distance. We remain interconnected with animals and people we are 'close' to, even when we are far away. We can affect people and animals by the way we look at them, even if they do not know we are there. We can retain a connection with our homes, however distant we are in a geographical sense. And we can be influenced by things that are about to happen in ways that defy our normal notions of causality.

We are on the threshold of a new understanding of the nature of minds.

Appendices

APPENDIX A

How to take part in research

There are few fields of science today where non-professionals can do exciting, hands-on research, whether they are students or adults. But most of the subjects covered in this book have been neglected by professional scientists. With a few notable exceptions,[1] they have also been ignored by psychical researchers, parapsychologists and veterinarians. The result is that this is an extraordinarily underdeveloped field of study. It is at the stage that many fields of science were in long ago, for example the study of magnetism in the early seventeenth century; fossils in the eighteenth century; genetics at the time of Mendel; or molecular biology in the 1950s.

Precisely because this is a field of enquiry in its infancy, there are remarkable opportunities for original, trailblazing investigations. For pioneering studies with pets, not much more than a notebook and pencil are needed. For more sophisticated research, video cameras and computers are very helpful, but these sophisticated technologies are now widely and inexpensively available.

Because the early stages of this research can be carried out on shoe-string budgets, there is no need for massive government funding, or indeed for any government funding at all. So far, there is no bureaucracy in charge of this research. The field is wide open. Such freedom in science is rare, and such periods do not last long.

The research described in this book is a preliminary attempt to chart the natural history of this almost unexplored field. There are several ways in which readers with experience of animals can take part in this enquiry. Those without animals can also make valuable contributions, as described below.

Please send me material concerning any of these areas of research to one of the addresses given at the end of this appendix.

Write about your own experiences with animals

If you have noticed any behaviour by your animals that you think would contribute to this ongoing research programme, please write about it. There is no need to write this account in any special format. An ordinary letter or e-mail will suffice, but please be sure to give your address and telephone number, so that I and my colleagues can contact you if we have any queries or need to ask for more details.

In particular, we are keen to know more about:

- Seemingly telepathic responses by camels, elephants, falcons and other animals not discussed in this book
- Any signs of uncanny behaviour by reptiles, amphibia, fish, or insects and other invertebrates
- Animals' sense of direction
- Pets finding their owners far away from home
- The feeling of being stared at by animals
- Animals feeling when they are being looked at
- Warnings of impending epileptic fits
- Warnings of impending disasters or deaths
- The sensing of danger
- Unusual behaviour prior to earthquakes

Write about your own experience

Most of the unexplained animal powers I have discussed in this book also occur in human beings, but almost nothing seems to be known about their natural history in the human realm. I would particularly like to hear about personal experiences of:

- Nursing mothers whose milk starts to flow when their baby needs to be fed, even if they are miles away
- The feeling of being looked at
- The ability to make others turn around by looking
- An unusual ability to find other people
- A well-developed sense of direction
- Premonitions of earthquakes and other disasters

Keep a log of your animal's behaviour

If your animal seems to react telepathically to your own or other people's intentions, or if it shows any other signs of uncanny perceptiveness, you can make a valuable contribution to this research by keeping a log. The simplest way to do this is to keep a special notebook for this purpose.

Note down the date and time at which your animal shows the response and also record all relevant information about the person or circumstances it is reacting to. For example, if it is responding to a person coming home, then the time at which they arrive should be noted, as should the time at which they set off, their mode of transport, whether or not they were coming at a routine time, and whether or not the people at home knew when to expect them. If the animal fails to respond, this should also be recorded.

The longer such logs are maintained and the greater the detail they contain, the more useful they are.

Build up your own database

My appeals for information from animal owners have mostly taken place in Britain, Ireland, France, the German-speaking countries and the United States. There is much scope for collecting information in other parts of the world, for example in Eastern Europe, Africa, Asia and South America, where people may well have a different range of experiences to report. Appeals can be made through newspapers, magazines and radio and TV stations. Some readers may also be able to investigate particular kinds of animal, for example parrots or ferrets, through specialist magazines, newsletters and clubs.

It is important to organize any collection of accounts in a systematic way so that the accounts can be retrieved, reviewed and compared, and for this purpose a computerized database is invaluable. You may want to set up your own database in your own format, but if you would like to follow the format I use myself, you can obtain the details through my world wide web site, www.sheldrake.org. If you use the same format as I do, this will facilitate the eventual merging of databases from different parts of the world, providing a major resource for future research.

Carry out your own survey of perceptive pets

The only random surveys of perceptive pets I know of are the four described in this book, carried out in England and California by myself and my colleagues. No one knows what patterns of results will be found in other places, and there is great potential for more surveys of this kind. If you follow the same procedure we have used, it will be possible to make direct comparisons of the responses. The details of our own surveys have been published in scientific journals,[2] and are also available on my web site.

Carry out experiments with your animals

Throughout this book, and especially in Chapter 2 and Appendix B, I have given examples of experiments with animals designed to find out whether their perceptive behaviour can be explained in terms of habit, routine and normal sensory information, or whether some other form of communication was involved. More experiments with dogs, cats, parrots, horses and other animals would be very desirable.

Such experiments need not necessarily be videotaped, but it is better if they are. The video provides an objective, time-coded record of the animal's behaviour which can be independently evaluated by a third party. It also provides far more detail than can be recorded by a human observer with a notebook.

You can base your experiments and data analysis on the methods used by myself and my colleagues. The details have been published in scientific journals[3] and are also available on my web site. Alternatively, you may want to develop your own methods and procedures.

Do research on the feeling of being stared at

In my book *Seven Experiments That Could Change the World*.[4] I outlined a simple experiment that people could do working in pairs, one of them sitting behind the other. In a series of trials, the 'looker' either looks at the back of the subject, or looks away and thinks of something else. I have developed new versions of this basic experiment, and have adapted the procedure for use in schools. Many experiments have already been carried out in schools in Britain, the United States and Germany.[5] The full instructions, including randomized score sheets, can be downloaded from my world wide web site, www.sheldrake.org

Study telepathic telephone calls

If you find that you often know when particular people are calling, then you can do research on this phenomenon by keeping a log of your intuitions. The simplest way to do this is to keep a log book by the telephone. (Of course, any electronic device that displays the telephone number of the caller should be switched off or put out of sight.) Every time you feel you know who is calling, write their name down in the log book before answering. Then after the call is over, make sure the date and time are filled in, and record whether your guess was right or wrong. Also note down whether the call was expected or not. This way you will be able to find out how often your intuitions were right or wrong.

If you are often right about particular people calling at unexpected times, then the next stage is to carry out simple experiments in which they are asked to call at times selected at random by procedures such as the throw of dice, or by an electronic random number generator. How often are you successful under these more rigorous conditions?

Addresses

You can write to me by post at either of the following addresses:

BM Experiments
London WC1N 3XX
England

The Institute of Noetic Sciences
475 Gate Five Road, Suite 300
Sausalito
CA 94965
USA

You can also communicate by e-mail via my world wide web site, www.sheldrake.org

APPENDIX B

Experiments with Jaytee

In Chapter 2, I summarized the main features of the many videotaped experiments carried out with the dog Jaytee, to study his behaviour when his owner, Pam Smart, was out and when she was on her way home. In these experiments, the video camera, mounted on a tripod, was switched on by Pam herself before she went out and the camera continuously filmed the area where Jaytee usually waited when she was coming home. Using a 120-minute film and the long play setting on the camera, up to 240 minutes of continuous filming were possible. In all experiments the timecode was recorded on the videotape, enabling Jaytee's behaviour to be timed to the nearest second.

Most of the experiments were carried out in the flat belonging to Pam's parents, adjacent to her own flat, in Ramsbottom, Greater Manchester. This is where she usually leaves Jaytee when she is out. Additional videotaped experiments, described below, were carried out with Jaytee left on his own in Pam's flat and in Pam's sister's house. In these experiments, when Pam went out she travelled from 4.5 to 14 miles away.

The videotapes were analyzed by writing down when Jaytee was in the target area near the window, and notes were made on his activities there: for example if he was barking at a passing cat, sleeping in the sun or sitting looking out of the window. These analyses were carried out by Pam herself and also carried out 'blind' by myself, Jane Turney or Dr Amanda Jacks, without our knowing any details of when Pam set off to come home or how long her journey took. These details were recorded separately by Pam. A comparison of the analyses by Pam herself and those carried out blind by others showed a remarkable agreement, with occasional differences of only a second or two. These slight differences had no significant effect on the overall results.

For the quantitative analysis of the data, all periods when Jaytee was present by the window were included, even if he was simply sleeping in the sun or barking at passing cats, as well as when he was showing his usual waiting behaviour. In this way any selective use of data was avoided, although the data were 'noisier' because they included visits to the window that had nothing to do with Pam's returns.

Analysis of data

I use two main ways of analyzing the data statistically. The first provides a simple way of comparing different experiments. For each experiment, the percentage of the time that Jaytee spends by the window is calculated for three periods:

1   The first ten minutes of Pam's journey home (the 'return period'). Only experiments with homeward journeys that lasted at least 13 minutes were included, and only the first ten minutes of her homeward journey was counted. Thus Jaytee's reactions when Pam was nearing home were disregarded, in case he could have been responding to the sounds of her car approaching. In fact most journey-times were more than 15 minutes long, so over five minutes of Jaytee's behaviour was excluded. For this statistical analysis, only the first ten minutes of the journey counted.
2   The ten-minute period prior to Pam's return (the 'pre-return' period).
3   The time when Pam was absent prior to the pre-return period (the 'main period'). This period varied in length from 60 to 200 minutes.

Examples of data analyzed in this way can be seen in Figure B.1.

Figure B.1 Jaytee's reactions to Pam's returns at times of her own choosing. The bars show the percentage of the time that Jaytee spent by the window during the main period of Pam's absence ('main period'), during the ten minutes prior to her setting off to come home ('pre-return') and during the first ten minutes of her journey home ('return'). (The standard error of each average is indicated by the bar at the top.) The data are from the same 30 experiments summarized in Figure 2.3A, but enable comparisons to be made as follows:

A: Experiments in the daytime (7) and in the evening (23).
B: 'Normal' experiments (23) and 'noisy' experiments (7), in which Jaytee was at the window for more than 15 per cent of the time in the main period of Pam's absence.
C: The first, second and third groups of ten experiments.
D: Long (13), medium (9) and short (8) experiments.

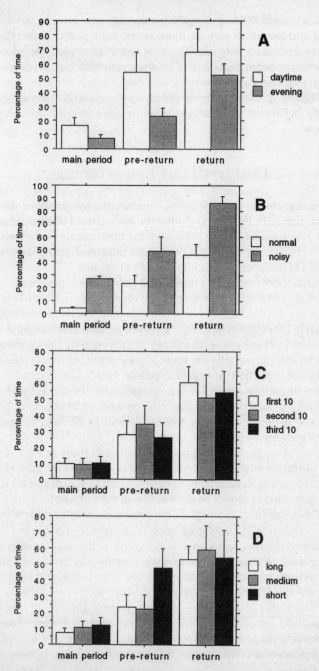

The second method of analyzing the data also involves ten-minute return and pre-return periods, but now the main period is also divided up into ten-minute intervals. The time Jaytee spent by the window, for whatever reason, in each of these ten-minute periods can then be plotted on a graph, as in Figure 2.4.

Neither of these methods depends on a subjective assessment of Jaytee's behaviour. They simply quantify how long he spent by the window.

Thirty ordinary homecomings

The average results from 30 ordinary homecomings at various times of day are shown in Figure 2.4. During the main period of Pam's absence, Jaytee was at the window 9 per cent of the time; during the ten minutes prior to her setting off, 29 per cent of the time, and during the first ten minutes of her return journey 55 per cent of the time.

A number of interesting details are hidden by this averaging process. First of all, although Jaytee spent more time at the window when Pam was on her way home on 24 occasions, on six occasions he did not. On five (all in the evening) he did not go to the window at all during the first ten minutes of her homeward journey. On the sixth (in the morning) he did so for only 10 seconds. On some of these occasions he was unusually inactive, and may have been exhausted after long walks, or sick. But irrespective of the reasons for his unresponsiveness, the fact is that he did not show his usual signs of anticipation on 6 out of 30 occasions. But on 24 out of 30 occasions, 80 per cent of the time, he *did* show this pattern of anticipation.

Second, in the daytime Jaytee was generally more active and alert than in the evening, and on average was at the window more (Figure B.1A). There was more activity outside for him to watch, and on sunny days, he tended to snooze by the window in the sunlight'

Third, the effect of 'noise' on the pattern of Jaytee's response can be examined directly by comparing 'noisy' experiments with the rest (Figure B.1B). By definition, Jaytee spends more time at the window during the main period of Pam's absence in noisy experiments. But he was still at the window more when she was preparing to go home, and most of all when she was actually on her way.

Fourth, the question of whether Jaytee's pattern of response changed with time can be examined by comparing the average of the first ten experiments (from May to September 1995) with the second and third batches of ten experiments (from September 1995 to January 1996, and from January to July, 1996, respectively). The pattern was similar in all three groups (Figure B.1C).

Finally, the length of time that Pam was away from home varied considerably. Did Jaytee behave in a similar way when she returned after short absences and after longer ones? To explore this question, I have divided the data up into three groups, long, medium and short absences[1] (Figure B.1D). The general pattern was similar, but in the short absences the experiments were noisier, and Jaytee showed more anticipation in the ten-minute period prior to Pam setting off.

One possibility is that Jaytee may simply have stayed more at the window the longer Pam was out. If so, he would automatically be at the window most in the period when she was returning, but not because of any psychic powers. The data in Figure 2.4 enable us to explore this possibility by looking at the time-courses of Jaytee's behaviour during short, medium and long absences by Pam. They do not support it. With short absences, Jaytee was at the window most during period 8, when Pam was on her way home, but there was no comparable increase in time at the window in the same period 8 of the medium and long absences. Likewise, the increased time at the window when Pam is on the way home during period 11 of medium absences does not show up in period 11 of the long absences. These differences were statistically very significant. (For period 8, when Pam was returning in the short experiments, Jaytee was at the window a very significantly higher proportion of the time than in period 8 of the medium and long duration experiments ($p=0.004$[2]). For period 11, Jaytee was at the window very significantly more in the medium-length experiments, when Pam was actually returning, than in the long experiments, in which she would not be returning for more than another hour ($p= 0.003$ [3])).

We also made a series of videotapes on evenings when Pam was not coming home until very late, or staying out for the night. These serve as controls or checks, and show that Jaytee did not to go the window more and more as the evening went on. (Figure B.2).

Videotaped experiments with randomly selected return times

The results of these experiments are shown in Figure 2.3. When Pam returned at randomly selected return times, in response to a telephone bleep from me, Jaytee was usually at the window far more of the time during her return journey than he was before she set off. This shows that his response to her coming home could not be explained in terms of

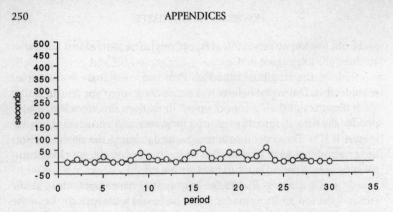

Figure B.2 Time spent by Jaytee at the window on evenings when Pam was not coming home. The first of the 30 ten-minute periods is from 5.50 to 6.00 pm, the last from 10.40 to 10.50 pm. The figures shown are averages from 10 evenings.

routine, or in terms of her parents knowing when she was coming and somehow passing on this expectation to Jaytee.

But there is a puzzling feature of these results. On some occasions, Jaytee started waiting at the window in the ten-minute period *before* Pam received the bleep. How could he have anticipated when I was going to bleep her?

It is conceivable that Jaytee was telepathically picking up my intention to bleep Pam from over 200 miles away. But I do not take this possibility very seriously. On one occasion[4] the bleeping was done not by myself but by someone neither Pam nor Jaytee had met, and Jaytee still responded in advance. It is also conceivable that Jaytee had a precognition of when Pam would be bleeped. But there may be a simpler explanation in terms of telepathy between Pam and Jaytee.

In all these experiments, Pam knew that she would be bleeped to come home within a particular time period. Ideally, her mind would have been entirely engaged with other concerns until the bleep came. But inevitably she was sometimes thinking about the signal to go home before it came, especially if it came towards the end of the time-window. She says that thoughts like 'It won't be long now' or 'I'll be setting off soon' were sometimes unavoidable. Jaytee may well have been picking up these anticipatory thoughts of hers, just as he seemed to respond to a fully-formed intention to go home.

A similar anticipation of Pam's setting off occurred in the experiments conducted by Richard Wiseman and Matthew Smith (Figure 2.5). Here again, Jaytee's anticipation may well have taken place in response to Pam's. She tells me that while she was with Matthew Smith, waiting for him to tell her when the randomly selected time came for them to return, it was impossible not to think about going home. Moreover, Matthew Smith himself knew when they were going to set off and he could well have communicated his anticipation to Pam unconsciously, for example through an increasing tenseness as the crucial moment approached.

If Jaytee was indeed responding to Pam's expectation that she would soon be receiving the signal to return, then this anticipatory effect would be expected to show up more when the bleep came towards the end of the 'window' period than at the beginning. To test this idea, I have compared the experiments in which Pam was bleeped early compared with those in which she was bleeped late (Figure B.3). There was indeed a difference, with less anticipation by Jaytee before early bleeps.

The numbers in Figure B.3 are averages, which of course mask differences between individual experiments. The results from each of the 12 bleeper trials are shown in Figure B.4 so that the patterns can be seen in detail. Of course there is much variation from trial to trial. But the patterns in the 'early bleep' and 'late bleep' trials look different. In four out of six of the 'early bleep' trials, Jaytee did not show any anticipation prior to Pam setting off. By contrast, there were signs of anticipation in all but one of the 'late bleep' trials. The exception was a trial in which Jaytee did not go to the window at all throughout the entire experiment.[5]

Thus Jaytee's anticipation of the bleep signalling Pam's return seems to be related to Pam's own anticipation of the bleep, which tended to be greater the later the signal came. This agrees with the idea that Jaytee's responses are telepathic.

Figure B.3 Comparison of the averages of six experiments in which Pam was bleeped to come home at randomly-selected times in the first half of the experimental period ('early bleep') and of six experiments in the second half ('late bleep').

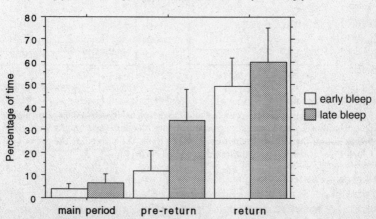

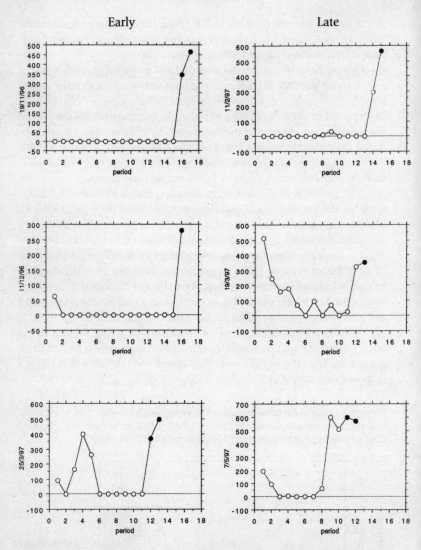

Figure B.4 The detailed time-course of all 12 experiments in which Pam came home at randomly-selected times in response to being bleeped. Experiments with early bleeps are on the left, with late bleeps on the right. The points for the periods in which she was returning are indicated by a filled circle (•).

Early   Late

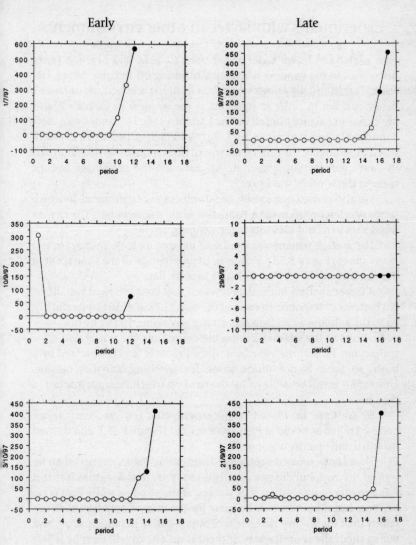

Experiments with Jaytee in other environments

Pam sometimes leaves Jaytee at her sister's house, and here too Jaytee often goes to the window when Pam is setting off to come home. Her sister, Cathie, usually knows when Pam is on her way because of Jaytee's behaviour. But in order to look out of the window in Cathie's house, Jaytee has to balance himself on the back of a sofa. He cannot wait there comfortably, and rarely stays for long. Nevertheless, in a series of video-taped experiments, the general pattern of his response was similar to that in Pam's parents' flat (Figure B.5A), although the percentage of time spent at the window was lower.

We also carried out a series of 50 videotaped experiments in which Jaytee was left on his own in Pam's flat while she went out. The camera was set up to record his visits to the window.

The average pattern was similar to the one we have already seen so many times (Figure B.5B). However, the percentage of the time spent at the window was lower than in Pam's parents' flat.

A closer analysis of the data revealed that Jaytee showed two different patterns of response. In most of the tests (35 out of 50) Jaytee did not go to the window when Pam was on her way home. In fact he made few or no visits to the window during the entire time she was absent. One reason may be that the view from the window is largely obscured by a bush, so there is not much scope for watching activities outside, although it is still possible to see the road on which Pam approaches in her car.

By contrast, in 15 out of 50 experiments (30 per cent), Jaytee behaved much as he did at Pam's parents' flat (Figure B.5C), and showed his usual anticipatory waiting.

Thus Jaytee seemed capable of anticipating Pam's returns when he was on his own, but did not usually do so. Why not? My guess is that it was a matter of motivation. His waiting at the window while Pam is on her homeward journey may be more for the sake of members of Pam's family than for his own sake. He is communicating his anticipation, and telling them she is on the way. If there is no one to tell, then he is less motivated to do it. Nevertheless, he sometimes does it anyway.

Figure B.5 Average results from experiments in which Jaytee was left in Pam's sister's house and alone in Pam's flat.

A: In Pam's sister's house. Average of 5 experiments.

B: Alone in Pam's flat. Average of 50 experiments

C: Alone in Pam's flat. Comparison of averages from 15 'positive' and 35 'negative' experiments.

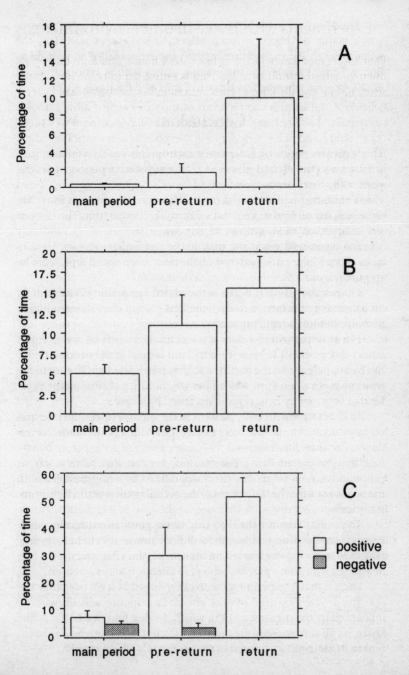

The difference in his behaviour in Pam's own flat and in her parents' was a matter of degree. In both places, he sometimes waited by the window when Pam was returning, and sometimes failed to wait there. But in Pam's parents' flat the waiting to not-waiting ratio was about 80:20, whereas when he was alone in Pam's own flat it was 30:70.

Conclusions

This extensive series of videotaped experiments with Jaytee confirms what Pam's parents had observed informally over a period of several years, and what systematic records of Jaytee's behaviour covering 100 of Pam's absences[6] had already showed. When he was at her parents' flat, Jaytee usually seemed to know when Pam was coming home, even when she returned at varying times of day, when she set off at randomly selected times, and when she travelled in unfamiliar vehicles. He also demonstrated the same pattern of behaviour when tested repeatedly by sceptics (Figure 2.5).

His reactions usually began in the ten-minute period before Pam set off, suggesting that he detected telepathically when she was intending to go home before she actually started her journey.

His anticipatory behaviour was less marked when he was at Pam's sister's flat, probably because he could not see out of the window easily, but had to balance on the back of a sofa. Nevertheless he still went to the window more when Pam was on her way home, and showed the same kind of anticipatory behaviour when tested by sceptics.

In Pam's flat on his own, he went to the window relatively little, and on most occasions did not react to Pam's travelling homewards. Nevertheless, he sometimes showed the same pattern of anticipatory behaviour that he did in Pam's parents' flat. Because this pattern was so pronounced, even when this effect was diluted by being averaged with the occasions when he did not react, the overall result was still significant statistically.

The results support the idea that Jaytee knew telepathically when Pam was coming home, although he did not always react to her returns.[7] He did so least when he was left on his own in Pam's flat, and most when he was left with Pam's parents, who paid attention to his reactions.

I expect that in experiments with other dogs that seem telepathically sensitive to their owners' returns, the dog's response will likewise be influenced by the circumstances in which the dog finds itself. If it is like Jaytee, it will react more in the presence of familiar people who pay attention to its anticipatory behaviour than when it is left on its own.

APPENDIX C

Morphic fields

Throughout this book, I have summarized some of the principal features of morphic fields. In this appendix, I explain this concept in more detail and discuss some of its implications.

My interest in these ideas first developed while I was doing research on the development of plants, at Cambridge University. How do plants grow from simple embryos into the characteristic form of their species? How do the leaves of willows, roses and palms take up their shapes? How do their flowers develop in such different ways? These are all questions to do with what biologists call *morphogenesis*, the coming-into-being of form (Greek: *morphe* = form; *genesis* = coming into being), which is one of the great unsolved problems of biology.

The naive approach to this problem is simply to say that all morphogenesis is genetically programmed. Different species just follow the instructions in their genes. But a few moments' reflection shows that this reply is inadequate. All the cells of the body contain the same genes. In your body, the same genetic programme is present in your eye cells, liver cells, and the cells in your arms and legs. But if they are all programmed identically, then how do they develop so differently?

Some genes code for the sequence of amino acids in proteins; others are involved in the control of protein synthesis. They enable organisms to make particular chemicals. But these alone cannot account for form. Your arms and your legs are chemically identical – if ground up and analyzed biochemically, they would be indistinguishable – but they have different shapes. Something over and above the genes and the proteins they code for is needed to explain their form.

This is easier to understand with the help of an architectural analogy. In a city street, there are buildings of different designs, but what makes them different is not the building materials. They could all be made of chemically identical bricks, concrete, timber and so on. If demolished and analyzed chemically, they might be indistinguishable. What makes them different are the architects' plans according to which they were built. These plans do not show up in any chemical analysis.

Biologists who study the development of form in plants and animals have long been aware of these problems, and since the 1920s many have adopted the idea that developing organisms are shaped by fields called *morphogenetic fields*. These are rather like invisible blueprints that underlie the form of the growing organism. But they are not, of course, designed by an architect, any more than a 'genetic programme' is supposed to be designed by a computer programmer. They are fields: self-organizing regions of influence, analogous to magnetic fields and other recognized fields of nature.

Although the concept of morphogenetic fields is widely accepted within biology, no one knows what these fields are or how they work. Most biologists assume that they will at some time in the future be explained in terms of regular physics and chemistry. But this is no more than an act of faith. After several years of wrestling with the problems of morphogenesis and thinking about morphogenetic fields, I came to the conclusion that these fields were not just a way of talking about standard mechanistic processes, but something really new.

This was the starting point for my own development of the idea of morphogenetic fields, first proposed in my book *A New Science of Life*[1] and further developed in my book *The Presence of the Past*.[2] There are three key features of this concept:

First, morphogenetic fields are a new kind of field, so far unrecognized by physics.

Second, like the organisms they shape, they evolve. They have a history, and contain an inherent memory given by the process I call morphic resonance.

Third, they are part of a larger family of fields called morphic fields.

These principles are the basis of what I call the hypothesis of formative causation.

The hypothesis of formative causation

In this hypothesis, I suggest that in self-organizing systems at all levels of complexity there is a wholeness that depends on a characteristic organizing field of that system, its morphic field. Each self-organizing system is a whole made up of parts, which are themselves wholes at a lower level

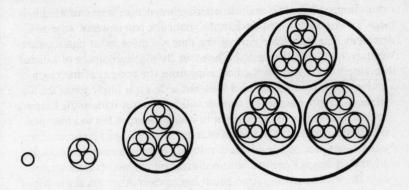

Figure C.1 Successive levels in a nested hierarchy of self-organizing systems. At each level the systems are wholes containing parts, themselves wholes containing lower-level parts. This diagram could represent subatomic particles, in atoms, in molecules, in crystals; or cells, in tissues, in organs, in organisms; or individuals, in family groups, in societies, in ecosystems. At each level the whole is organized by a morphic field.

(Figure C.1). At each level, the morphic field gives each whole its characteristic properties, and makes it more than the sum of its parts.

In plants and animals the fields responsible for the development and maintenance of bodily form are called morphogenetic fields. In the organization of perception, behaviour and mental activity they are called perceptual, behavioural and mental fields. In crystals and molecules they are called crystal and molecular fields. In the organization of societies and cultures they are called social and cultural fields.[3] All these kinds of organizing fields are morphic fields.[4]

Morphic fields, like the already-recognized fields of physics, are regions of influence in space-time, located within and around the systems they organize. They work probabilistically. They restrict, or impose order upon, the inherent indeterminism of the systems under their influence. They embrace and connect together the various parts of the system they are organizing. Thus a crystal field organizes the way in which the molecules and atoms are arranged inside the crystal. A sea-urchin field shapes the cells and tissues within the growing sea-urchin embryo, and guides its development towards the characteristic adult form of the species. A social field organizes and coordinates the behaviour of individuals within the social group, for example the way individual birds fly within a flock.[5]

Morphic fields guide the systems under their influence towards characteristic goals or end-points. The British biologist C.H. Waddington gave the name *chreode* to the canalized pathways of change organized by morphogenetic fields, and visualized chreodes in terms of channels down which balls rolled towards the goal.[6] The ball represents the development of a particular part of the embryo towards its characteristic mature form, for example the heart or liver. Disturbances of normal development may push the ball away from the bottom of the channel and up the side of the channel wall, but unless it is pushed over the top of this wall into another channel, it will find its way back to the bottom of the channel, not to the point from which it started, but to a later position in the canalized pathway of change. This represents embryonic regulation, the process by which a developing organism can reach a normal adult form in spite of disturbances during the process of development.

The mathematician René Thom has made mathematical models of morphogenetic fields in which the end-points towards which systems develop are defined as *attractors*. [7] In the branch of mathematics known as dynamics, attractors represent the limits towards which dynamical systems are drawn. They provide a scientific way of thinking about ends, purposes, goals or intentions.

The most controversial feature of this hypothesis is the proposal that morphic fields themselves evolve. They are not fixed for all time by eternal mathematical equations in some kind of transcendent Platonic realm, or by a read-only program in a cosmic compact disc. Their structure depends on what has happened before. They contain a kind of memory. Through repetition the patterns they organize become increasingly probable, increasingly habitual.

The first field of any given type, say the field of the first insulin crystals, or the field of a new idea, such as Darwin's theory of evolution, comes into being through a creative jump. The source of this evolutionary creativity is unknown. Maybe it is a matter of chance. Maybe it is an expression of some inherent creativity in mind and nature.[8]

Whatever the explanation of its origin, once a new field, a new pattern of organization, has come into being, then through repetition this morphic field becomes stronger. The same pattern becomes more likely to happen again. The more often patterns are repeated, the more probable they become; the fields contain a kind of cumulative memory and become increasingly habitual. Fields evolve in time and form the basis of habits. From this point of view nature is essentially habitual. Even the so-called 'laws of nature' may be more like habits.[9]

The means by which information or an activity-pattern is transferred from a previous to a subsequent system of the same kind is called morphic resonance. Morphic resonance involves the influence of like upon like, the influence of patterns of activity on subsequent similar patterns of activity, an influence that passes through or across space and time. These influences are assumed not to fall off with distance in space or time, but they come only from the past, not the future. The greater the degree of similarity, the greater the influence of morphic resonance.

Morphic resonance is the basis of the inherent memory in fields at all levels of complexity. Any given morphic system, say a giraffe embryo, 'tunes in' to previous similar systems, in this case previous developing giraffes. Through this process each individual giraffe draws upon, and in turn contributes to, a collective or pooled memory of its species. In the human realm, this kind of collective memory is closely related to what the psychologist C.G. Jung called the 'collective unconscious'.

This hypothesis predicts that morphic resonance should be detectable in the realms of physics, chemistry, biology, psychology and the social sciences. However, old-established systems, such as hydrogen atoms, salt crystals and haemoglobin molecules, are governed by such strong morphic fields, such deep habits, that little change can be observed. They behave *as if* they are governed by fixed laws. By contrast, new systems – new crystals, new forms of organism, new patterns of behaviour, new ideas – should show an increasing tendency to come into being the more often they are repeated. They should become increasingly probable, ever more habitual. Morphic resonance involves non-local effects in both space and time.

Here is a summary of the hypothetical properties of morphic fields, as set out in *The Presence of the Past*:[10]

1   They are self-organizing wholes.
2   They have both a spatial and a temporal aspect, and organize spatio-temporal patterns of vibratory or rhythmic activity.
3   They attract the systems under their influence towards characteristic forms and patterns of activity, whose coming-into-being they organize and whose integrity they maintain. The ends or goals towards which morphic fields attract the systems under their influence are called attractors.
4   They interrelate and co-ordinate the morphic units or holons that lie within them, which in turn are organized by morphic fields. Morphic fields contain other morphic fields within them in a nested hierarchy or holarchy.
5   They are structures of probability and their organizing activity is probabilistic.
6   They contain a built-in memory given by self-resonance with a morphic unit's own past and by morphic resonance with all previous similar systems. This memory is cumulative. The more often particular patterns of activity are repeated, the more habitual they become.

In *A New Science of Life* and *The Presence of the Past*, I discussed a variety of experimental tests of morphic resonance. All these tests depended on detecting changes in the ease or probability with which the repeated pattern recurs. In other words, I concentrated on the aspect of the hypothesis of formative causation summarized in point 6 above. I did not at first propose experiments to test the more general aspect of the hypothesis of formative causation, namely the existence of the spatially extended fields themselves, as summarized in points 1–5. That is the question I addressed in my book, *Seven Experiments That Could Change the World*[11] and discuss on pp. 263-264 below.

Connections with quantum physics

Experiments to test for the spatial aspects of morphic fields imply a kind of non-locality that is not at present recognized by institutional science. Nevertheless, it may turn out to be related to the non-locality or non-separability that is an integral part of quantum theory, implying connections or correlations at a distance undreamt of by classical physics. Albert Einstein found the idea of 'spooky action at a distance' implied by quantum theory deeply distasteful; but his worst fears have come true.[12] Recent experimental evidence shows that these connections lie at the heart of physics. Their wider implications are still unclear – they may be related to what I call morphic fields – but no one yet knows.

Non-locality is one of the most surprising and paradoxical aspects of quantum theory in that parts of a quantum system that have been connected together in the past retain an instantaneous connection even when very far apart. For example, two photons, by definition travelling at the speed of light, moving in opposite directions from an atom that has emitted them, retain an immediate non-local connection, such that if the polarization of one is measured, the other will instantly have the opposite polarization, even though the polarization of each particle was not determined until the moment the measurement was taken. This is also called 'quantum entanglement'.

The two parts of the same system separated in space are linked by a quantum field. This is not a field in ordinary space, but is represented mathematically as a multi-dimensional space of possibilities.

Just as in atoms and molecules, the members of social groups are parts of the same system. They share food, breathe the same air, are interlinked through their minds and senses and interact continually. When they are separated, the parts of the social system may retain a non-local or non-separable connectedness comparable to that observed in quantum physics.

If this is the case, then morphic fields could be reinterpreted in terms of quantum theory. This would involve an enormous extension of quantum theory to cover biological and social organization. It may well be a step that physics needs to take.

I discussed with the quantum physicist David Bohm the connection between the idea of morphic fields and his theory of the implicate order, an 'enfolded' order underlying the explicate order, the unfolded world that we experience. His theory, based on the non-separability of quantum systems, turned out to be extraordinarily compatible with my own proposals.[13] These connections have also been explored by the American quantum physicist Amit Goswami[14] and by the German quantum physicist Hans-Peter Dürr.[15]

However, it is also possible that morphic fields represent a new kind of field altogether, not already described in any way by physics. Nevertheless, they would still have more in common with the fields of quantum theory than with gravitational fields or electromagnetic fields.

I now turn to a consideration of evidence relating to the spatial aspect of morphic fields, and then to evidence concerning morphic resonance.

Experiments on morphic fields

I have not been able to think of potentially decisive experiments to test directly for the existence of morphic fields *within* molecules, crystals, micro-organisms, plants and animals. Morphic fields act along with known kinds of fields and gradients, and in general it is difficult to separate morphic-field effects from possible effects of chemical gradients, genes, electromagnetic fields, and other known kinds of causation. However, the occurrence of morphic resonance effects (discussed below) would imply the existence of such fields, and thus provide indirect evidence for their existence.

The easiest way to test for morphic fields *directly* is to work with societies of organisms. Individuals can be separated in such a way that they cannot communicate with each other by normal sensory means. If information can still travel between them, this would imply the existence of bonds or interconnections of the kind provided by morphic fields.

When I started looking for evidence of field-like connections between members of a social group, I found that I was moving into realms very little understood by science. For example, no one knows how societies of termites are co-ordinated in such a way that these small, blind insects can build complex nests with an intricate internal architecture.[16] No one understands how flocks of birds or schools of fish can change direction so quickly without the individuals bumping into each other.[17] Likewise, no one knows what is the nature of human social bonds.

One particularly promising area for this kind of research concerns the bonds between people and domesticated animals, as discussed in this book.

According to the hypothesis of formative causation, morphic fields extend beyond the brain into the environment, linking us to the objects of our perception, and making us capable of affecting them through our intention and attention.[18] This is another aspect of morphic fields that lends itself to experimental testing. Such fields would mean that we can affect things just by looking at them, in ways that cannot be explained in terms of conventional physics. For example, we may be able to affect someone by looking at them from behind, when they have no other way of knowing that we are staring at them.

The sense of being stared at from behind is in fact a common experience. Experiments already indicate that it is a real phenomenon (Chapter 16).[19] It does not seem to be explicable in terms of chance coincidence, the known senses, or fields currently recognized by physicists.[20]

The unsolved problems of animal navigation, migration and homing may also depend on invisible fields connecting the animals to their destinations. In effect, these could act like invisible elastic bands linking them to their homes. In the language of dynamics, their home can be regarded as an attractor.[21]

Morphic resonance in biology

Both the form and behaviour of organisms involve an inherent memory, if the idea of morphic resonance is correct. As with morphic resonance effects in general, long-established patterns of morphogenesis and of instinctive behaviour will be so deeply habitual that few changes will be observable. It is only in the case of new patterns of development and of behaviour that the build-up of habits can be observed experimentally.

There is already evidence from experiments with fruit flies that such effects may be occurring in the realm of morphogenesis.[22]

There is also much circumstantial evidence that animal behaviour can evolve rapidly, as if a collective memory is building up through morphic resonance. In particular, large-scale adaptations have been observed in the behaviour of domesticated animals all over the world.

For example, Roy Bedichek, in his day a well-known Texas naturalist, wrote in 1947 of changes in the behaviour of horses that he had seen in his lifetime:

> It was freely predicted fifty years ago that barbed wire could never be used for horse pastures. Horses in fear or frolic dashed right into it, cut their own throats, tore great slugs of flesh from their breasts, while wounds not fatal or mere scratches became infested with screwworms. I can remember the time when there was hardly a horse to be found in Texas farming or ranching sections that were not scarred up from encounters with barbed wire . . . But in half a century the horse has learned to avoid barbed wire. Colts rarely dash into it. The whole species has been taught a new fear.
>
> When automobiles first appeared, horse-drawn traffic was disorganized . . . Many a vehicle was wrecked and many the neck broken in making the introduction of horse to automobile and establishing his tolerance for it. Loud were the demands for laws to keep automobiles in their place . . . [But] domestic stock generally have lost their original fear of both the locomotive and the automobile.[23]

This change is not simply a matter of colts learning from their mothers. Even if they have not previously been exposed to barbed wire or cars and are separated from older and more experienced horses, the young do not generally react today in the ways that their predecessors did a hundred years ago.

Another example concerns cattle grids. Ranchers throughout the American West have found that they can save money on cattle grids by using fake ones instead, consisting of stripes painted across the road. Real cattle grids (known as cattle guards in the US) are made of a series of parallel steel tubes or rails with gaps in between, which make it difficult for cattle to walk across them, and even painful to try. However, present-day cattle do not usually even try to cross them. The illusory grids work just like the real ones. When cattle approach them, they 'put on brakes with all four feet', as one rancher expressed it to me.

Is this just because calves learn from older cattle that they should not try to cross? Apparently not. Several ranchers have told me that herds not previously exposed to real cattle grids will avoid the phoney ones. And Ted Friend, of Texas A & M University, has tested the response of several hundred head of cattle to painted grids, and has found that naive animals avoid them just as much as those previously exposed to real grids.[24] Sheep and horses likewise show an aversion to crossing painted grids. This aversion may well depend on morphic resonance from previous members of the species that have learned to avoid cattle grids the hard way.

There are many such examples. There are also data from laboratory experiments on rats and other animals showing that such effects occur. The best known involves a series of experiments in which subsequent generations of rats learned how to escape from a water maze. As time went on, rats in laboratories all over the world were able to do this quicker and quicker.[25]

Only one specifically designed experimental test for morphic resonance has so far been carried out in the realm of animal learning. This experiment involved day-old chicks, and was carried out in the laboratory of a sceptic, Steven Rose, at the Open University in England.

Day after day, newly hatched batches of chicks were shown a small yellow light (a light-emitting diode or LED), and pecked at it, as they tend to peck at any small prominent object in their environment. After they had pecked at it, they were injected with a chemical that made them feel queasy. They associated feeling ill with pecking at the yellow light, and afterwards avoided pecking it when they were shown it again. (This rapid form of learning is called conditioned aversion.) As a control, an equal number of chicks were shown a small chrome bead. After pecking it they were given a blank injection which had little or no effect on them, and produced no aversion to pecking at the chrome bead when they were shown it again.

The idea was that by morphic resonance, subsequent batches of newly hatched chicks should show an increasing aversion to pecking at the yellow light when they were first shown it, because of morphic resonance from their predecessors. They would draw on a collective memory of aversion, and the more chicks that were made averse to the yellow light, the stronger this effect should become. No such aversion to the chrome bead would be expected in the control chicks.

In fact subsequent batches of chicks exposed to the yellow light did indeed become increasingly averse to it, as predicted on the basis of morphic resonance.[26] This effect was statistically significant.

Morphic resonance in human learning

Morphic resonance has many implications for the understanding of human learning, including the acquisition of languages. Through the collective memory on which individuals draw, and to which they contribute, it should in general be easier to learn what others have learned before.

This idea fits well with the observations of linguists like Noam Chomsky, who propose that language learning by young children takes place so rapidly and creatively that it cannot be explained simply in terms of imitation. The structure of language seems to be inherited in some way. In his book *The Language Instinct* Steven Pinker gives many examples to support this idea.

This process is particularly striking in the evolution of new languages, which can occur very rapidly. When speakers of different languages need to communicate but do not learn each other's language, they develop a makeshift called a pidgin, choppy strings of words borrowed from the language of the colonizers, with little in the way of grammar. But in many cases, pidgins have been transformed into a full complex language, a creole, at one fell swoop. All it takes is for a group of young children to be exposed to the pidgin at the age when they acquire their mother tongue. Historically, this probably happened in groups of children of slaves tended collectively by a worker who spoke to them in pidgin. 'Not content to reproduce the fragmentary word strings, the children injected grammatical complexity where none existed before, resulting in a brand new, richly expressive language'.[27]

Even more remarkable is the evolution of new sign languages. For example, in Nicaragua there were no sign languages at all until recently, because deaf people were isolated from each other. When the Sandanistas came to power in 1979 the first schools for the deaf were created.

> The schools focused on drilling the children in lip reading and speech, and as in every case where that is tried, the results were dismal. But it did not matter. On the playgrounds and school buses the children were inventing their own sign system, pooling the makeshift gestures that they used with their families at home. Before long the system congealed into what is now called the Lenguaje de Signos Nicaragüense (LSN).[28]

This pidgin sign language is now used by young deaf adults, who joined the school when they were ten or older. But younger people, who joined the school about the age of four, when LSN was already around, are quite different. They speak a far more complex and expressive language, referred to by a different name, Idioma de Signos Nicaragüense (ISN). This creole language with its consistent grammar was created in one leap. As Pinker remarks, 'A language has been born before our eyes.'[29]

The inherited plans that facilitate both the learning of existing languages and the evolution of new ones are not merely general principles that for logical reasons have to be present in all languages. They are more like arbitrary conventions, that could have been different. In Pinker's words: 'It is as if isolated inventors miraculously came up with identical standards for typewriter keyboards or Morse code or traffic signals.'[30]

Both Chomsky and Pinker assume that the ability to learn language must depend on a coding in the DNA of the genes for universal structures common to all languages. They take it for granted that all hereditary information is inscribed in the genes, and are forced to assume the existence of a universal grammar because young children of any ethnic group seem to be able to learn any language; for example, a Vietnamese baby adopted by a Finnish family easily learns Finnish.

Morphic resonance provides a simpler explanation. The young child resonates with the speakers around it, and with millions of speakers of the language in the past. Morphic resonance facilitates its learning of the language, just as it facilitates other kinds of learning. Likewise, morphic resonance facilitates the acquisition of sign languages by the deaf, who tune in to past users of these languages. There is no need to suppose the existence of genes for ordinary languages and for sign languages lying latent in everyone's DNA.

Of course this interpretation of language acquisition in terms of formative causation is speculative. But so is the theory of genes for a hypothetical universal grammar. As Pinker himself remarks, 'No one has yet located a grammar gene.'[31]

Changes in human performance over time

One way of studying possible effects of morphic resonance on a large scale is provided by existing bodies of quantitative data on human performance over the years. Does human performance show a tendency to improve as time goes on? Obviously it does in skills such as snowboarding and computer programming. But such improvements are rarely documented quantitatively, and the situation keeps changing through technical innovations, increased availability of equipment, better teachers, social and economic forces, and so on. Any morphic resonance effects would be hard to disentangle from all these other factors, even if quantitative data existed.

One of the few areas in which detailed quantitative data are available over periods of decades is in the scores of IQ (Intelligence Quotient) tests. Around 1980, I realized that if morphic resonance occurs, average performance in IQ tests should be rising, not because people are becoming more intelligent, but because IQ tests should be getting easier to do as a result of morphic resonance from the millions who have done them before. I searched for data that would enable this prediction to be tested, but could not find any suitable published figures, nor could I find any discussion of this question. I was therefore intrigued when, in 1982, it turned out that average IQ test scores in Japan had been increasing by three per cent a decade since the Second World War.[32] Soon afterwards, it turned out (to the relief of many Americans) that IQs had been rising at a similar rate in the United States.

This effect was first detected in America by James Flynn in his study of the testing of intelligence by the US military authorities. He found that recruits who were merely average when compared with their contemporaries were above average when compared with recruits in a previous generation who had taken exactly the same test (Figure C.2). No one had noticed this trend because testers routinely compared an individual's score with others of the same age tested at the same time; at any given time the average IQ score is set at 100 by definition.[33]

Flynn has now established that comparable increases have occurred in twenty other countries, including Australia, Britain, France, Germany and Holland.[34] Many attempts have been made to explain this 'Flynn effect', but none has succeeded.[35] For example, very little of this effect can be ascribed to practice at doing such tests. If anything, such tests have become less common in recent years. Improvements in education cannot explain it either. Nor, as some have suggested, can increasing exposure to television. IQ scores began rising decades before the advent of television in the 1950s, and as Flynn has commented wryly, television

Figure C.2 The rise in IQ scores in the USA between 1918 and 1989, an example of the 'Flynn effect'. The scores have been calibrated according to 1989 levels (after Horgan, 1995).

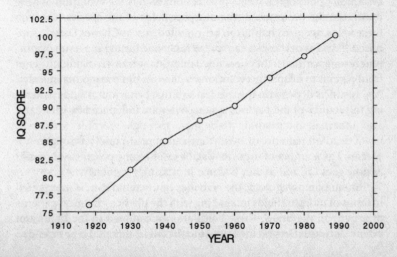

was usually considered 'a dumbing down influence until this effect came along'.[36] The more research there has been, the more mysterious it has become. Flynn himself describes it as 'baffling'.[37] But morphic resonance could provide a natural explanation.

If the Flynn effect is indeed explicable in terms of morphic resonance, it shows that such resonance effects are relatively small. If millions of people taking IQ tests lead to increased scores of only a few per cent, then in experiments involving a few hundred people, or at most a few thousand, the morphic resonance effects may be too small to detect against the 'random noise' due to wide variations in performance from subject to subject.

Implications

The hypothesis of formative causation has far-reaching implications in all branches of science.

In chemistry, crystallography and molecular biology, molecular and crystalline forms can be seen to evolve and to have a kind of memory within them, instead of being determined by eternal, unchanging laws. The exploration of memory in the molecular and crystalline realm could ultimately lead to major technological applications, including new kinds of computers interconnected by morphic resonance and with global collective memories.

In biology, the development of animals and plants can be seen as shaped by invisible organizing fields, the carriers of ancestral habits. The evolution of biological forms involves not merely the evolution of gene pools, but the evolution of the morphic fields of the species. Through these fields, acquired habits can be inherited, just as Charles Darwin supposed.[38] And as new habits can spread faster and further as a result of morphic resonance than if they depended only on the transfer of mutant genes from parents to offspring, evolutionary changes can occur more quickly.

Instincts depend on the species' habitual behavioural fields patterning the activity of the nervous system. They are influenced by genes and also inherited by morphic resonance. Through morphic resonance, newly learned patterns of behaviour can spread rapidly throughout a species. The learning of these new skills can become progressively easier as time goes on, and as they become increasingly habitual.

In human psychology, the activities of the mind can be interpreted in terms of morphic fields interacting with the physico-chemical patterns of activity in the brain. These fields are not confined to the brain, but extend outwards beyond the body into the environment. These extended mental fields underlie perception and behaviour. They also enable 'para-normal' phenomena, such as telepathy and the sense of being stared at, to be interpreted in such a way that they seem normal.

Personal memory can be understood in terms of self-resonance from a person's own past; it is no longer necessary to suppose that all memories need to be stored as elusive material 'traces' in the brain.[39] A less specific resonance with countless other people in the past connects each of us to the collective memory of our society and culture, and ulti-mately to the collective memory of all humanity.

Personal habits and collective habits do not differ in kind, but in degree; both depend on morphic resonance. This novel approach to memory could give a new impetus to the understanding of learning in general, and could well have major educational applications. Teaching methods that maximize morphic resonance from those who have learned the same thing in the past could lead to more efficient and rapid learning.

The morphic fields of social groups would help to explain many otherwise mysterious aspects of social organization, including the behaviour of social insects, flocks of birds and human societies.

The social sciences could receive a new theoretical foundation, and new avenues of research would open up. The understanding of cultural forms in terms of morphic fields would likewise revolutionize our understanding of cultural inheritance, and the influence of the ancestors. Richard Dawkins has given the name 'meme' to 'units of cultural trans-mission',[40] and such memes can be interpreted as morphic fields. Mor-phic resonance also sheds new light on many religious practices, including rituals.[41] Even scientific paradigms can be seen as morphic fields, stabilized by morphic resonance, with a tendency to become increasingly habitual and unconscious the more often they are repeated.[42]

The entire cosmos now seems to be evolutionary. The fields of atoms, molecules, crystals, planets, stars and galaxies are evolving; and like the morphic fields of biological organisms, their evolution is subject to natural selection. The hypothesis of formative causation provides a way of exploring the evolutionary process in all nature, not just in the biological realm.

But however wide its implications, this hypothesis has a major inherent limitation. It helps explain how patterns of organization are repeated; but it does not explain how they come into being in the first place: it leaves open the question of evolutionary creativity. Formative causation is compatible with several different theories of creativity, rang-ing from the idea that all novelty is ultimately a matter of chance to explanations in terms of divine creativity.[43]

Notes

Preface

1 Sheldrake (1994).

Introduction

1 Serpell (1986).
2 For a discussion of the mechanistic theory of life and of alternatives to it, see Sheldrake (1988a, 1990).
3 Pfungst (1911), p.10.

Chapter 1: The domestication of animals

1 Karsh and Turner (1988).
2 Godwin (1975); Marx et al. (1988).
3 Leakey and Lewin (1992); Mithen (1996).
4 Ehrenreich (1997).
5 Ibid.
6 Eliade (1964); Burkert (1996).
7 Eliade (1964), p. 94.
8 Masson (1997).
9 Morell (1997).
10 Paxton (1994).
11 Fiennes and Fiennes (1968).
12 Serpell (1983).
13 Ibid.
14 Galton (1865).
15 Kerby and Macdonald (1988).
16 Clutton-Brock (1981), p. 110.
17 Kiley-Worthington (1987).
18 For an interesting discussion of the evolution of the Lassie stories, see Garber (1996).
19 Galton (1865).
20 Fiennes and Fiennes (1968).

21 In the USA in 1996 there was an average of 2.2 cats per cat-owning house-hold, compared with 1.7 dogs per dog-owning household. (Source: Humane Society of America, Washington, DC.)
22 Darwin (1875).
23 Kiley-Worthington (1987).
24 Kerby and Macdonald (1988).
25 Sheldrake (1988a).
26 Francis Huxley has pointed out that Darwin's most famous book would more appropriately be called 'The Origin of Habits' (Huxley, 1959).
27 Sheldrake (1981, 1988a).
28 For a mathematical model of communication through a morphic field, see Abraham (1996).

Chapter 2: Dogs that know when their owners are coming home

1 Serpell (1986).
2 Fogle (1995), p. 41.
3 Shiu, Munro and Cox (1997); Munro, Paul and Cox (1997).
4 Boone (1954), Chapter 7.
5 Serpell (1986), pp. 103–4.
6 Sheldrake and Smart (1997); Brown and Sheldrake (1998); Sheldrake, Lawlor and Turney (1998).
7 www.sheldrake.org
8 Sheldrake and Smart (1997); Brown and Sheldrake (1998); Sheldrake, Lawlor and Turney (1998).
9 Matthews (1994).
10 For the linear correlation between journey time and Jaytee's reaction time, $p < 0.0001$ (Sheldrake and Smart, 1998).
11 On 20 out of 55 occasions, Jaytee reacted at the time Pam set off, or within 2 minutes of this time. But sometimes Jaytee reacted before Pam set off and sometimes after: in 9 cases he reacted more than 3 minutes early, and in 26 cases he reacted more than 3 minutes late. Is this variation merely a matter of chance? Or could some of this variation be due to biases in the way the data were recorded? There could have been at least two sources of bias, work-ing in opposite directions. First, some of the data on Jaytee's behaviour may be biased towards lateness. If Mr and Mrs Smart were not in their sitting room, or if they were distracted, for example by visitors, by telephone calls or television programmes, they would not have noticed Jaytee's reactions immediately. Thus, on some of the occasions when Jaytee's reported reac-tions began after Pam set off to come home, he may in fact have reacted ear-lier, closer to the time she set off. Second, on some of the occasions on which Jaytee reacted early, this earliness could be an artefact arising from the way in which Pam's time of setting off was defined. The setting-off times recorded by Pam were those at which she actually began her car journey. But some-times she started getting ready to go 10 minutes or more beforehand, taking time to say goodbye to the people she was with, or chatting as she was leav-

ing. And sometimes she was thinking about leaving before she made a move to do so. If Jaytee was reacting to her intentions, then he would tend to react *before* she set off in the car.

12 Sheldrake and Smart (1998).

13 Ibid.

14 Ibid.

15 A videotape showing sequences from this experiment is commercially available: Sheldrake, R. (1997) *Seven Experiments That Could Change the World: The Video.* Wellspring Media, 65 Bleecker Street, New York, NY 10012, USA.

16 Sheldrake (1994).

17 $p < 0.000001$.

18 During the period in which Pam could be bleeped it was important for her to be free to come home straight away. Thus, for example, we could not do one of these experiments while she was at the dentist, or in the middle of a important meeting. Most of them took place when she was visiting friends or members of her family, at the library or in a café or pub. Of course, both Pam and I both had to know in advance during what window of time the bleep would occur.

19 $p < 0.000001$.

20 For example, Matthews (1995).

21 Wiseman, Smith and Milton (1998).

22 There is no dispute about the facts. But there is a dispute about the interpretation of the facts. Richard Wiseman and Matthew Smith invented a criterion of their own by which to judge Jaytee's success. They decided that Jaytee's 'signal' for Pam's return was to be the first time he visited the window for more than two minutes for no obvious external reason. They disregarded all the data subsequent to these so-called signals. In fact, in their experiments at Pam's parents' flat, although Jaytee went to the window several times during Pam's absence, he spent a far higher proportion of the time at the window when Pam was actually on the way home. On average, Jaytee was at the window only 4 per cent of the time for the main part of Pam's absence; in the ten minutes prior to her return, 48 per cent, and while she was actually returning, 78 per cent. This pattern of results, discussed in more detail in Appendix B, is similar to my own (Figure 2.3), and is statistically significant. However, Wiseman and Smith decided to ignore most of their own data and to disqualify Jaytee if he did not meet their arbitrary two-minute criterion, and thus they were able to claim that Jaytee had failed the test. They announced this conclusion through press releases, television and newspapers. For details of this controversy, see Sheldrake (1999a), Wiseman, Smith and Milton (2000) and Sheldrake (2000).

Chapter 3: Cats

1 Deag, Manning and Lawrence (1988).

2 Kerby and Macdonald (1988).

3 Turner (1995).

4 Males make up 54 per cent and females 46 per cent of the total number of stories where the gender of the cat is given.

Chapter 4: Parrots, horses and humans

1 A statistical analysis using the paired-sample t test showed a significance of p=0.03.
2 Barber (1993).
3 von Frisch (1975).
4 Pet Food Manufacturers Association (UK), 1997.
5 van der Post (1958).
6 Inglis (1977), p.18.
7 Lang (1911).
8 Hygen (1987).
9 For example, Haynes (1976), pp. 208–9.
10 Knowles (1996).

Chapter 5: Animals that comfort and heal

1 Partridge (1958), p. 475.
2 For the most influential statement of this point of view, see Dawkins (1976).
3 The most systematic exposition of this theory is that of Wilson (1980).
4 For a discussion of the extent to which giving alarm signals can be dangerous for the individual though beneficial to the group, see Ridley (1996).
5 But if pets and people help each other to survive, then they are genetically co-dependent, and remain so over many generations. They would therefore have been subject to selection for inter-species altruism.
6 Karsh and Turner (1988).
7 Ibid.
8 Hart (1995); Dossey (1997).
9 Lynch and McCarthy (1969).
10 Friedmann (1995).
11 Hart (1995); Rennie (1997).
12 Hart (1995).
13 Serpell (1991).
14 Hart (1995).
15 Dossey (1997).
16 For example, Paul and Serpell (1996).
17 For example, Summerfield (1996).
18 For example, Phear (1997).
19 Ormerod (1996).
20 Rennie (1997).
21 Susan Chernak McElroy (1997) in her book *Animals as Teachers and Healers* gives many examples of healing and comforting by dogs and other animals, including dogs that visit the sick and dying.
22 Metzger (1998).
23 Garber (1997), pp. 137–8.

24 Edney (1992).
25 McCormick and McCormick (1997).
26 Stewart (1995).
27 Ibid.
28 Masson (1997).
29 Michell and Rickard (1982), p. 127.
30 Ibid., p. 128

Chapter 6: Distant deaths and accidents

1 Masson (1997), p. 144.
2 Bradshaw and Nott (1995).
3 Morris (1986), p. 17.
4 Steinhart (1995), p. 24.
5 Gurney, Myers and Podmore (1886); Broad (1962).
6 Stevenson (1970).

Chapter 8: Telepathic calls and commands

1 Woodhouse (1992), p. 54.
2 Sheldrake and Smart (1997); Sheldrake, Lawlor and Turney (1998); Brown and Sheldrake (1998); Sheldrake (1998a).
3 Ibid.
4 Ibid.
5 Bechterev (1949; translated from an article originally published in 1924 in *Zeitschrift für Psychotherapie*).
6 Bechterev (1949) p. 175.
7 But some preliminary and rather inconclusive laboratory experiments were carried out with cats by Osis (1952) and Osis and Foster (1953).
8 Kiley-Worthington (1987), pp. 88–9.
9 Roberts (1996).
10 Blake (1975).
11 Ibid., p. 131.
12 Ibid., p. 94.
13 Ibid., p. 129.
14 Patanjali: *Yoga Sutras*, iii, 36.
15 Smith (1989).
16 Myers (1997).
17 St Barbe Baker (1942), p. 41.
18 Steiger and Steiger (1992), p. 16.
19 The surveys were carried out by telephoning households selected at random from telephone directories. In Bury, 65 per cent of the people questioned said they had telephoned someone who said they were just thinking about telephoning them. Fifty per cent of the people questioned said they themselves had known who was telephoning them before they answered the telephone, without any possible clue. Significantly more women than men had had these experiences. (The statistical significance of the difference between men

and women was p< 0.02.) Over a third of the people who had these experiences said they happened often. In London, a random sample of the population was asked: 'Have you ever felt that someone was going to telephone you just before they did?' Fifty-eight per cent said they had had this experience.

Chapter 9: Animal-to-animal telepathy

1 Wilson (1971).
2 Hölldobler and Wilson (1994), pp. 109–110.
3 von Frisch (1975).
4 Ibid., p. 150.
5 Marais (1973).
6 Sheldrake (1994).
7 Wilson (1980).
8 Ibid., pp. 207–8.
9 Partridge (1981).
10 Ibid., pp. 493–4.
11 Mathematical models of fish schooling have to take into account synergistic or cooperative effects over the entire school, which are one way of representing the field of the school. See for example Huth and Wissel (1992); Niwa (1994).
12 Selous (1931), p. 9.
13 Ibid., p.10.
14 Potts (1984).
15 For a summary of recent research on flock behaviour and the mathematical modelling of animal groups, see Parrish and Hammer (1997). Models using local interactions between birds and their neighbours have been constructed on the basis of cellular automata programs by Craig Reynolds and others, the best known being Reynolds' 'Boids' program (details on his world wide web site: http://hmt.com/cwr/boids/html). These are able to simulate some properties of flock behaviour. But some new models are far better predictors of flock behaviour than the original 'boids'. These models are based on field phenomena, such as the the fields that order the magnetic spin of the atoms within a magnet, or the fields of flow of fluids. But none of these computer models goes into the details of how bird-to-bird communication occurs in reality. Observational data from high-speed cinematography show that this interaction is too rapid to be explained by visual stimuli from neighbours. The birds react quicker than their nerve impulses would allow if they were just reacting to neighbours (Sheldrake, 1988). Rather, they seem to be reacting to the pattern of change in the moving flock as a whole. Waves can pass through these flock fields (Schecter, 1999). These new, improved field versions of boids imply some kind of rapid information transfer through fields, and agree well with a field model of the kind I am suggesting.
16 Long (1910), pp.101–105.
17 Blake (1975).
18 Ostrander and Schroeder (1970).
19 Rogo (1997).

20 Wylder (1978).
21 Peoc'h (1997).

Chapter 10: Incredible journeys

 1 Burnford (1961).
 2 Young (1995).
 3 Lemish (1996), p. 220.
 4 Haldane: *Drovers' Roads of Scotland*.
 5 Herrick (1922).
 6 Schmidt (1932).
 7 Schmidt (1936), pp. 188–9.
 8 Ibid., p. 192.
 9 Thomas (1993), p. 7.
10 Ibid., p. 8.
11 A report was broadcast on *Out of this World* on BBC 1 on 6 August 1996.
12 McFarland (1981).
13 Steinhart (1995), p. 16.
14 Boitani et al. (1995).
15 Kerby and Macdonald (1955).
16 Liberg and Sandell (1955).
17 Carthy (1963); Matthews (1968).
18 Matthews (1968).
19 Carthy (1963).
20 Gould (1990).
21 Schmidt-Koenig and Ganzhorn (1991).
22 Walraff (1990).
23 Schmidt-Koenig (1979).
24 This was a lesson learnt through various attemps to determine longitude at
    sea, of great importance in naval navigation. See Sobel (1996).
25 Keeton (1981).
26 Schmidt-Koenig (1979); Wiltschko, Wiltschko and Jahnel (1987).
27 Moore (1988); Walcott (1991).
28 van der Post (1962), p. 235.
29 Forster (1778).
30 For a summary of research findings, see Baker (1989).

Chapter 11: Migrations and memory

 1 Brower (1996).
 2 Berthold (1991).
 3 Keeton (1981).
 4 Able (1982).
 5 Wiltschko and Wiltschko (1995, 1999).
 6 Skinner and Porter (1987).
 7 Able and Able (1996).
 8 Sobel (1996).

9 Hasler, Scholz and Horrall (1978).
10 Papi and Luschi (1996).
11 Ibid.
12 Lohmann (1992).
13 Jouventin and Weimerskirsch (1990); Weimerskirsch et al. (1993).
14 Papi and Luschi (1996).
15 Sheldrake (1981, 1988a).
16 Helbig (1996).
17 Perdeck (1958).
18 Ibid.
19 Ibid.
20 Baker (1980).
21 Helbig (1996).
22 On this hypothesis, when birds of different migratory races are crossed, for example blackcaps from eastern and western Europe, their offspring would tune in to both sets of migratory habits. In fact, when such hybrid birds are tested at the beginning of the migratory season to see which way they hop in cages, they show a much wider variation than birds of the parental races. Caged birds of the eastern race tend to hop towards the southeast; the western race southwest; and the hybrids on average hop in an intermediate direction, southwards. (Helbig, 1993, 1996). In real life, if the hybrids persisted on a southward course, they would not follow either of the traditional migratory paths from Europe to Africa, with short sea crossings over the Straits of Gibraltar or the Bosphorus, and would either perish or have to find a new wintering place.
23 Bowen and Avise (1994).

Chapter 12: Animals that know when they are nearing home

1 Thomas (1993), p. 143.

Chapter 13: Pets finding their people far away

1 The details are given in a nineteenth-century account, published in St Gallen, entitled Zollikofer und sein Hund, a copy of which was kindly given me by Prof. C. Zollikofer of the University of Zurich, a descendant of the ambassador.
2 Cooper (1983), p. 149.
3 Geller (1998).
4 Rhine (1951).
5 Rhine and Feather (1962).
6 Ibid.
7 Ibid.
8 Ibid.
9 Whitlock (1992).
10 Pratt (1964).
11 Reprinted in World Farming Newsletter, 1983.

12 'Cow's long march.' *Soviet Weekly*, 24 January 1987.
13 Long (1919), p. 95.
14 Ibid., pp. 97–9.

Chapter 14: Premonitions of fits, comas and sudden deaths

1 For an enlightening discussion of the emotion of fear, see Masson (1996).
2 Hölldobler and Wilson (1994).
3 Brown (1975).
4 Chandrasekeran (1995).
5 Price (1998).
6 Edney (1993).
7 Smith (1997).
8 Support Dogs, PO Box 447, Sheffield S6 6YZ, England.
9 National Service Dog Center, 289 Perimeter Road E, Renton, WA 98055-1329, USA. A training programme has also been established as part of the Prison Pet Partnership Program, 9601 Bujacich Road, PO Box 17, Gig Harbor, WA 98335-0017, USA.
10 Chandrasekeran (1995).
11 At the time of writing, research programmes are being considered by at least two centres in the United States: The Epilepsy Institute, 257 Park Avenue South, New York, NY 10010, USA; and in the Department of Physiological Sciences, College of Veterinary Medicine, University of Florida, PO Box 100144, Gainesville, FL 32610-0144, USA.
12 Lim et al. (1992).
13 Williams and Pembroke (1989).

Chapter 15: Forebodings of earthquakes and other disasters

1 I am grateful to Anna Rigano for these reports.
2 Tributsch (1982), p. 13.
3 Ibid.
4 Bardens (1987).
5 Wadatsumi (1995).
6 Geller et al. (1997).
7 Tributsch (1982), p. 9.
8 Ibid., p. 10.
9 Evernden (1976).
10 Hui (1996).
11 Hui and Kerr (1997).
12 Hui (1996).
13 Otis and Kautz (1981).
14 Probabilities of the results being due to chance were as low as $p < 0.00005$.
15 Tributsch (1982), Chapter 5.
16 Otis and Kautz (1981).
17 Ikeya et al. (1997).
18 Lighthill (1996).

19 Time Research Institute, PO Box 620198, Woodside, CA 94962, USA.
20 Ikeya, Takaki and Takashimizu (1996); Ikeya, Matsuda and Yamanaka (1998).
21 Cooper (1983).
22 Ibid., p. 128.
23 Peter (1994).
24 Parson (1956).
25 Inglis (1985), p. 74.
26 Radin (1997), p. 112.
27 Dunne (1958).
28 Radin (1997), Chapter 7.

Chapter 16: Animal powers and human minds

1 For two such stories about the bushmen by Laurens van der Post, see p.67 and p. 158.
2 Lang (1911).
3 In our own surveys, more women than men said they had had a psychical experience, and more had experienced seemingly telepathic telephone calls: Sheldrake and Smart (1987); Sheldrake, Lawlor and Turney (1998); Brown and Sheldrake (1998).
4 Baker (1989).
5 The most striking exception is the pioneering work of Rhine and Feather (1962). For a review of research by parapsychologists on this subject, see Morris (1977).
6 Peoc'h (1988a, b).
7 Peoc'h (1988c).
8 Peoc'h (1997b).
9 Jahn and Dunne (1987); Radin (1997).
10 For a discussion of the effects of intention and their relationship to positive thinking and prayer, see Sheldrake and Fox (1996).
11 Cottrell, Winer and Smith (1996).
12 Sheldrake (1994); Cottrell, Winer and Smith (1996).
13 Elsworthy (1898).
14 Dundes (1981).
15 Sheldrake (1994).
16 Sheldrake (1998b, 1999b).
17 Braud, Shafer and Andrews (1993a, b); Schlitz and LaBerge (1997). However, one investigator failed to find positive effects when he himself or his sceptical colleagues were doing the staring: Richard Wiseman. One of the people who consistently obtained positive results in this experiment was Marilyn Schlitz, of the Institute of Noetic Sciences in Sausalito, and she travelled to Wiseman's laboratory in England to carry out the experiment under his conditions, with a group of volunteer participants who were allocated at random either to Schlitz or Wiseman. In these experiments, when Schlitz was the looker her participants' emotional state changed, as revealed by

changes in their skin resistance, in a statistically significant manner. When Wiseman was the looker, his participants showed no significant difference (Wiseman and Schlitz, 1997). This shows a clear 'experimenter effect', whereby the expectations and abilities of experimenters can affect the results of their experiments. But whereas it is easy to understand how a sceptic could cause an experiment to fail, the results of Marilyn Schlitz cannot be explained in a similar way. Her belief in the reality of this effect could not have made the participants feel she was looking at them unless there was some real influence of her mind at a distance.

18 The morphic field concept might perhaps be able to account for precognitions if it were developed further to take into account the way that waves and vibrations are spread out in time, with no sharp cut-off between past, present and future, as discussed by Sheldrake, McKenna and Abraham (1998).

19 For a discussion of some of these implications, see Sheldrake, McKenna and Abraham (1998).

20 I am grateful to David Jay Brown for suggesting this line of thought to me.

21 Barrow (1988), p. 361.

22 Davies and Gribbin (1991), p. 217. A recent experimental development of the principle of non-locality is the achievement of 'quantum teleportation' (Bouwmeester et al., 1997).

Appendix A: How to take part in research

1 For example, Rhine and Feather (1962); Edney (1993); Peoc'h (1988a, b, c; 1997a, b).

2 Sheldrake and Smart (1997); Sheldrake, Lawlor and Turney (1998); Sheldrake and Brown (1998); Sheldrake (1998a).

3 Sheldrake and Smart (1998, 1999).

4 Sheldrake (1994).

5 Sheldrake (1998b, 1999).

Appendix B: Experiments with Jaytee

1 For this purpose, long means more than 3 hours; medium, 1 hour 50 minutes to 2 hours 50 minutes; and short, 1 hour 20 minutes to 1 hour 40 minutes.

2 F value (df 2, 27)= 8.84.

3 F value (df 1, 22)= 11.31.

4 On 1 July, 1997.

5 On 29 August, 1997.

6 Sheldrake and Smart (1998).

7 For a detailed account of these experiments with Jaytee, see Sheldrake and Smart (2000).

Appendix C: Morphic fields

1 Sheldrake (1981).

2 Sheldrake (1988a).

3 Sheldrake (1981).

4 Sheldrake (1988a).

5 Ibid., Chapters 13 and 14.

6 Waddington (1957).

7 Thom (1975, 1983).

8 For a discussion of alternative theories of creativity, see Sheldrake (1988a), Chapter 18.

9 Sheldrake (1988a, 1990).

10 Sheldrake (1988a), pp. 316-7.

11 Sheldrake (1994).

12 Davies and Gribbin (1991).

13 Bohm and Sheldrake (1985): Morphogenetic fields and the implicate order. In: Sheldrake (1985), p. 234.

14 Goswami (1997).

15 Dürr (1997).

16 Sheldrake (1994).

17 Sheldrake (1988a).

18 Sheldrake (1981), section 9.6.

19 Sheldrake (1994; 1998b; 1999).

20 Abraham, McKenna and Sheldrake (1992); Sheldrake (1994).

21 For a discussion of this idea, see Sheldrake, McKenna and Abraham (1998), Chapter 4.

22 Sheldrake (1988a), Chapter 8.

23 Bedichek (1947; reprinted 1961), pp. 157-8.

24 Sheldrake (1988b).

25 Sheldrake (1988a), Chapter 9.

26 Sheldrake (1992a). Perhaps inevitably, Rose and I disagreed about the interpretation of the data. He remained sceptical (Rose, 1992), but his conclusions were based on an erroneous set of data, and on ignoring the results from the control chicks (Sheldrake, 1992b). See also Mikulecky (1996).

27 Pinker (1994), p. 33.

28 Ibid., p. 36.

29 Ibid., p. 37.

30 Ibid., p. 41.

31 Ibid, p. 46.

32 Anderson (1982).

33 Flynn (1983, 1984).

34 Flynn (1987).

35 Neisser et al. (1995); Horgan (1995).

36 Horgan (1995).

37 Ibid.

38 Darwin (1875).

39 Sheldrake (1988a).

40 Dawkins (1976).

41 Sheldrake and Fox (1996).

42 Sheldrake (1988a).

43 Sheldrake (1981; 1988a; 1990). Ibid., p. 94.

References

Able, K.T. and Able, M.A. (1996) The flexible migratory orientation system of the Savannah sparrow. *Journal of Experimental Biology* 199, 3–8.

Able, K.T. (1982) The effects of overcast skies on the orientation of free-flying nocturnal migrants. In: Papi, F. and Wallraff, H.G. (eds) *Avian Navigation*. Springer, Berlin.

Abraham, R. (1996) *Vibrations: communication through a morphic field*. Visual Math Institute, Santa Cruz.

Abraham, R., McKenna, T. and Sheldrake, R. (1992) *Trialogues at the Edge of the West*. Bear and Co., Santa Fe.

Anderson, A.M. (1982) The great Japanese IQ increase. *Nature* 297, 180–1.

Ash, E.C. (1927) *Dogs: Their History and Development*. Benn, London.

Baker, R. (1980) *The Mystery of Migration*. MacDonald, London.

Baker, R. (1989) *Human Navigation and Magnetoreception*. Manchester University Press, Manchester.

Barber, T.X. (1993) *The Human Nature of Birds*. St Martin's Press, New York.

Bardens, D. (1987) *Psychic Animals: An Investigation of their Secret Powers*. Hale, London.

Barrow, J. (1988) *The World Within the World*. Clarendon Press, Oxford.

Bekhterev, W. (1949) 'Direct influence' of a person upon the behaviour of animals. *Journal of Parapsychology* 13, 166-76.

Bedichek, R. (1947) *Adventures with a Texas Naturalist*. Reprinted 1961, University of Texas Press, Austin.

Berthold, P. (1991) Spatiotemporal programmes and the genetics of orientation. In: Berthold, P (ed.) *Orientation in Birds*. Birkhäuser, Basel.

Blake, H (1975) *Talking with Horses: A Study of Communication Between Man and Horse*. Souvenir Press, London.

Bloxham, J. and Gubbins, D. (1985) The secular variation of the Earth's magnetic field. *Nature* 317, 777–81.

Bohm, D. and Sheldrake, R. (1985) Morphogenetic fields and the implicate order. In: Sheldrake, R. *A New Science of Life*, second ed. Blond, London.

Boitani, L., Francisci, F., Ciucci, P. and Andreoli, G. (1995) Population biology and ecology of feral dogs in central Italy. In: Serpell, J. (ed.) *The Domestic Dog*. Cambridge University Press, Cambridge.

Boone, J.A. (1954) *Kinship With All Life*. Harper and Row, New York.

Bouwmeester, D., Pan, J.W., Mattle, K., Eibl, M., Weinfurter, H. and Zellinger, A. (1997) Experimental quantum teleportation. *Nature* 390, 575–9.

Bowen, B.W. and Avise, J.C. (1994) Tracking turtles through time. *Natural History* 12, 5–6, 38–39.

Bradshaw, J.W.S. and Nott, H.M.R. (1995) Social and communication behaviour of companion dogs. In: Serpell, J. (ed.) *The Domestic Dog*. Cambridge University Press, Cambridge.

Braud, W., Shafer, D. and Andrews, S. (1993a) Reactions to an unseen gaze (remote attention): A review, with new data on autonomic staring detection. *Journal of Parapsychology* 57, 373–90.

Braud, W., Shafer, D. and Andrews, S. (1993b) Further studies of autonomic detection of remote staring: replications, new control procedures, and personality correlates. *Journal of Parapsychology* 57, 391–409.

Broad, C.D. (1962) *Lectures on Psychical Research*. Routledge and Kegan Paul, London.

Brower, L.P. (1996) Monarch butterfly orientation. *Journal of Experimental Biology* 199, 93–103.

Brown, D.J. and Sheldrake, R. (1998) Perceptive pets: a survey in north-west California. *Journal of the Society for Psychical Research* 62, 396–406.

Brown, J.L. (1975) *The Evolution of Behavior*. Norton, New York.

Burkert, W. (1996) *The Creation of the Sacred: Tracks of Biology in Early Religions*. Harvard University Press, Cambridge, Mass.

Burnford, S. (1961) *The Incredible Journey*. Hodder & Stoughton, London.

Carthy, J.D. (1963) *Animal Navigation*. Unwin, London.

Chandrasekeran, R. (1995) Epileptic owners swear by seizure-alerting dogs. *Washington Post*, 31 July.

Clutton-Brock, J. (1981) *Domesticated Animals From Early Times*, Heinemann, London.

Cooper, J. (1983) *Animals in War*. Imperial War Museum, London.

Cottrell, J.E., Winer, G.A. and Smith, M.C. (1996) Beliefs of children and adults about feeling stares of unseen others. *Developmental Psychology* 32, 50–61.

Darwin, C. (1875) *The Variation of Animals and Plants Under Domestication*. Murray, London.

Davies, P. and Gribbin, J. (1991) *The Matter Myth*. Viking, London.

Dawkins, R. (1976) *The Selfish Gene*. Oxford University Press, Oxford.

Deag, J.M., Manning, A. and Lawrence, C.A. (1988) Factors influencing the mother-kitten relationship. In: Turner, D.C. and Bateson, P. (eds) *The Domestic Cat*. Cambridge University Press, Cambridge.

Dossey, L. (1997) The healing power of pets: a look at animal-assisted therapy. *Alternative Therapies* 3, 8–15.

Dundes, A. (ed.) (1981) *The Evil Eye: A Casebook*. University of Wisconsin Press, Madison.

Dunne, J.W. (1958; third edition) *An Experiment With Time*. Faber and Faber, London.

Dürr, H.P. (1997) Sheldrakes Vorstellungen aus dem Blickwinkel der modernen Physik. In: Dürr, H.P. and Gottwald, F.T. (eds) *Rupert Sheldrake in der Diskussion*. Scherz Verlag, Bern.

Edney, A.T.B. (1992) Companion animals and human health. *Veterinary Record* 130, 285–287.

Edney, A.T.B. (1993) Dogs and human epilepsy. *Veterinary Record* 132, 337–338.

Ehrenreich, B. (1997) *Blood Rites*. Metropolitan Books, New York.

Eliade, M (1964) *Shamanism: Archaic Techniques of Ecstasy*. Princeton University Press, Princeton.

Elsworthy, F. (1898) *The Evil Eye*. Murray, London.

Evernden, J.R. (ed.) (1976) *Abnormal Animal Behavior Prior to Earthquakes*. US National Earthquakes Hazards Reduction Program, Conference 23–24 September.

Fiennes, R. and A. (1968) *The Natural History of the Dog*. Weidenfeld & Nicholson, London.

Flynn, J.R. (1983) Now the great augmentaton of the American IQ. *Nature* 301, 655.

Flynn, J. R. (1984) The mean IQ of Americans: massive gains 1932 to 1978. *Psychological Bulletin* 95, 29–51.

Flynn, J. R. (1987) Massive IQ gains in 14 nations. *Psychological Bulletin* 101, 171–191.

Fogle, B. (1994) Unexpected dog ownership findings from Eastern Europe. *Anthrozoos* 7, 270.

Fogle, B. (1995) *The Encyclopedia of the Dog*. Dorling Kindersley, London.

Forster, J.R. (1778) *Observations Made During a Voyage Around the World*. Robinson, London.

Friedmann, E. (1995) The role of pets in enhancing human well-being: physiological effects. In: Robinson, I. (ed.) *The Waltham Book of Human-Animal Interaction: Benefits and Responsibilities of Pet Ownership*. Pergamon Press, Oxford.

Galton, F. (1865) The first steps towards the domestication of animals. *Transactions of the Ethnological Society of London, New Series* 3, 122–38.

Garber, M. (1996) *Dog Love*. Hamish Hamilton, London.

Geller, R.J., Jackson, D.D., Kagan, Y.Y. and Mulargia, F. (1997) Earthquakes cannot be predicted. *Science* 275, 1616–7.

Geller, U. (1998) Uri Geller's Weird Web, *The Times*, 27 May.

Godwin, R.D. (1975) Trends in the ownership of domestic pets in Great Britain. In: R.S. Anderson (ed.) *Pet Animals and Society*. Balliere Tindall, London.

Goswami, A. (1997) Eine quantentheoretische Erklärung von Sheldrakes morphischer Resonanz. In: Dürr, H.P. and Gottwald, F.T. (eds) *Rupert Sheldrake in der Diskussion*. Scherz Verlag, Bern.

Gould, J.L. (1990) Why birds (still) fly south. *Nature* 347, 331.

Gurney, E., Myers, F. and Podmore, F. (1886) *Phantasms of the Living*. Trubner, London.

Hart, L.A. (1995) Dogs as human companions: a review of the relationship. In: Serpell, J. (ed.) *The Domestic Dog*. Cambridge University Press, Cambridge.

Hasler, A.D., Scholz, A.T. and Horrall, R.M. (1978) Olfactory imprinting and homing in salmon. *American Scientist* 66, 347–55.

Haynes, R. (1976) *The Seeing Eye, The Seeing I*. Hutchinson, London.

Helbig, A.J. (1993) What do we know about the genetic basis of bird orientation? *Journal of Navigation* 46, 376–82.

Helbig, A.J. (1996) Genetic basis, mode of inheritance and evolutionary changes of migratory direction in palearctic warblers. *Journal of Experimental Biology* 199, 49–55.

Herrick, F.H. (1922) Homing powers of the cat. *Science Monthly* 14, 526–39.

Hölldobler, B. and Wilson, E. O. (1994) *Journey to the Ants: A Story of Scientific Exploration*. Harvard University Press, Cambridge, Mass.

Horgan, J. (1995) Get smart, take a test: a long-term rise in IQ scores baffles intelligence experts. *Scientific American*, November, 10–11.

Hui, L. (1996) China's campaign to predict quakes. *Science* 273, 1484–6.

Hui, L. and Kerr, R.H. (1997) Warnings precede Chinese tremblors. *Science* 276, 526.

Huth, A. and Wissel, C. (1992) The simulation of the movement of fish schools. *Journal of Theoretical Biology* 156, 365–85.

Huxley, F. (1959) Charles Darwin: life and habit. *The American Scholar* (Fall/Winter), 1–19.

Hygen, G. (1987) *Vardøger: Vårt Paranormale Nasjonalfenomen*. Cappelens Forlag, Oslo.

Ikeya, M., Matsuda, T. and Yamanaka, Y. (1998) Reproduction of Mimosa and clock anomalies before earthquakes. *Proceedings of the Japanese Academy* 74B, 60–64.

Ikeya, M., Takaki, S., Matsumoto, H., Tani, A. and Komatsu, T. (1997) Pulsed charge model of fault behavior producing seismic electrical signals. *Journal of Circuits, Systems and Computers* 7, 153–64.

Ikeya, M., Takaki, S. and Takashimizu, T. (1996) Electric shocks resulting in seismic animal anomalous behaviors. *Journal of the Physical Society of Japan* 65, 710–12.

Inglis, B. (1977) *Natural and Supernatural*. Hodder & Stoughton, London.

Inglis, B. (1985) *The Paranormal: An Encyclopedia of Psychic Phenomena*. Granada, London.

Jahn, R.J. and Dunne, B. (1987) *Margins of Reality*. Harcourt Brace, New York.

Jouventin, P. and Weimerskirsch, H. (1990) Satellite tracking of wandering albatrosses. *Nature* 343, 746–8.

Karsh, E.B. and Turner, D.C. (1988) The human-cat relationship. In: Turner, D.C. and Bateson, P. (eds) *The Domestic Cat*. Cambridge University Press, Cambridge.

Keeton, W.T. (1981) Orientation and navigation of birds. In: Aidley, D.J. (ed.) *Animal Migration*. Society for Experimental Biology Seminar Series 13, Cambridge University Press, Cambridge.

Keller, O. (1913) *Antike Tierwelt*. Engelmann, Leipzig.

Kerby, G. and Macdonald, D.W. (1955) Cat society and the consequences of colony size. In: Turner, D.C. and Bateson, P. (eds) *The Domestic Cat*. Cambridge University Press, Cambridge.

Kiley-Worthington, M. (1987) *The Behaviour of Horses*. J.A. Allen, London.

Knowles, O.S. (1996) Letter. *Psi Researcher* 21, 24

Lang, A. (1911) Second sight. *Encyclopaedia Britannica* (11th ed.). Cambridge University Press, Cambridge.

Leakey, R. and Lewin, R. (1992) *Origins Reconsidered*. Little, Brown and Co., London.

Lemish, G.H. (1996) *War Dogs: Canines in Combat*. Brassey, Washington.

Liberg, O. and Sandell, M. (1955) Spatial organization and reproductive tactics in the domestic cat and other felids. In: Turner, D.C. and Bateson, P. (eds) *The Domestic Cat*. Cambridge University Press, Cambridge.

Lighthill, J. (ed.) (1996) *A Critical Review of VAN*. World Scientific, Singapore.

Lim, K., Wilcox, A., Fisher, M. and Burns-Cox, C.J. (1992) Type 1 diabetics and their pets. *Diabetic Medicine* 9, Supp 2, S3.

Lohmann, K.J. (1992) How sea turtles navigate. *Scientific American*, January, 75–82.

Long, W. (1919) *How Animals Talk*. Harper, New York.

Lynch, J.J. and McCarthy, J.F. (1969) Social responding in dogs: heart rate changes to a person. *Psychophysiology* 5, 389–93.

Marais, E. (1973) *The Soul of the White Ant*. Penguin Books, London.

Marx, M.B., Stallones, L., Garrity, T.F. and Johnson, T.P. (1988) *Anthrozoos* 2, 33–7.

Masson, J.M. (1996) *When Elephants Weep*. Delta, New York.

Masson, J.M. (1997) *Dogs Never Lie About Love*. Jonathan Cape, London

Matthews, G.V.T. (1968) *Bird Navigation* (second ed.). Cambridge University Press, Cambridge.

Matthews, R. (1994) Animal magic or mysterious sixth sense? *Sunday Telegraph*, 24 April.

Matthews, R. (1995) Psychic dog gives scientist a lead. *Sunday Telegraph*, 15 Jan.

McCormick, A. and D. (1997) *Horse Sense and the Human Heart*. Health Communications, Deerfield Beach, Florida.

McElroy, S.C. (1997) *Animals as Teachers and Healers*. Ballantine Books, New York.

McFarland, D. (ed.) (1981) Navigation. *The Oxford Companion to Animal Behaviour*. Oxford University Press, Oxford

Metzger, D. (1998) Coming home. In: Peterson, B., Metzger, D. and Hogan, L. (eds) *Intimate Nature: The Bond Between Women and Animals*. Ballantine Books, New York.

Michell, J. and Rickard, J.M. (1982) *Living Wonders: Mysteries and Curiosities of the Animal World*. Thames & Hudson, London.

Mikulecky, M. (1996) Sheldrake versus Rose. *Biology Forum* 89, 469–78.

Mithen, S. (1996) *The Prehistory of the Mind: A Search for the Origins of Art, Religion and Science*. Thames & Hudson, London.

Moore, B.R. (1988) Magnetic fields and orientation in homing pigeons: the experiments of the late W.T. Keeton. *Proceedings of the National Academy of Sciences, USA* 85, 4907–9.

Morell, V. (1997) The origin of dogs: running with the wolves. *Science* 276, 1647–8.

Morris, D. (1986) *Dogwatching*. Jonathan Cape, London.

Morris, R.L. (1977) Parapsychology, biology and ANPSI. In: *Handbook of Parapsychology* (ed. Wolman, B.B.). Van Nostrand Reinhold, New York.

Munro, K.J., Paul, B and Cox, C.L. (1997) Normative auditory brainstem response data for bone conduction in the dog. *Journal of Small Animal Practice* 38, 353–6.

Myers, A. (1997) *Communicating with Animals*. Contemporary Books, Chicago.

Neisser, U. (1995) *Intelligence: Knowns and Unknowns.* American Psychological Association Report.

Niwa, H.S. (1994) Self-organizing dynamic model of fish schooling. *Journal of Theoretical Biology* 171, 123–36.

Ormerod, E. (1996) Pet programmes in prisons. *Society for Companion Animal Studies Journal* 8 (4), 1–3.

Osis, K. (1952) A test of the occurrence of a psi effect between man and the cat. *Journal of Parapsychology* 16, 233–56.

Osis, K. and Forster, E.B. (1953) A test of ESP in cats. *Journal of Parapsychology* 17, 168–86.

Ostrander, S. and Schroeder, L. (1970) *Psychic Discoveries Behind the Iron Curtain.* Abacus Books, London.

Otis, L.S. and Kautz, W.H. (1981) *Biological premonitors of earthquakes: a validation study.* Annual report prepared for the US Geological Service.

Papi, F. and Luschi, P. (1996) Pinpointing 'Isla Meta': the case of sea turtles and albatrosses. *Journal of Experimental Biology* 199, 65–71.

Parrish, J.K. and Hammer, W.M. (eds) (1997) *Animal Groups in Three Dimensions.* Cambridge University Press, Cambridge.

Parson, N.A. (1956) *Guided Missiles in War and Peace.* Harvard University Press, Cambridge, Mass.

Partridge, B. (1981) Schooling. In: McFarland, D. (ed.) *The Oxford Companion To Animal Behaviour.* Oxford University Press, Oxford.

Partridge, E. (1958) *Origins: A Short Etymological Dictionary of Modern English.* Routledge and Kegan Paul, London.

Paul, E.S. and Serpell, J.A. (1996) Obtaining a new pet dog: effects on middle childhood children and their families. *Applied Animal Behaviour Science* 47, 17–29.

Paxton, D. (1994) Urban animal management. *Proceedings of the Third National Conference on Urban Animal Management in Australia,* Australian Veterinary Association, Canberra.

Peoc'h, R. (1988a) Action psychocinétique des poussins sur un générateur aléatoire. *Revue Française de Psychotronique* 1, 11–24.

Peoc'h, R. (1988b) Chicken imprinting and the tychoscope: an ANPSI experiment. *Journal of the Society for Psychical Research* 55, 1–9.

Peoc'h, R. (1988c) Psychokinetic action of young chicks on an illuminated source. *Journal of Scientific Exploration* 9, 223–9.

Peoc'h, R. (1997a) Telepathy experiments between rabbits. *Fondation Odier de Psycho-Physique Bulletin* 3, 25–8.

Peoc'h, R. (1997b) Telekinesis experiments with rabbits. *Fondation Odier de Psycho-Physique Bulletin* 3, 28–36.

Perdeck, A.C. (1958) Two types of orientation in migrating starlings and chaffinches as revealed by displacement experiments. *Ardea* 46, 1–37.

Peter, M. (1994) Fliegerangriff! Tauben schlugen Alarm. *Kronen Zeitung,* Vienna, 26 November.

Pfungst, O. (1911) *Clever Hans: A Contribution to Experimental Animal and Human Psychology.* Henry Holt & Co., New York.

Phear, D. (1997) A study of animal companionship in a day hospice. *Society for Companion Animal Studies Journal* 9 (1), 1–3.

Pinker, S. (1994) *The Language Instinct*. Penguin, London.

Potts, W.K. (1984) The chorus line hypothesis of manoeuvre co-ordination in avian flocks. *Nature* 309, 344–5.

Pratt, J.G. (1964) *Parapsychology: An Insider's View of ESP*. W.H. Allen, London.

Price, P. (1998) Back from the dead. *The Times*, 21 February.

Radin, D. (1997) *The Conscious Universe: The Scientific Truth of Psychic Phenomena*. Harper, San Francisco.

Rennie, A. (1997) The therapeutic relationship between animals and humans. *Society for Companion Animal Studies Journal* 9 (4), 1–4.

Rhine, J.B. (1951) The present outlook on the question of psi in animals. *Journal of Parapsychology* 15, 230–51.

Rhine, J.B. and Feather, S.R. (1962) The study of cases of 'psi-trailing' in animals. *Journal of Parapsychology* 16, 1–22.

Ridley, M. (1996) *The Origins of Virtue*. Viking, London.

Roberts, M. (1996) *The Man Who Listens to Horses*. Hutchinson, London.

Rogo, D.S. (1997) Do animals have ESP? In: *Psychic Pets and Spirit Animals*. Llewellyn Publications, St Paul, MN.

Rose, S. (1992) So-called 'formative causation': a hypothesis disconfirmed. *Biology Forum* 85, 445–53.

Schechter, B. (1999) Birds of a feather. *New Scientist*, 23 January, 30–3.

Schlitz, M.J. and LaBerge, S. (1997) Covert observation increases skin conductance in subjects unaware of when they are being observed: a replication. *Journal of Parapsychology* 61, 185–96.

Schmidt, B. (1932) Vorläufiges Versuchsergebnis über das hundliche Orientierungsproblem. *Zeitschrift für Hunderforschung* 2, 133–56.

Schmidt, B. (1936) *Interviewing Animals*. Allen and Unwin, London.

Schmidt-Koenig, K. (1979) *Avian Orientation and Navigation*. Academic Press, London.

Schmidt-Koenig, K. and Ganzhorn, J.U. (1991). On the problem of bird navigation. In: Bateson, P.P.G. and Klopfer, P.H. (eds) *Perspectives in Ethology*, Vol. 9. Plenum Press, New York.

Selous, E. (1931) *Thought Transference or What? in Birds*. Constable, London.

Serpell, J. (1983) Best friend or worst enemy: cross-cultural variation in attitudes to the domestic dog. *Proceedings of the 1983 International Symposium of the Human-Pet Relationship*. Austrian Academy of Sciences, Vienna.

Serpell, J. (1986) *In the Company of Animals*. Cambridge University Press, Cambridge.

Serpell, J. (1991) Beneficial effects of pet ownership on some aspects of human health and behaviour. *Journal of the Royal Society of Medicine* 84, 717–20.

Sheldrake, R. (1981; second ed. 1985) *A New Science of Life: The Hypothesis of Formative Causation*. Blond and Briggs, London.

Sheldrake, R. (1988a) *The Presence of the Past: Morphic Resonance and the Habits of Nature*. Collins, London.

Sheldrake, R. (1988b) Cattle fooled by phoney grids. *New Scientist* 11 Feb, p. 65.

Sheldrake, R. (1990) *The Rebirth of Nature: The Greening of Science and God*. Century, London.

Sheldrake, R. (1992a) An experimental test of the hypothesis of formative causation. *Biology Forum* 85, 431-443.

Sheldrake, R. (1992b) Rose refuted. *Biology Forum* 85, 455–60.

Sheldrake, R. (1994) *Seven Experiments That Could Change the World: A Do-It-Yourself Guide to Revolutionary Science*. Fourth Estate, London.

Sheldrake, R. (1998a) Perceptive pets with puzzling powers: three surveys. *International Society for Anthrozoology Newsletter* 15, 2–5.

Sheldrake, R. (1998b) The sense of being stared at: experiments in schools. *Journal of the Society for Psychical Research* 62, 311–23.

Sheldrake, R. (1999a) Commentary on a paper by Wiseman, Smith and Milton on the 'psychic pet' phenomenon. *Journal of the Society for Psychical Research*, 63, 306-311.

Sheldrake, R. (1999b) The 'sense of being stared at' confirmed by simple experiments. *Biology Forum* 92, 53-76.

Sheldrake, R. (2000) The 'psychic pet' phenomenon. *Journal of the Society for Psychical Research* 64, 126-128.

Sheldrake, R. and Fox, M. (1996) *Natural Grace: Dialogues on Science and Spirituality*. Bloomsbury, London.

Sheldrake, R., Lawlor, C. and Turney, J. (1998) Perceptive pets: a survey in London. *Biology Forum* 91, 57–74.

Sheldrake, R., McKenna, T. and Abraham, R. (1998) *The Evolutionary Mind*. Trialogue Press, Santa Cruz.

Sheldrake, R. and Smart, P. (1997) Psychic pets: a survey in north-west England. *Journal of the Society for Psychical Research* 61, 353–64.

Sheldrake, R. and Smart, P. (1998) A dog that seems to know when its owner is returning: preliminary investigations. *Journal of the Society for Psychical Research* 62, 220–32.

Sheldrake, R. and Smart, P. (2000) A dog that seems to know when its owner is returning: videotaped experiments and observations. *Journal of Scientific Exploration* 14, 233-256.

Shiu, J.N., Munro, K.J. and Cox., C.L. (1997) Normative auditory brainstem response data for hearing threshold and neuro-otiological diagnosis in the dog. *Journal of Small Animal Practice* 38, 103–107.

Skinner, B.J. and Porter, S.C. (1987) *Physical Geology*. Wiley, New York.

Smith, H. (1997) My psychic bunny's a lifesaver. *News of the World Magazine* , 8 June.

Smith, P. (1989) *Animal Talk: Interspecies Telepathic Communication*. Pegasus Publications, Point Reyes, CA.

Sobel, D. (1996) *Longitude*. Fourth Estate, London.

St Barbe Baker, R. (1942) *African Drums*. Lindsay Drummond, London.

Steiger, B. and Steiger, S.H. (1992) *Strange Powers of Pets*. Fine, Inc., New York.

Steinhart, P. (1995) *The Company of Wolves*. Knopf, New York.

Stevenson, I. (1970) *Telepathic Impressions*. University Press of Virginia, Charlottesville.

Stewart, M. (1995) Dogs as counsellors? *The Society for Companion Animal Studies Journal* 7 (4), 1–4.

Summerfield, H. (1996) Pets as therapy. *Society for Companion Animal Studies Journal* 8 (4), 9.

Thom, R. (1975) *Structural Stability and Morphogenesis*. Benjamin, Reading, MA.

Thom, R. (1983) *Mathematical Models of Morphogenesis*. Horwood, Chichester.

Thomas, E.M. (1993) *The Hidden Life of Dogs*. Houghton Mifflin, Boston.

Tributsch, H. (1982) *When the Snakes Awake*. MIT Press, Cambridge, MA.

Turner, D.C. (1995) The human-cat relationship. In: *The Waltham Book of Human-Animal Interaction* (ed. I. Robinson). Pergamon, Oxford.

van der Post, L. (1962) *The Lost World of the Kalahari*. Penguin Books, London.

von Frisch, K. (1975) *Animal Architecture*. Hutchinson, London.

Wadatsumi, K. (1995) *Witnesses 1519 Prior to Earthquake*. Tokyo Publishers, Tokyo (in Japanese).

Waddington, C.H. (1957) *The Strategy of the Genes*. Allen and Unwin, London.

Walcott, C. (1991) Magnetic maps in pigeons. In: Berthold, P. (ed.) *Orientation in Birds*. Birkhäuser, Basel.

Walraff, H.G. (1990) Navigation by homing pigeons. *Ethology, Ecology and Evolution* 2, 81–115.

Weimerskirsch, H., Salamolard, M., Sarrazin, F. and Jouventin, P. (1993) Foraging strategy of wandering albatrosses through the breeding season: a study using satellite telemetry. *Auk* 110, 325–41.

Whitlock, R. (1992) How do they do it? *Guardian Weekly*, 4 December.

Williams, H. and Pembroke, A. (1989) Sniffer dogs in the melanoma clinic? *Lancet*, April, p. 734.

Wilson, E.O. (1971) *The Social Insects*. Harvard University Press, Cambridge, Mass.

Wilson, E.O. (1980) *Sociobiology*. Harvard University Press, Cambridge, Mass.

Wiltschko, R. and Wiltschko, W. (1995) *Magnetic Orientation in Animals*. Springer-Verlag, Berlin.

Wiltschko, R. and Wiltschko, W. (1999) Das Orientierungssystem der Vögel: I. Kompassmechanismen. *Journal für Ornithologie* 140, 1–40.

Wiltschko, W., Wiltschko, R. and Jahnel, M. (1987) The orientation behaviour of anosmic pigeons in Frankfurt a. M., Germany. *Animal Behaviour* 35, 1328–33.

Wiseman, R. and Schlitz, M. (1997) Experimenter effects and the remote detection of staring. *Journal of Parapsychology* 61, 197–207.

Wiseman, R., Smith, M. and Milton, J. (1998) Can animals detect when their owners are returning home? An experimental test of the 'psychic pet' phenomenon. *British Journal of Psychology* 89, 453–62.

Wiseman, R., Smith, M. and Milton, J. (2000) The 'psychic pet' phenomenon: a reply to Rupert Sheldrake. *Journal of the Society for Psychical Research* 64, 46-49.

Woodhouse, B. (1992) *How Your Dog Thinks*. Ringpress, Letchworth.

Wylder, J. (1978) *Psychic Pets: The Secret World of Animals*. Stonehill, New York.

Young, R. (1995) Dog walks 60 miles home to its master. *The Times*, 9 September.

Index of Names

Most people cited in this book were happy for their real names to be used; some asked to be referred to by pseudonyms, indicated by asterisks.

Index of Subjects